MY YUENDUMU STORY

YURNTUMU NGAJU-NYANGU YIMI

FRANK BAARDA

This edition 2022
fdbaarda@gmail.com

Cover photograph- Mt. Eclipse (Yikupali)- Blim Nolan- edited Jason Woods, PAW
Media, Yuendumu.
Photos (page 65, 141, 278, 327) - Jennifer Baarda
Drawings (page 13, 67, 127, 175) - Quentin Cockburn
Please note- This book mentions and contains images of people who have passed away.
This may cause distress to some readers.

A catalogue record for this
book is available from the
National Library of Australia
NATIONAL
LIBRARY
OF AUSTRALIA

This story is dedicated to
Yurntumu-wardingki yapa-patu.

The Warlpiri people of Yuendumu.

FOREWORD

Nyampu Jungarrayi-kirlangu yimi Yurntumu-kurlu ngulaju junga-nyayirni manu manyu-kurlu yirrarnu, kujarlpa-rnalu milya-pinyi yinka-kurlu, kuja kangalpa manyu-manyu ngarlarrinjaku ngurrju-mani. Nyampuju pina-maninjaku kardiya-patuku Warlpiri jaru-kurluku, manu kujalu ngalpa government-wardingkirli muku puntarnu yapaku nyiya-kanti-kanti.

Ngaju karna milya-pinyi Jungarrayi manu Nangala tarnngangku-juku, kujalu ngalpa purntu yukaja yapa Warlpiriki nyampurla.

Jungarrayi's story about Yuendumu is true and amusing.

We remember with a smile and it makes us laugh. This story teaches whitefellas about Warlpiri ways and how the governments have taken everything away from Yapa.

I have known Jungarrayi and Nangala for a long time, since they came and formed a warm friendship with Warlpiri people here.

Warren Japanangka Williams

MY YUENDUMU STORY

Countless Brilliant Fragments

Martin Flanagan, the former Melbourne Age's Sports Writer, visited Yuendumu in 1987. After a return visit in 2009 Martin wrote an article which included:

> *"Three of the most momentous days of my life occurred in 1987 when I attended a football carnival at Yuendumu on the Warlpiri tribal lands north-west of Alice Springs. In three days, the glass tower of my preconceptions about Aboriginal Australia was shattered. I could tell a dozen stories as to why, each as important as the last…And I went to a party where a traditional man with initiation scars all down his chest played the electric guitar like Jimi Hendrix and a white geologist who lived in Yuendumu accompanied him like a jazzman on a trumpet. In that room, that night, Aboriginal people and white people mingled in a spirit of fraternal respect. Walking back to the car I was sleeping in, I thought there has to be some way of taking that spirit to the rest of Australia."*

The guitarist was Micah Jampijinpa Hudson, and I was the trumpet player. The occasion was my 44th birthday party.

In Martin Flanagan's original 1987 article, the glass tower of his preconceptions about Aboriginal Australia, had been shattered into countless brilliant fragments.

Black Fella/White Fella....

Neil Murray and George Rrurrampu 1985

The Yurntumu-wardingki, the people of Yuendumu, refer to Aborigines as Yapa and to whitefellas as Kardiya.

Yapa and Kardiya share a common humanity. We are more alike than we are different. Yet it is the differences between us, this diversity, that our Australian nation ought to be celebrating. We sometimes brag about our multiculturalism but invariably omit the First Australians and their descendants from this vision of an inclusive and fair society.

This story was initially sub-titled 'Glimpses across a cross cultural gulf'.' Too pretentious to my liking, so I dropped it.

Reading Alexis Wright's essay 'What Happens When You Tell Somebody Else's Story', (Meanjin Quarterly, Summer 2016) has reinforced my awareness of the minefield that is cross-cultural writing. So let me make it clear at the outset, that this is a story told by a Kardiya; perish the thought I'd claim it to be otherwise. Any occasional pearl of wisdom in this story is a Kardiya pearl, albeit one formed inside a Yapa oyster shell.

Yuendumu - the place

Yuendumu lies at the southern edge of the Tanami Desert, 293 km northwest of Alice Springs. The Tanami is not a barren desert. Even the northern half has ground cover, just mostly no trees. Here in the southern part we have plenty of trees, mulga forests, open country with bloodwoods, dogwoods, ghost gums, and many acacias, useful trees with edible seeds, good wood for cooking and keeping warm and excellent wood for boomerangs, spears, clapsticks and anything else you would need for a happy hunting life.

Central Australia is classified as semi-arid, with an average annual rainfall of 200 to 250 mm. This average is misleading and rather meaningless, in that some years there is virtually no rain and sometimes, with almost no warning, there is a deluge. It is hot in summer, over 40°C most days in mid-Summer, but the evenings and nights are pleasant and cool. Night time is socialising time for many Warlpiri. The heat of day is for sleeping. In winter the days are perfect, 25°C to 35°C most days, and although nights are cold, down to zero, by 8:00 a.m. short sleeves and sandals are all you need. The winter evenings are too cold unless you have a good fire and even then, you have to rotate yourself, like a rotisserie chicken.

Housing for Kardiya was luxury compared to mining camps, or Darwin with only fans and no air cooler. We have always had 'swampies', evaporative coolers which work very well in the dry heat and we have few muggy days. Even on the hottest days, under some shady trees there is always a little breeze. A smouldering fire, a little upwind, disperses the flies.

When I was an active radio amateur operator I was forever being told that in Japan it was very "crowdy" (cloudy), to which I would triumphantly respond with *"koko-ni itenkidesu"*, (here it is good weather).

There is another season, *"karapurda"* when the gusty, dusty west winds come to waken up the goannas from their hibernating slumber. It's spring, birds are nesting, emu chicks break out of their eggs and follow their fathers in a line. In a wet year masses of wild flowers, and even in a dry year there are always some flowers.

When looking through photo albums, colour photos from Yuendumu and Central Australia instantly stand out. They are so much brighter and the stark vibrant colours make elsewhere look grey and dull. The usually clear skies are so blue that we've even had a visiting scientist who studied and measured the blueness. The rusty red ground and rocky hills glow at sunrise and just before sunset.

Many Kardiya fall in love with the desert and keep coming back every few years. Yapa are overjoyed to see them again. They are soul mates because they share a love of Warlpiri country.

The climate here is changing, fewer zero nights, longer stretches of over 40°C and more muggy days, but I would still say this is paradise.

Aerial photo- Yuendumu 1970s

Yuendumu - the people

Yuendumu was established as a postwar ration depot in 1946 by the Native Affairs Branch of the Australian Government's Department of the Interior. Yuendumu has a shifting population of around 800 to 1,000 predominantly Warlpiri people whose mother tongue is the Warlpiri language.

When destiny steered my wife Wendy, our children and me towards Yuendumu, we didn't have a clue what to expect. What we found is the most friendly, generous, openhearted, dignified, nonjudgmental, interesting, welcoming people we are ever likely to meet. This is despite, as we were to learn, that less than half a century earlier and within living memory, they had been subjected to the random killings of the Coniston massacre.

The Warlpiri were among the last freely roaming Aboriginal tribes in Australia, some of the last to be dispossessed of their lands, to be subjected to a foreign invasion, and be systematically subjugated and herded like cattle onto missions and settlements.

I've come across Kardiya who seem to think all aborigines look the same and are the same. Nothing could be further from the truth. From early childhood Yapa are allowed to be themselves, however different. There is no pressure on them to conform to standards. They have very distinct individual facial features, expressions and ways of walking.

I've also heard it said that people who immerse themselves in another culture, are dissatisfied with their own culture. In fact we find that Warlpiri culture has made us more aware and appreciative of our European heritage. Customs and habits we took for granted, almost didn't notice, or thought were unnesessary, now appear as essentials of our own culture, quite precious and without which we would be lost sheep. We need some everyday rituals, protocols, morals, things to revere, some rules for interpersonal relations, and some celebrations.

The Warlpiri have so much to teach us. There is much we can learn about ourselves by looking into the mirror they hold up to us. And they have a great sense of humour. Hardly a day goes by where we don't share a laugh.

Story time
(photo @Bunbadgee)

My memory diamonds

*"Elke herinnering werd een diamant en zij sleep er telkens nieuwe
kanten aan." (Every memory became a diamond and forever more she
polished new facets onto them.)*
A quote my sister found in a boring since discarded old Dutch book.

Telling my Yuendumu story is the least I could do to express my gratitude to the Warlpiri people of Yuendumu, who have tolerated and
welcomed us in their midst, thereby greatly enriching our lives.

But I have never kept a diary, so these stories are from my treasure
trove of memory-diamonds. Inevitably, when experience is put into
words some of these diamonds are more polished than others and
retelling always adds new facets. My family and friends have heard
some of these stories many times. But I have been told I tell them well!

It was widely assumed that my wife Wendy and I would 'go down
South' when we retired. That is what Kardiya do. They go 'back
home'. That is what we thought we'd do, but after nearly half a century
living in Yuendumu, home is here and we are staying.

Often people would say to me, *"You must have seen a lot of
changes, you should write a book"*. Which is what I'm setting out to do
but, as I explore my kaleidoscopic memory, it soon becomes apparent
to me, that seemingly irrelevant events that happened far away and
long ago, and which moulded me and shaped my way of seeing, have a
place in my Yuendumu story. I don't quite know where to begin, so I
ask you to stick with me as we take this corrugated and potholed road
from 1973 to 2021. Yuendumu is a very special place I'd like to show
you, so switch off your TV, computer and mobile phone, pull up a chair
at my dinner table or sit down at my campfire, join my friends, as, like
the Ancient Mariner, I hold you with my glittering eye and tell you my
tale of Yuendumu.

The muster

There are not many, if any, people alive today who clearly remember as far back as 1946, when Yuendumu settlement was first established. Only snippets of Yuendumu's early days can be garnered from what people have experienced or been told. Searching the academic literature and written memoirs and official records yields a confused and at times somewhat contradictory picture, which I will not even attempt to comprehensively unravel. What can be fairly stated however, is that the limited availability of water resources and the competition for such from the pastoral industry, played a pivotal role in the destiny of the Warlpiri people.

Post-war, the authorities embarked on what can best be described as a mustering exercise. Yapa having been subjugated by the whims and terror of colonial power could be pushed from pillar to post with ne'er a whimper, just like cattle or sheep. On the other hand much movement of Warlpiri people in the early days of contact had been prompted by bad seasons and other factors, and was driven by Yapa initiative and resourcefulness rather than by Kardiya coercion. By the time Yuendumu Settlement was started, the largest concentration of Warlpiri people was at the wolfram mine near Old Mount Doreen homestead, fifty-five kilometres north west of Yuendumu. † Uni Nampijinpa told Wendy that she and her family had been tricked onto a truck and, instead of going hunting, as promised, they were hijacked to Yuendumu and subsequently put to work on clearing the airstrip, no ifs no buts.

There are stories about people being sent out like bell cows, to persuade other distantly scattered groups to return with them to the settlement. For example one group is known to have been brought in from distant Ethel Creek, west and well outside of Mt. Doreen Pastoral Lease. The Yapa man who told us this story felt that † Garden Jack Japanangka, the man who had taken the Kardiya out to find this group, ought to be recognised as playing an important part in the history of Yuendumu. Why there was this imperative to gather these isolated small groups who were minding their own business on land no one else wanted, was a bit of a mystery to me until †Harry Jakamarra Nelson told me it was the missionaries who were behind this herding. Of course! They were shepherds gathering their flock, the biblical parable of the lost sheep in action. There are Yapa who think this was a good thing and perhaps it was. It wasn't so good for the bilbies, burrowing bettongs and bandicoots which, without fire management of their habitat, were doomed, roasted in their burrows to extinction.

In 1946 a small settlement at Rock Hill Bore (Wakurlpa), ten kilometres north of Yurntumu, very quickly grew and was moved to present day Yuendumu. By the end of 1946, officially there were approximately 400 Yapa at Yuendumu Native Settlement. Further movement occurred prompted by the successful drilling of Penhall's Bore at 4-mile (Ramarra-kujurnu), seven kilometres south of Yuendumu. At some stage there was a group camping at White Point Bore (Kanaji), west of 4-mile, just north of the present day bore field, which supplies Yuendumu with water. No clear picture emerges about these first years of Yuendumu settlement, insufficient water and family disputes being the official reasons given for these meanderings. In 1952, an area of 850 square miles (over 2,000 square kilometres), was officially declared as the Yuendumu Aboriginal Reserve.

By 1948 a Native Reserve had been declared at Catfish Block, approx. 600 km north of Yuendumu. The name, Hooker Creek, was soon adopted which years later was changed to Lajamanu. That same year it had become abundantly clear that Yuendumu could not sustain its growing population and an initial group of twenty people were trucked to this new paddock, and placed on agistment. In 1952, another 150 or so people were trucked to Hooker Creek from Yuendumu. Warlpiri people from other places such as The Granites and Warrabri augmented the Hooker Creek population. That Hooker Creek was not on Warlpiri land doesn't seem to have worried the possibly unaware authorities. British based Vestey Brothers had failed to renew their pastoral lease on the block and water had been found in a bore and that is all that mattered as far as they were concerned.

It is interesting to note that the indicated population figures for Hooker Creek fall short of the number of people recorded as having been trucked there. In 1954 anthropologist M. J. Meggitt in his 1962 book 'Desert People' estimated the number of Warlpiri people at Hooker Creek to be 165.

It is well known in Yuendumu, that whole families had walked back from Hooker Creek to Yuendumu. To put the approx. 600 km walking distance into perspective, this is twice the distance from the top to the bottom of the Netherlands, my country of birth, where you would never die of thirst. I've even heard that some families walked back twice.

On Mt. Doreen cattle-station in the summer of 1955, Meggitt saw a group of men, women and children en route to Yuendumu, who had walked from Hooker Creek in what he called 'appalling heat'. Ellen Kettle, who had been Yuendumu's first Kardiya nurse, mentioned in her 1967 book 'Gone Bush' that in 1952 'Willie' with his two wives and two babies had walked from Hooker Creek. Their babies had perished on the way and so had their dogs. This family was † Little Willie Japanangka and his wives † Lorna and † Jorna Napurrurla Williams who were fifteen and sixteen years old at the time of the tragedy. Tommy Jangala Watson told me of three Japanangka men and their families, who had walked back from Lajamanu. These were † Pompy, † Barney and the very same aforementioned † Little Willie. Barney famously returned with his wife on horseback.

This Hooker Creek exodus seems to have embarrassed the officials as there appear to be no official records of it. The number of returnees was significant. They were middle aged when we arrived in Yuendumu, and have mostly been written out of history. It is worth mentioning that the officials perceived these exiles as having voluntarily mounted the trucks that transported them to Hooker Creek. No coercion had been applied when docile Yapa had, like lambs to the slaughter, and with little if any objection, let themselves be loaded onto trucks. I suspect that, at least in part, this subservient obedience was a result of vestigial fear resulting from the Coniston killings, which had taken place a mere two decades earlier and were still fresh in the communal memory. Yet many Yapa embarked on an arduous and perilous return journey on foot.

Tells you something about cross cultural communication at the time, let alone the power imbalance.

Then the heav'n espie...

In 1973, Central Pacific Minerals N.L.(CPM), the company for which I'd been working in the Darwin/Pine Creek region, transferred me to their Alice Springs office. CPM was exploring for uranium in the Ngalia Basin. On a map I spotted Yuendumu on the northern margin of the Ngalia Basin, so I rang the Department of Education to ask if there was a school in 'Yuwen-doo-moo' which our eldest son, Donovan who had just turned five, would be able to attend. I was told that Don would only be allowed to attend Yuendumu school if he lived there, but that there was no housing available except for community staff. Wendy had qualified as a teacher during our Canadian stint so I asked if there were any vacant teaching positions in Yuendumu. The fellow at the other end, as much as jumped through the phone. Yuendumu had a very high turnover of Kardiya teachers and had just lost a few. It was thus that Wendy got a job at Yuendumu School.

CPM was one of only a few mineral exploration companies that employed Yapa. Because of this many of CPM's Kardiya staff and contractors left the region with a greater respect for Warlpiri people and their culture. Central Pacific Minerals is known by those Yapa who can remember as 'Syphic'. Sounds more like a disease than a mineral exploration company. CPM no longer exists. CPM appointed †Murray Japangardi Wood as my offsider. Murray became a friend and mentor. He was my first Warlpiri teacher. As we ranged over the Ngalia Basin as a two man exploration team, we had a lot of laughs whilst Murray gradually taught me bits of the Warlpiri language and opened my eyes and gave me my first insights into the Warlpiri parallel universe that was to captivate me.

♫ ♫ ♫

A man that looks on glasse, On it may stay his eye;
Or if he pleaseth, through it passe, And then the heav'n espie...
The Elixir-George Herbert (1633)

† Paddy Japanangka Doolan was another of CPM's Yapa employees. Paddy and I were sitting on a rocky outcrop near CPM's exploration camp at Wanipi. Paddy told me that the majestic *wapurnungku*, the ghost gum tree at the camp, is a fellow who is spying on a group of women who are grinding seeds in a green grassy enclosure below the Wanipi escarpment. These women are 'wrong skin' and thus forbidden for the Peeping Tom who is turned into a bird and has to fly away. For a few brief seconds in my mind the escarpment ceased to be the Vaughan Springs Quartzite and at its base a group of women were grinding grass seeds. Then Paddy said something I'll never forget. Pointing at the ghost gum he said: ' *'Him still there''*. Perving for eternity.

It was the first instance in which the timelessness of the dreamtime, the Jukurrpa, was made evident to me. The 'dreamtime' or 'dreaming' are highly inadequate translations of Jukurrpa. To Warlpiri people Jukurrpa is everything. Jukurrpa is such a complex multifaceted concept that I can't begin to explain it nor can I claim to even begin to comprehend it. I can only glimpse in wonder across this crosscultural gulf. The closest English translation of Jukurrpa I can think of is 'Cosmology'.

Wendy recalls that, when she and some friends visited Wanipi camp, the women and children had dug up a large quantity of *janmarda* in the grassy enclosure where the dreamtime ladies are forever grinding seeds and being perved on. *Cyperus bulbosus*, the so-called bush onions, are in serious decline as a result of the introduction and rapid spread of buffel grass. Just as buffel grass is choking the *janmarda*, so too is Kardiya society choking Yapa culture.

Exotic beings

"To see ourselves as others see us is a most salutary gift. Hardly less important is the capacity to see others as they see themselves."
Aldous Huxley, The Doors of Perception

On 12th May 1873, the explorer Peter Warburton camped near a pointy hill south west of Yuendumu. There was a lunar eclipse that night. Warburton put the hill on his maps and named it Mount Eclipse. In his diary Warburton described the area as uninhabited. Long before Warburton passed through the region the non-inhabitants had named the pointy hill Yikupali. I wonder what the non-inhabitants were thinking as from the next ridge they observed Warburton and his party. Perhaps that is the genesis of a story handed down, about when Kardiya first entered Warlpiri land and Yapa, watching from a distance, thought they were seeing two headed beings, which then mysteriously split in two. These exotic beings were men on camels. Today you can see Yikupali without travelling by camel. It's on the cover of this book.

Murray Wood taught me the names of the places near where we were looking for radioactivity in the Carboniferous Mount Eclipse Sandstone. Names such as, *Pikilyi, Yurnmaji, Warnalyurrpa, Wijinpa, Raparlpa, Palkura, Wanipi, Patumungkala, Kunalka, Warlukurlangu, Kanaji, Kirrirdi, Yipiri, Mijil-parnta, Ramarra-kujurnu, Rukurri, Ngama* and indeed, *Yikupali*!

Some of my first friendships forged in Yuendumu were the result of my having bothered to learn these place names. It was a way of better fitting into Yuendumu society both physically and mentally.

I used air photos in my job with 'Syphic'. Some Warlpiri men showed an intense interest in these so I laid down an air photo of Yuendumu on the ground and was immediately corrected. One of the men turned the photo around so its orientation matched the orientation of the real landscape the photo depicted. I then laid out air photos in a row due west all the way to Vaughan Springs. Within minutes the men excitedly were reading these photos and naming every little hill and creek. We had no television back then and most of these men had never been up in an aircraft. Drones didn't yet exist. So much for von Daniken's 'Chariots of the Gods?' Little green men in flying saucers had had nothing to do with the innate Warlpiri skill at air photo interpretation.

Recently I read a very beautiful illustrated book 'Desert Lake: Art, Science and Stories from Paruku', edited by Steve Morton, Mandy Martin, Kim Mahood and John Carty- CSIRO Publishing 2013.

Paruku is the Walmajarri name for Lake Gregory in Western Australia. The chapter written by geologist Jim Bowler includes:

"When we looked at a satellite image the Mulan people read it in a way that would put most students of geology to shame. The Walmajarri ability to recognise and translate subtle features on the image to real places on the ground revealed a different sense of spatial perceptions to my own"

As you can see I'm not alone in being intrigued and enthralled when realising that Yapa have a 'different sense of spatial perceptions'.

Back in 1964 at Melbourne University I had been one of Jim Bowler's students who the people of Mulan had, as he put it, 'put to shame'. I recall Jim telling our small geomorphology class to go and see the film 'Lawrence of Arabia', not for its historical significance, but because in it all the desert land-forms on the curriculum are beautifully filmed, including Jim's beloved crescent dunes, which led him to discover Mungo Man.

Pleased to meet you

♫ ♫ ♫

Sympathy for the Devil-Jagger/Richards 1968

Let me introduce myself. I was born in occupied Holland in 1943. My full name is Franklin Delano Baarda, I was named after F. D. Roosevelt America's wartime President. After the war my father got a job with a Dutch bank in Argentina where I spent nine years of my happy childhood. We briefly returned to the Netherlands and two years later, in 1958, we emigrated to Australia. English is my third language. I met my wife Wendy at Melbourne University where I studied geology. We married in 1966 and arrived in Yuendumu in 1973 with our three children.

Wendy came from the Western District of Victoria, which to me was effectively a foreign place. Sensing my anxiety and puzzlement at this different world, a mutual friend gave me Margaret Kiddle's 'Men Of Yesterday: A Social History Of The Western District Of Victoria, 1834-1890' to read. This historical background brought sense to the beliefs and attitudes of the remnants of that squattocratic enclave I was confronted with. It is fair to say that Wendy and I took part in a cultural exchange which changed both our worldviews which would undergo further radical changes after we settled in Yuendumu.

The main reason I had chosen to study geology, apart from liking rocks, is that I saw it as giving me the opportunity to travel to foreign places. I mean this in the nicest of ways when I say that it doesn't get much more foreign than Yuendumu. We are the longest ever Yuendumu resident Kardiya. Sam McKell comes a close second. *Inshallah*, hopefully, we'll be here many more years to come.

When Wendy got her teacher's job, she and the children were on a Tiwa bus en route to Yuendumu. The Tiwa bus service was one of many pioneering Aboriginal owned and run enterprises which sprang up in a window of opportunity and optimism during the so-called Whitlam Era. Tiwa Buses, through lack of support and other reasons, went the way of most such enterprises, the victim of industrial infanticide. It sank into the morass of historical amnesia. It was ahead of its time. After a long hiatus without buses, we again have a regular bus service. A fleet of government subsidised flash new buses now crisscross Central Australia. It is an entirely Kardiya owned and run enterprise. Yapa have once again been relegated to being clients and customers to be 'serviced' (my use of this double entendre is deliberate). But I digress.

It was a drizzly morning when I plonked my family on the bus in Alice Springs, and I was told later that the bus hadn't arrived in Yuendumu until well after dark. Heavy recent rain meant the bus had to plough through mud to Napperby Station, and then more mud to Mt. Allan Station before finally reaching Yuendumu. Ranches in Australia are known as Stations. Wendy and the kids didn't get to see much of the landscape, the bus windows were covered in mud. Wendy hadn't yet learned to orientate herself and by the time the bus arrived at its destination she didn't have a clue where she was. Sometime later she told me she was glad I'd got her the job. She liked Yuendumu. She still does, and now most definitely knows where east, north, west and south are, at least in and around Yuendumu.

Soon after we arrived in Yuendumu, Wendy's parents ventured into the outback and paid us a visit. Not long after their arrival, Wendy's mother answered a knock on the door. My mother-in-law was not expecting to be confronted by a Warlpiri man. Shocked, she waved him away as she exclaimed: *"This is Wendy's house, shoo, shoo!"*

E.O., Wendy's dad, came back from having been shown around the men's museum and wanted to know what 'dum-dum' meant. My father-in-law thought 'dum-dum' might have some deep spiritual meaning because † Darby Jampijinpa Ross who had guided him through the museum, had several times solemnly used the phrase

'Dum-dum in the dreamtime.' Darby had been speaking Aboriginal English: '*Sometime in the dreamtime!*'

Aboriginal English, contrary to popular belief, is not bad or simple English. It is quite varied over Australia, is complex and subtle and follows grammatical rules. I've heard one of our granddaughters switch back and forth seamlessly between Aboriginal English (just for fun) with her friends and Australian Standard English, when talking to us, her grandparents. It was fascinating to listen to and reminded me of when a friend in Montreal had switched seamlessly from French to Quebecois depending on who she was talking to.

Before passing value judgements on Aboriginal English, Kardiya would do well to consider that, whereas nearly all Yapa speak English, almost no Kardiya speak Warlpiri.

I'd gone back to work "out bush" when Wendy's mother decided to wait at home, while Wendy, her dad and the kids went to church to hear a visiting missionary from New Guinea. During their absence the power went off. When they came home they found Wendy's mum had locked herself in and barricaded the doors whilst crouching in fear all alone in the dark. They soon lit a Tilley lamp and candles, but the power stayed off for several days and the meat in the freezer, a whole cut up bullock, defrosted. My mother-in-law felt compelled to save the meat and spent much of her stay making curries and casseroles, which would keep. The power stayed on after that and we were able to enjoy the fruits of her labour long after she had left.

Power outages were quite a common occurrence in those days, especially around breakfast time, but Tony Juttner or †Michael Japangardi Poulson would race to the powerhouse, and usually break the eerie silence by quickly restoring the electricity. Once I'd started working in Yuendumu, whenever the power went out, I would hurry outside and give a few blasts on my trumpet. Soon and out of the blue from the south side of town my reveille style trumpet calls would be echoed. A ritual, I like to think not entirely unlike the call-and-response shouts and hollers of the American slave era cotton fields, evolved between Yuendumu Housing Association manager †Blue Priestley on his bugle and myself on the trumpet. It didn't take long for observant Yapa children to conclude that it was the trumpet and bugle combination that made the power come back on.

Switching on the power (photo - Neil Murray)

Not a good place to be - 1932

Our interaction with a new environment is very much shaped by the circumstances under which we grew up. I had a very fortunate and varied childhood and upbringing which prepared me to embrace, enjoy and appreciate other cultures and languages.

My grandparents on both sides were Dutch born socialists. My father was born in 1917 in Amsterdam, but grew up in a region known as the Ruhrgebiet, the industrial hub of Germany. My grandmother went to stay with her sister in Amsterdam to await the birth of her son (my dad), after which she returned to her home in Mülheim an der Ruhr where the Ruhr river runs into the Rhine river. Dad went to school in an ever increasingly xenophobic Germany, and learnt much about the nature of bullying, prejudice, elitism, authority, control, fascism, racism, sadism, patriotism, extremism, fanaticism, national-ism, totalitarianism, militarism and just plain mean spirited ignorance. Knowledge he passed on to us, his children. At the age of fifteen in 1932 my dad told my grandparents *"This is not a good place for us foreigners to be"* and he ran away from home to return to the Nether-lands. That in the process he kidnapped his two year old sister is another story. During the war, in occupied Holland, my father was involved in some significant acts of sabotage and resistance. He got away with these because of his absolute command of the German language, his second language, which he loved, and his thorough understanding of the German psyche. He fooled the Germans into thinking he was 'one of them'.

Growing up with my parents' stories of their wartime experiences has given me an acute awareness, short of experiencing it, of what it is like to live under occupation, to be dominated and controlled by invaders of another culture, invaders having a different world view, a different *Weltanschauung* as Germans call it, and speaking a different language. I therefore see places like Yuendumu to be under occupation, controlled and dominated by foreigners with a different language and culture. Whilst I recognise that I speak the language and grew up with the values of the oppressor, I think it likely, that if I'd left Yuendumu, whoever replaced me would have been more destructive of Warlpiri culture than me, less likely to notice and appreciate the countless brilliant fragments. My parents also taught me much about the often subtle nature of passive resistance, the pervasive presence of which I perceive to exist in Yuendumu.

Occasionally I tread on thin ice and invoke the Nazi horrors and Fascism to draw attention to what is happening to remote Aboriginal Australia and this often provokes a hostile reaction. How can I possibly compare what is happening in the Northern Territory of Australia to what took place in Sobibor where 34,313 Netherlands citizens were gassed, or in Bergen-Belsen concentration camp? Whilst the reality of that evil abomination called the Holocaust bears no comparison to anything, it should be recognised however, that Aboriginal Australia suffered a decimation of its own.

It is vaguely estimated that the land we now call Australia held 750,000 inhabitants at the time of the First Fleet's arrival in 1788, after which it took less than a year for half the prior inhabitants of the Sydney Basin to die of smallpox. How many died from this disease as it spread inland we will never know. A history of countless massacres of Aborigines by shooting or poison, the so called Frontier Wars, has been hidden from mainstream Australian society and is only recently being revealed and openly discussed.

♪ ♪ ♪

You can say it didn't happen, You can say it's long ago.
You can say it wasn't us, You can say we didn't know,

The last officially recorded massacre in Australia, the Coniston Massacre, a series of punitive raids that took place in 1928, started at Yurrkuru, a mere fifty five kilometres northeast of Yuendumu. The repercussions of these 'killing times' as Yapa refer to them were severe and widespread. †Shorty Jangala Robertson, who was four years old at the time, told us how his family had been camped at Jila (Chilla Well) when news reached them that Kardiya were shooting Yapa. Jila is 130 kilometres northwest of Yuendumu. Shorty's panic stricken family immediately moved a considerable distance further west. After the killings, small groups of Yapa avoided 'civilisation' for a long time at scattered remote places.

A seismic event rocked Yuendumu society when in 2007, the Howard Government in a nasty act of electoral desperation and political opportunism ambushed Clare Martin's Northern Territory Government and launched the Northern Territory Emergency Response, soon to become known as the 'Intervention', upon the N.T. socio-political landscape. This Intervention was the culmination of a couple of centuries of colonial conquest and oppression in Australia.

So strongly do I feel about the injustices to which Aboriginal Australia has been and continues to be subjected, that I'm often unable to restrain myself and put a sock in it. At the beginning of the Intervention, in a letter to the editor of the Centralian Advocate, a prominent Aborigine referred to me as *"that loud whitefellow who claims to speak for my people"* which was rather unfair as I have never made such a claim. There have been occasions I've been silenced or ignored because I'm not a local Aborigine. Such silencing or ignoring was usually done by Kardiya who are even less local than I am, or by Yapa quislings. There have also been occasions on which I'd made erroneous assumptions and Yapa friends have had to pull me up and tell me I was mistaken, as well as instances when I've been rightly accused of being racist. Our ethnocentricity dictates that none of us are entirely devoid of racism but this does not make it right nor excusable.

I told Wendy that I was having second thoughts about including the allusion to Nazism and Fascism in this story. Some may miss the point I try to make and just be offended. As Basil Faulty put it *"Don't mention the war"*. But Wendy was adamant it was part of my story:

"We are all ethnocentric to some extent which is normal and probably necessary. But the Nazis took ethnocentrism to grossly brutal extremes and we need to keep remembering this. We need to learn from this

history. We must remain alert to the acceptance of unfair treatment, unjust laws, racist language and the creeping slide towards dehumanisation of other races, cultures or religions. If we don't, all of those people have died in vain."

And don't get me wrong, I'm very much aware of the many other atrocities, the Rape of Nanking, the Cambodian Killing Fields, the Armenian and Rwandan genocides to mention just a few. I've focused on Nazi Germany because it happens to be what my parents experienced and told me about.

My father, who as I mentioned grew up in pre-Nazi Germany, was an astute witness to the descent into barbarity. He told me that when the Nazis first stood for election they got 3% of the vote. He told me how they systematically dehumanised their scapegoats thereby normalising the abnormal and justifying the unjustifiable. He always maintained that if it could happen in the land that gave us Goethe, Schiller and Schubert it could happen anywhere and anytime. To me this was confirmed by what happened in Argentina, the cosmopolitan country I grew up in, with its so-called 'Dirty War' from 1976 to 1983.

Dad didn't consider Australia to be immune either, and neither do I.

Not a good place to be - 1943

On the 16th April 1943 a few months before I was born, the RAF carried out a bombing raid on the railway yards near the suburb of Haarlem, where my parents lived. The raid claimed eighty five lives and there were forty three severely wounded civilians. In the street of my birth many homes were destroyed. According to historical information the raid failed to hit the target because of inadequate weather reports. No 'smart bombs' back then. The Gimpels were good friends of my parents. Margot Gimpel was expecting her first child at the same time as my mother was expecting me. The house opposite Margot's received a direct hit. Dad raced around the corner to Margot's house and found her slumped in the shower where she'd sought refuge. She looked peaceful and unharmed. A piece of shrapnel had pierced her in the neck and she'd neatly bled to death down the plughole.

Destruction in the Teding van Berkhoutstraat - the street I was born in and where we lived- 1943

As Dad told it to me:

"At great risk, we had a radio mounted under the dinner table. We listened to the Dutch broadcasts of Radio Orange out of London. We were told that the railway workshop in Haarlem had been totally destroyed. In our close vicinity fifty six people had been killed. I helped with loading the corpses onto trucks. Not a single bomb had fallen on the railway yards."

Not surprisingly, Dad often didn't believe what he was told when he listened to the news. He'd been like that ever since I can remember. He infected all of us with such scepticism. Almost none in our immediate family ever thought that there were weapons of mass destruction in Iraq. How do you move and hide a tunnel? As for Colin Powell's child like drawings of chemical weapons factories on the back of trucks? Say no more!

Twelve Lockheed Ventura bombers from RAF 487E squadron took part in the bombing raid.

Setting the scene...

Stereotyping, stigmatisation, propaganda and misinformation or 'fake news', as it is now known, are nothing new under the sun. Since 1788, there has been a huge Communication Gap between the First Australians and the new arrivals. The Gap of Aboriginal disadvantage that the assimilationists have defined and are failing to close, (more on the government's 'Closing the Gap' later), pales into insignificance when compared to the gap author Bruce Pascoe calls, "*the gulf of incomprehension*" this abyss of ignorance, misunderstanding and deliberate deceit.'

Malthus' Essay on the principles of population published in 1826 sets the scene:

> "*...A native with his child, surprised on the banks of the Hawkesbury river by some of our colonists, launched his canoe in a great hurry, and left behind him a specimen of his food, and of the delicacy of his stomach. From a piece of water-soaked wood, full of holes, he had been extracting and eating a large worm. The smell both of the worm and its habitation was in the highest degree offensive. These worms, in the language of the country, are called Cah-bro; and a tribe of natives dwelling inland, from the circumstance of eating these loathsome worms, is named Cah-brogal...*"

That these "loathsome worms" were probably mangrove worms which are not a worm at all, but a filter feeding mollusc, and taste like oysters, is a moot point.

In a second hand book shop in Lorne in Victoria, I chanced upon 'Our Australian Colonies', by Samuel Mossman, an interesting and charming little book published in 1866 by the Religious Tract Society of London. I quote from page 108:

> "*...Shall it be said then that this fair and fertile portion of our common mother earth was destined by the Lord Almighty to be perpetually occupied by the indolent savage? Such a conclusion*

would be contrary to His mandate, where He commands us to 'multiply and replenish the earth' ..."

Stereotyping had begun. How could indolent loathsome-worm consuming savages possibly have a deep spiritual connection to the land? How could they possibly own the unfenced land?

'Terra Nullius' is often misunderstood to mean that the Australian continent was regarded as uninhabited, whereas it is actually a legal construct of British colonialism and means the land has been declared to "*have no ownership and no government*" thus justifying its annexation, especially when mandated to do so by the Almighty.

Loathsome worms

A deliberate act...

....Pour your pitcher of wine into the wide river, and where is your wine? There is only the river... From Assimilation-No!
A poem by Oodgeroo Noonuccal (Kath Walker)

On the 19th November 2010 at the University of New South Wales, they held a National Indigenous Policy and Dialogue Conference. Professor Patrick Dodson, one of Aboriginal Australia's better known deep thinkers, gave the keynote address. Patrick Dodson's speech was titled 'Can Australia Afford Not to be Reconciled?' and included:

"The strategy for the assimilation of our peoples is not a mistake made by low-level bureaucrats on behalf of successive governments who didn't know better. It was and continues to be a deliberate act orchestrated at the highest levels in our society, and no amount of moral posturing can hide that reality. This Assimilation I talk of has not been evidenced by equality, but by further control, incarceration and subjugation to norms and values without our consent."

I couldn't agree more with Patrick Dodson's insightful assertion, it bloody well is deliberate, and now seventy-seven years after I might have been killed in the womb by a 'collateral damage' bomb, which Allied propaganda would have strenuously denied ever having missed its intended target, I don't have to look very far to perceive Pat Dodson's *"This assimilation I talk of..."* in action, nor the propaganda machine that foments it.

As the Bob Dylan song says,

"You don't need a weatherman to tell which way the wind blows"

The Commonwealth Government's assimilation policy was implemented in the 1930s, and replaced the 'smooth the dying pillow' or Protection policy, all being policies that laboured under the erroneous illusion that Aboriginal Australia could be made to conveniently disappear. Assimilation was originally applied only to mixed race people born of Aboriginal and non-aboriginal parentage. Then in 1962, the assimilation policy was rolled out to all Aboriginal people. The Whitlam Government, advised by Nugget Coombs, officially scrapped the policy a decade later in 1972. At the coal face however, the assimilation imperative never ceased to be applied and continues unabated albeit not officially.

Economist H.C.'Nugget' Coombs had been appointed the inaugural Chairman of the Council for Aboriginal Affairs. The council had been set up on the coattails of the now famous and celebrated 1967 Referendum, in which over 90% of voters voted 'yes' to changes to the constitution, which inter alia, formally included Aborigines as part of Australia's population. Whitlam valued the knowledge his friend Nugget had gained from that appointment and, despite his cabinet's resentment, made the most of Nugget as a trusted adviser. Nugget largely wrote the Whitlam Government's policy on Aboriginal affairs, in particular, the commitment to Aboriginal Land Rights.

Starting in the 1960s the introduction of equal wages and the gradual replacement of stockmen on horseback by helicopters, motor bikes and stock trucks, resulted in many Aboriginal people being driven off their lands where on cattle stations they had found refuge and a purpose to their lives. The luckier ones ended up on missions or on Government settlements such as Yuendumu. The more unfortunate ones became fringe dwellers in larger population centres, often away from their traditional lands. For most of the latter, their children had to learn another language and the deep ties to their Jukurrpa were seriously disrupted and damaged if not obliterated. Some languages have disappeared. Others are down to the last few speakers.

Pervasive child removal never ceased albeit a different modus operandi evolved. A complex web of laws and regulations and protocols is now used to ensnare Indigenous children, a web once caught in, it is very difficult to break free from. Child removal has grown into a significant industry.

From Martín Fierro- a 19th. Century classic Argentine epic poem by José Hernández (1872& 1879):

La ley es tela de araña en mi inorancia lo explico
no la tema el hombre rico
nunca la tema el que mande
pues la rompe el bicho grande y solo enrieda a los chicos

The law is like a spider's web, In all 'umility I explain:
the rich man fears it not
neither he that is in command.
The large beetles break free and only the small insects are
ensnared

Authorities refer to child 'protection', 'safety' and 'welfare'. They're too gutless to call it kidnapping.

On Native Reserves and Missions and even in larger towns, de facto segregation reigned. Often a Superintendent or Missionary would, with the best of intentions, rule with an iron fist or with benevolent patronising strictness.

Paul Kelly's song - *(In the land of the) Little Kings*

♫ ♫ ♫

Deliberate policies limiting the number of Kardiya on settlements prevailed, as both missionaries and bureaucrats jealously guarded their condescending and moralistic grip on what they referred to as "our natives". Under Native Welfare rules, Warlpiri people had to get permission from the superintendent to come and go from their community and it was forbidden for Kardiya to enter a settlement without authorisation.

These strict control measures were much motivated by a justified concern for miscegenation. It was a common occurrence for white men to freely molest and force themselves on native women and for Kardiya society and law enforcement to turn a blind eye. So called 'gins' and 'lubras', euphemistically referred to as 'black velvet', were considered fair game, and there wasn't much Yapa men could do about it, and if they did they'd do so at their peril.

Just as sovereignty of Aboriginal land was never ceded, so too the authorities never ceded their protection and assimilation agendas and haven't done so to this day. 'Protection' is a euphemism for control, 'assimilation' is the single-minded policy that dare not speak its real name.

As luck would have it…

On 11th February 1958, my dad's forty-first birthday, the Baarda family arrived in Melbourne on the *MS Johan van Oldenbarnevelt*. I was fourteen years old and eager to embrace language number three and develop a third identity. That same year Minister for Territories Paul Hasluck, a strong believer and supporter of assimilation, paid a visit to Yuendumu. Unlike at present, when visitors and politicians often arrive at our airstrip to be met by no one and then have to summon a ride 'into town' by mobile phone, back then the far fewer important visitors were met with anticipation and some pomp and ceremony.

A group of respected old men had been issued with new long sleeved white shirts, neckties, ironed shorts, long white socks and shiny black shoes. The importance of the visitor had been impressed upon them. A favourable impression would be the key to future federal funding for Yuendumu. There they were gathered at the dusty airstrip all standing in line. Hasluck's plane taxied in, a door opened, an equerry installed some steps and raised a small Australian flag and the Minister descended from the plane, at which point an excited Jimmy Jungarrayi broke ranks, strode forward and with an extended welcoming hand exclaimed: *"Money! Money!"*

Ted Egan (Japangardi) is now the only person alive to have witnessed this emblematic cross-cultural interaction and he tells me that Hasluck was most impressed by his reception. So what has changed? Apart from a massive explosion in rules and administrative requirements which in turn necessitated the abandonment of the policies of limiting the number of Kardiya on communities, as the French say:

Plus ça change, plus c'est la même chose - the more things change, the more they stay the same.

We still have Yapa under the stranglehold of Kardiya power and control clamouring: *"Money! Money!"*.

*Jimmy Jungarrayi at the 1959 Alice Springs Bangtail Muster. Berger
Paints used the photo in an advertising campaign, and paid Jimmy £20
which was equivalent to 40 weeks Yapa wages at the time.
(Photo provided by Ted Egan)*

"Take it right back cause I don't want it in here"

🎵 🎵 🎵

Sung by Bessie Smith Composed by Evelyn Wilson 1929

Ted Egan was the Superintendent at Yuendumu from 1957 to 1963. In 1958 Ted sent the first semi-trailer load of Kingstrand house kits to arrive in Yuendumu back to whence it came. Ted told the distraught driver (*"I'll lose my job!"*) not to worry, as Ted himself would take full responsibility. Ted told me that the Kingstrands were ovens in the summer and freezers in the winter and that they were assembled and installed by Kardiya contractors who invariably denigrated Yapa.

Ted got stonemason Arthur Hutchins, with local labour, to build a stone house at the 4-mile farm. They'd even set up a lime kiln in which they produced quicklime by burning naturally occurring calcrete to cement the natural stones; no need for expensive cement sourced half a continent away. Sending back the Kingstrands wasn't the only time Ted put his job on the line. Unsolicited, Ted had been sent a large quantity of galvanised irrigation pipes with instructions to install these at the farm. Watering the veggie garden at the farm by hand kept many Yapa usefully and convivially occupied. The irrigation pipes proved ideal for building cattle yards. This Ted did with an almost all Yapa workforce. Ted was ahead of his time as self-determination wasn't yet official policy.

Almost three decades later a convoy of trucks loaded with building material arrived in Nyirrpi, 160 Km west of Yuendumu. The building contractors had unloaded the trucks, when they were confronted by †Paul Quinlivan, the Nyirrpi community adviser. Paul waved a copy of the contract at them and pointed out the local employment clause. The contract had been granted on the condition that the contractors employ locals. By unloading the trucks without local involvement they had already shown they had no intention of complying with this contractual obligation. When Paul made it plain that they weren't to be exempted from this clause, the contractors immediately reloaded their trucks and departed and reneged on the contract. This was the last time such a showdown was to occur in Yuendumu or Nyirrpi. No one stood in their way when all subsequent building construction by outside contractors didn't, with a few exceptions, contribute anything to local participation nor the local economy.

When Wendy started work as a teacher in Yuendumu, she was initially installed into a Health Department flat with our children. The Matron told her that she shouldn't allow native children into the flat. Those 'native children' were Wendy's pupils and they had names and they came to play with our children whom they'd befriended at school. At a barbecue Wendy was told by Barry Lambshed, the Superintendent *"You'll love this community, there is no one here over thirty"*. Shocked, she asked: *"What? Do people here die that young?"* Barry had been talking only about Kardiya, as if Yapa didn't exist. For a while I continued to work 'out bush' for Central Pacific Minerals. I came home as often as I could and was tolerated as a 'house husband', but I wasn't part of the long white socks brigade, the colonial expatriate clique, which was soon to disappear.

In hindsight, the long white socks Native Welfare employees seem benign compared to present day Kardiya contractors and government employees. For all their assumption of superiority, their racist attitudes and blatant use of racist terms, they actually had a higher opinion of Yapa skills and abilities than their successors. They expected Yapa to work and trusted them to do so and never saw them as useless and helpless clients. And they knew or gave them their names.

Traditional dancing

Paul Hasluck wasn't to be the only Minister of the Crown to visit Yuendumu, many followed.

In the late 1970s, a much anticipated visitor was Minister for Aboriginal Affairs Ian Viner. Minister Viner was flying down from Yirrkala (East Arnhem Land) where he had presented the first title deeds issued under the new NT Land Rights Act. Yuendumu was next.

At the Men's Museum where a magnificent ground painting had been prepared for the Minister, Sam Brown asked me for a lift to the airstrip.

Sam Brown was employed as a plumber by Yuendumu Council, He had a prominent nose which left legendary Hollywood character Schnozzle Durante's nose for dead. We all knew him as *Mulyuwiri* (big nose). Furthermore alcoholic Sam's nose was bright red, like Rudolph's.

In hindsight taking Sam to the airstrip was a serious mistake. The men were getting themselves painted up ready to welcome the Minister. When the plane landed, as the Minister stepped out of the plane, the men seated on the ground started to chant accompanied by clicking boomerangs, when suddenly, a painted up drunken Kardiya with a prominent nose sprung up frantically waving a pair of boomerangs and doing a Saint Vitus dance.

This was the biggest, to use Aboriginal English "shame job" I can recall.

Incidentally, Ian Viner and Fred Chaney are in my opinion the best Aboriginal Affairs Ministers we've ever had. Both are from Western Australia.

The next day, †Tim Japangardi Langdon asked me to come along as a witness when Mulyuwiri was called on the mat. There was our plumber, facing our council of elders. *"We are very sorry for you, old man,"* was the opening remark. Warlpiri capacity for forgiveness never ceases to amaze me. Reading between the lines, I knew that the elders were prepared to give Mulyuwiri a second chance. Mulyuwiri however couldn't read between the lines, nor am I sure he could read at all, *"If you're going to be like that, I won't be fixing any more taps, blah blah blah..."* he angrily raved. Once again, *"We are very sorry for you, old man,"* hint hint, to no avail. In the end, he left them no option but to sack him.

In Mulyuwiri's short Yuendumu career, I don't think he fixed a single tap.

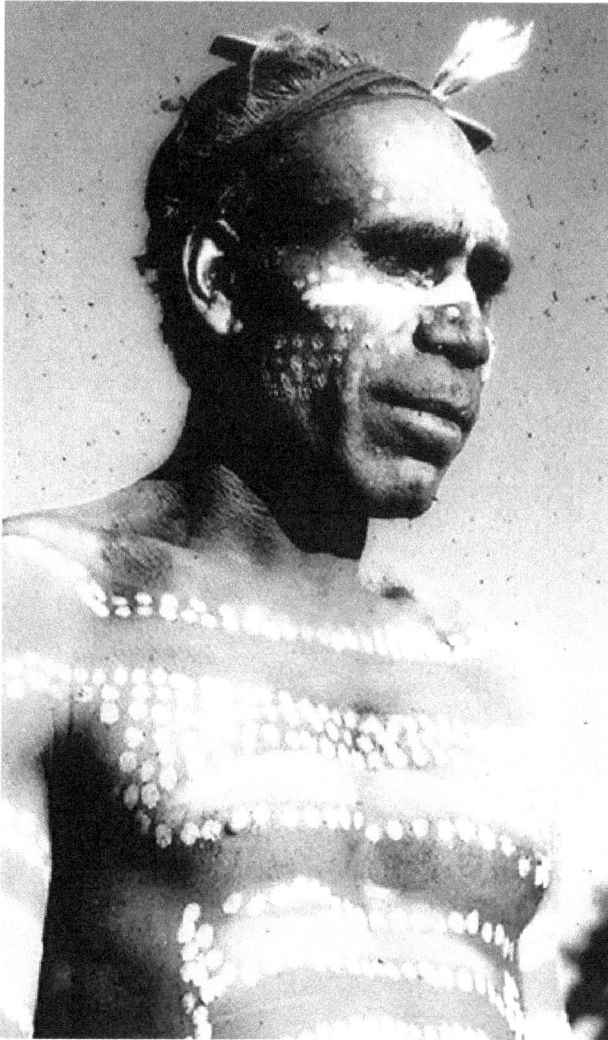

Tim Japangardi Langdon (photo: Ted Egan)

Will the circle be unbroken?...

♫ ♫ ♫

A.P.Carter-1935

The Warlpiri use what anthropologists call a matrilineal kinship system. At the risk of making your eyes glaze over, I'll try to explain the system because so-called skin-names are an integral and important part of Yapa social fabric. By all means skip the next few pages and, if you wish, come back to them after you've read further.

Skin-name is a corruption of 'kin-name' derived from the anthropological 'kin naming system', the latter English phrase being rather meaningless to Yapa. The Warlpiri have eight male skin-names starting with the letter J, e.g. Jangala, and eight equivalent female skin-names starting with the letter N, Nangala. Jangala and Nangala are siblings.

Everyone is related to everyone. In all, a simultaneously complex yet simple system of social glue. A truly wonderful system of social and mathematical beauty. Everyone has others they are obligated to care for, others who are obligated to care for them. They have authority over and the right to discipline some others and there are others who have authority over them and the right to discipline. Mutual communal obligation and privilege. No man is an island.

This non-hierarchical system is a perfect inoculation against the corruption of power. From the moment Yapa are born they have a predetermined skin-name. It is not only who they are, but also what they are, how they relate to others, and others relate to them, who they should marry and who they should not. It determines how they relate to the land passed down from their father's father. Passed down from their mother's family is their role as guardians and carers of their mother's family land. It is a part of their identity, of their very being.

Kardiya who stay on Warlpiri land will sooner or later be assigned a skin-name. Often, but not always, such naming results from a friendship or mark of reciprocal respect or as an expression of Yapa generosity. This is not a feather in the cap, but the cap itself. Wendy was assigned the skin-name Nangala and this automatically made me Jungarrayi and our children Japaljarri and Napaljarri. Thus functions the system.

If a Kardiya is assigned a skin-name, all that Kardiya's relatives are automatically named by default, the assigned skin-names being determined by how they are related to that Kardiya. It goes without saying that these potentially numerous Kardiya are mostly oblivious to their newly assigned skin-names. Kardiya need to have a skin-name, to make it easier for Yapa to relate to them and include them into the framework of Yapa society. When my sister's daughter came to visit I introduced her as Nampijinpa because introducing her as Mrs. Hunter would have meant nothing to Yapa. As soon as I introduced her as Nampijinpa everyone immediately knew how she was related to me and how they were related to her.

A skin-name is a label, like a wedding ring or a Polynesian flower in the hair, but it is much more than that. As I said it is social glue, a scaffolding, an integral part of Warlpiri social fabric and existence.

Kardiya reaction to be "given" a skin-name ranges from total disinterest to ecstatic exhilaration. At one end of this spectrum there is, *"I was made a member of the tribe!"*, which of course is a bit of nonsense. If someone addresses me as Señor Baarda this doesn't make me a Spaniard!

I asked Margit Bowler, a linguist who resides in the USA, and who keeps returning to Yuendumu at every opportunity she gets, to tell me what she likes about Yuendumu and this is some of what she wrote:

> *"It still makes me happy every time someone asks for my skin-name which is Napangardi and then when I tell them, they immediately work out and name our relationship. When I first came to Yuendumu, I was worried that I would feel very isolated in the desert, since I didn't know anyone when I arrived. I didn't expect this feeling of interconnectedness which is so precious. Of course, if everyone is family and everyone is related, you will feel obligated to look out for*

each other more... It's such a simple idea, but so different from western ideas of kinship and social structures. I really miss it when I go away."

Whilst the skin-name Margit, an only child, was assigned, can in no way be said to have made her a member of the tribe, it did give her the extended family she had always yearned for.

This year, the pandemic prevented Margit from returning.

Brett, a volunteer youth worker, was chuffed and felt honoured when he was given an Aboriginal name. The name he was given was 'Mangarri', the Warlpiri word for bread. Some of Wendy's pupils at Yuendumu school called her 'Mrs. Jara' and thought this was very funny. Took us a while to figure that one out. *Jara* means fat and includes butter. Baarda sounds like butter. Brett sounds like bread. What is orange and sounds like a parrot? Of course: a carrot!

Warlpiri children and I share a love of word-play which is so much more enjoyable when it crosses language barriers.

Wendy is Nangala, Wendy's sister Diane is also Nangala. Wendy and Diane's mother Zette was Napangardi. Diane's daughters, Lisa and Sophie are both Napaljarri. The Warlpiri word for the maternal grand-mother/granddaughter relationship is *jaja*. The term is reciprocal, Zette would have called Lisa and Sophie *jaja*, and Lisa and Sophie would have called Zette *jaja*. Lisa and Sophie's daughter's daughters, if they have them, will again be Napangardi, like Zette.

To try and get your head around this think of the seasons. Now it is winter, two seasons from now it will be summer. So what was it two seasons ago? Yes sir, winter. You go to the past and you go to the future and you end up in the same place. Back to the future. Those mathematically inclined will discern the circular nature of this.

El tiempo:
> *No tuvo nunca principio ni jamás acabará,*
> *porque el tiempo es una rueda, y rueda es eternidá.*
> (Time never had a beginning, nor will it ever end,
> because time is a wheel, and a wheel is eternity.)

From previously quoted Argentine poem 'Martín Fierro'

The skin-name system is timeless. Yapa society is a 'time's cycle' society. We Kardiya are 'time's arrow' people. Neither is better or worse than the other, just different. Vastly different. To get a deeper insight into this difference I can recommend † Stephen Jay Gould's priceless book, 'Time's Arrow, Time's Cycle - Myth and Metaphor in the Discovery of Geological Time.'

I'm often asked what the purpose of the skin-name system is. Why did it evolve? I don't think everything necessarily needs to have a raison d'etre. I suspect that one advantage of the system is that it minimises inbreeding in a society which practised endogamy, marriage within a closed system. I am told for instance that colour blindness was non-existent in pre-contact Yapa society. Hope you're still with me, I realise the skin-name system is rather confusing and not all that interesting to many who are unfamiliar with it. Like Chinese writing.

Warlpiri Skin Name Circle

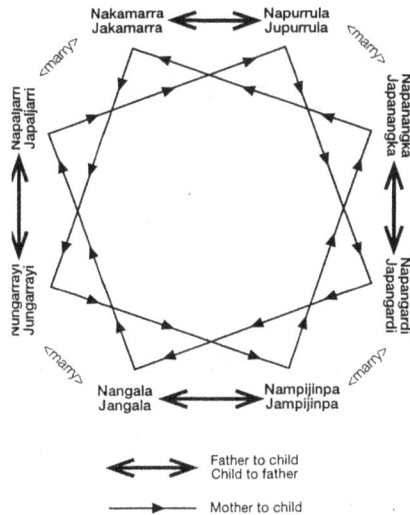

Natives (Los pueblos originarios)

Like so many 'western' children I grew up barely aware of the existence of the cornucopia of indigenous languages and cultures. In the 1950's Argentina of my childhood, Argentinian 'natives' did not exist. We were oblivious to the fact that a significant proportion of the population have the black shiny hair, high cheekbones, almond eyes and bronze skins of the original inhabitants.

My brother and I regularly used to banter with the Paraguayan labourers who dug the sewerage trenches. We children were amused by their sing-song Guarani conversations, and by their high pitched laughter when we repeated what were undoubtedly rude Guarani words.

But these were not Argentinian Indians and thus didn't count. The history books taught us that General Rosas, or was it General Roca?, had defeated the Indians and in our minds they had been wiped out and no longer existed. Just like later I was to 'learn' that Truganini was Tasmania's last surviving Aborigine.

It was indeed Juan Manuel de Rosas I learnt about in primary school. (Image - Wikipedia)

What's in a name?

When in 1958 we settled in Moe (pronounced Ma-oo-wee) in Victoria, indigenous people were irrelevant to our daily lives. A common belief in Moe was that Moe is an Aboriginal name. Wikipedia tells me it is in Kurnai, the local Australian Aboriginal language. In the Moe of the late 1950's Aborigines effectively did not exist and there was nothing to indicate that they ever had except for the assumed origin of the town's name.

Dad and I were postage stamp collectors and the only Aboriginal thing I can remember from back then was the iconic Australian stamp which featured the image of an Aboriginal man. A similar image can now be found on the Australian two dollar coin. Recently I found out that the Aboriginal man in question was 'One-pound Jimmy' Tjungarrayi†, also known as '*Kwatje*' the Arrernte word for water.

Jungarrayi had been chained to a tree but subsequently escaped during the raids of the Coniston Massacre. Tommy Watson further enlightened me about 'One-pound Jimmy'. So intertwined are Yapa relationships that it turns out that some of my own grandchildren are the great grandchildren of that Jungarrayi's youngest brother. I'll be darned.

Older Yapa remember Jimmy who was famous Aboriginal artist †Clifford Possum's father. My informants told me Jimmy had ended up living on Narwietooma Station, not far from the Tanami Road's Papunya turn-off. Narwietooma, approximately 150 km distant from Yuendumu, was owned by well known aviation pioneer Eddie Connellan. Connellan's airline Connair regularly flew a mail and passenger service to Yuendumu until 1980. Eddie Connellan's ancient and beautiful Rolls Royce is prominently displayed in a glass case at Alice Springs airport.

Less than an hour's drive north of Moe there is the old gold mining town of Walhalla, and not far from Walhalla there is Mt. Erica and the small town of Erica which was named after it. Valhalla is the Norse mythical place where warriors slain in battle end up. Erica is the female equivalent of Eric, a name which has its origins in Old Norse.

The poets and writers Jørgen Engebretsen Moe and Peter Christen Asbjørnsen collected Norse fairy tales, myths and stories during the nineteenth century and are credited with having had a crucial influence in developing the Norwegian language and identity. Moe's Post office was opened in 1862. So is Moe an Aboriginal place name or was Moe named after a Norwegian poet?

First contact…

"…And although the little presents which we had left there before had not yet been taken away, we left other of somewhat more value, consisting of cloth, looking glasses, combs, and beads, and then went up into the country…but we only saw one of the people, who the moment he discovered us ran away." .

James Cook 1st May 1770 (during his first Pacific voyage)
(Which begs the question as to what the unclaimed little presents of lesser value might have been).

My first brief encounter with Aboriginal Australia was in 1965 at Roebourne, in the Pilbara region of Western Australia. I hired an Aboriginal man as a guide during a reconnaissance of known copper occurrences in the region. At the dust-blown Roebourne Native Reserve some kilometres out of town I was taken aside by the Superintendent who quietly told me I shouldn't overpay the man lest I upset the status quo apple cart.

Then in 1966 when I was 23 years old, the same age my father had been when the German Wehrmacht (armed forces) occupied Holland, the firm of consultant geologists I had joined upon graduation, sent me to Mount Anderson Station in the Fitzroy Trough of the Canning Basin.

Mount Anderson Station in the Kimberley region of Western Australia had been bought cheaply after a drought. The lucky new owner owned a green flourishing station when some fortuitous rains arrived soon after his purchase. Our exploration team was camped in the wool shed. We were looking for bituminous coal. Mount Anderson Station was a mixed cattle and sheep station.

A party of Oklahomans arrived complete with their own fancy saddles and wearing expensive Red Wing cowboy boots. They had purchased the station but weren't interested in paying for the sheep. I overheard one of the cowboys ask the station owner ''*What about these here niggras?"* The station owner reassured him not to worry, the 'niggras' would soon be gone.

The station owner was given a short period of time to sell the sheep. The owner was over the moon when he sold the sheep to neighbouring Liveringa Station for two pounds a head.

I asked one old 'niggra' what was he going to do when the new bosses took over. He smiled at me and with his bottom lip protruding and his chin pointing eastward he gave a far away look and said in a languid tone of voice, *"Me go langa Liveringa."*

The first truck load of sheep was dispatched and thus Liveringa Station now had a flock of mixed brand sheep. The Mt. Anderson Station owner couldn't find any more sheep. In desperation he got up in his single engine plane and searched all over his property, to no avail. Distraught he said he somehow had lost 3,000 sheep. Perhaps I jumped to conclusions when I reckoned the 3,000 missing sheep were set free *'langa Liveringa'* together with the 'niggras'.

In 1973 an excision from the Liveringa Pastoral Lease was granted to local Aborigines which became the community of Looma (a blue tongue lizard Jukurrpa). I can't claim to know very much about Looma, but I did notice when finding it on Google Earth that Looma's largest building is labelled the 'Multi-Functional Police Facility' and thus it has this in common with Yuendumu which also has a large Police Complex. The Yuendumu Police Complex was also intended to be multi-functional, which didn't happen however. Yuendumu Police Station's only function, that I am aware of, is to uphold Kardiya law and to send a significant number of Yapa residents to prison.

In 2014 Gina Rinehart, Australia's richest woman acquired a 50% stake in Liveringa Station. The station no longer runs sheep. It has 22,000 head of cattle. In 2019 a mass death of over 40 critically endangered sawfish took place on Liveringa Station. The possibility that the over one billion litres of water pumped out of a nearby tributary of the Fitzroy River for irrigation purposes may have had anything to do with the mass death has not been investigated, yet Gina Rinehart and her cronies are applying for a 300 fold increase in the amount of water they are allowed to pump annually out of the Fitzroy River, the damming of which is being promoted by several parties. Surprise, surprise, Looma Yapa are opposed to these developments!

On my return from the Kimberlies Wendy and I got married in Melbourne in December, after she completed her studies and I had complied with my future father-in-law's stipulation that I had at least $2,000 in the bank. Donovan, our oldest son was conceived at Lake Carey between Leonora and Laverton in Western Australia. Our second son Joseph, was born in Roebourne. This was the time of the Nickel Boom, and for the first time in Australia, due to a shortage of geologists, women were allowed in exploration camps. Male geologists refused to go 'bush' without their spouses.

I was hired out to Newmont and towing a caravan ranged over the Western Australian Goldfields and Nullarbor regions on various drilling and mapping projects. Wendy came along as the unpaid cook, and Newmont appointed †Didla Graham, a Wongai man from Kalgoorlie, as my offsider. Didla very soon reversed our roles and made me his apprentice in bush skills. He showed me what sandalwood shrubs looked like so we often enjoyed scented campfires. He made me drive and taught me how to retrieve a vehicle sunk to the axles in a clay pan. He also taught me how by observing the vegetation not to get bogged in the first place. He taught us how racism often in subliminal ways manifests itself in Australian society. It was 1967 the year of the aforementioned referendum. Didla asked what the referendum was all about. We told him:*"Well, it means your mob will be counted."* *"Big deal,"* retorted Didla, *' 'We have been counted and measured many times over."* Didla had been issued with a so-called 'dog tag' which meant he was no longer registered as a ward of the state and was thus entitled to drink at a pub without getting arrested. He was twice my age and received half my salary.

When I was transferred to the Pilbara, (hired out to U.S.Steel) Wendy got a job at Weeriana Hostel in Roebourne, where Aboriginal children were boarded so they would attend school. Wendy joined Rosie and Eve, two young Aboriginal women working in the kitchen. Rosie and Eve secretly taught themselves each other's language. 'Talking in lingo' was forbidden at the hostel for both children and staff. Although the couple running the hostel had the best of intentions, the Hostel System had a disastrous effect on Western Australian languages.

This is how Wendy remembers the hostel:

"There were 60 children and about six staff. The children ranged in age from 4 to 16 years. They came off stations and the reserve. Some had itinerant parents who were too far away to pick them up when the hostel closed for Christmas. These children went to the reserve where a good Christian Aboriginal woman looked after a number of children. The aim of the hostel was to ensure they went to school. It was run on a shoestring, cabbage, potato, pumpkin every night, plus a bit of variety in meat or fish. It was a government hostel but was run by a very Christian couple who managed very well with few resources. It was tough, especially for the little children who tried so hard to tell us things but we couldn't understand them. The older girls did their best to comfort them."

Glowing in the dark...

After our stint in Nickel Boom Western Australia we spent a year and a half in Canada. In 1971 we returned to Australia, firstly by road to Panama, and then by ship. When MV Tahitien reached Sydney, as Wendy walked down the gangplank carrying a guitar, a wharfie sang out *"Gissa chune on ya banjo luv."* We knew then we were back home. Australia the land of the Fair Go.

There followed a year in pre-cyclone Darwin. It was in Darwin that I became an Australian citizen. The Vietnam war, which we considered to be a terrible mistake, was still raging and we'd heard there were a lot of Vietnamese babies awaiting adoption. Considering all the damage we had done as a nation, adopting a war orphan seemed the least we could do. When we went to the Darwin adoption agency we were told they didn't handle international adoptions and we were presented with a list of about ten Aboriginal babies who were in foster care and up for adoption. It felt weird to be offered a choice, a bit like shopping. We only looked at one baby. That is when we adopted our then ten month old Yapa daughter Jenny.

We finally arrived at Yuendumu in January 1973.

Central Pacific Minerals N.L. (CPM) was in joint venture with the Italian Agip Australia Ltd. and the German Urangesellschaft MbH. CPM was a small Australian company at risk of running out of exploration money before finding and developing a commercial ore body. Both overseas partners on the other hand, because they were not in danger of running out of money, were far more interested in adding to their worldwide inventory of uranium resources rather than to aim for commercial development. These poles apart imperatives resulted in the parties not being able to agree on a budget and programme.

An emergency budget, so as to meet the minimum requirements of the Department of Mines & Energy (DME) to maintain the tenements in good standing, was brought into play. Large areas were covered by car-borne radiometric surveys. These surveys were highly inefficient and time consuming as compared to higher budget airborne surveys but they put lots of numbers on maps submitted to the DME. This is not unlike numerous reports dealing with the socalled 'Aboriginal Problem', reports which are relatively meaningless but fill many pages with drivel to satisfy the bureaucracy.

Murray Wood and I were to survey an area west of Napperby Creek. Murray drove and I recorded scintillometer readings every 100 metres. Scintillometers measure radioactivity and have replaced geiger counters. I told Murray that he was to head west and, that seeing he was the driver, it would be his responsibility to fix tyre punctures. I gave Murray permission to deviate if he so desired to prevent punctures, which he did with consummate skill. All our lines when plotted onto a map were exactly parallel and deviated six degrees from true west, which was where the sun was setting that time of year. The lines measured 10% longer than the distance on the map, easily dealt with when plotting the readings. Murray had weaved in and out and continuously compensated so the end result was an accurately aimed straight line. Instantaneous sub-conscious puncture-less vector addition.

Meanwhile Urangesellschaft's representative had spent a day or so installing and calibrating a dashboard mounted compass. This was not an easy task because a vehicle is essentially a lump of steel on wheels. Later we would hear him on the radio to the Alice Springs office: *"Oond I need sree tayas oond faive teeoobes oond faive peckets of tayah petches."* He had ploughed through the mulga scrub, in a straight line, eyes firmly fixed on the compass. Like a Panzer Division.

Murray and I were the first to stumble onto the Bigrlyi uranium prospect, sixty five kilometres west of Yuendumu. Now I wish we had never found it and I hope it never gets mined, but at the time it was very exciting.

Vaughan Springs -Yapawaraji is by far the best permanent surface water source on Warlpiri land and occurs on the lower eastern slope of the large and long Mt. Davidson. Mt. Doreen station's current homestead is at Vaughan Springs. The uranium prospect stretches in a parallel line just south of the Treuer Range at the western end of which is Mt. Davidson. The Warlpiri name for Mt. Davidson is Pikilyi after which Bigrlyi prospect was named. My Warlpiri spelling back then left much to be desired.

† John Ivanac, Central Pacific Minerals' chief geologist liked the name very much because the German and Italian joint venture partners, with whom he was having somewhat acrimonious relations at the time, would never be able to pronounce Bigrlyi. As far as I know they never did pronounce Bigrlyi correctly. You try it, in a German or an Italian accent!

Sitting on a hillside overlooking the discovery valley just before heading home to Yuendumu, in the setting sun shadows, we noticed that there was something different about the rocks down below than those we'd been traversing on foot when taking what had been low monotonous scintillometer readings. We descended into the valley and when we came to what would eventually be anomaly № 7 the scintillometer went crazy. Within days we'd outlined from west to east anomalies № 1 to № 14 and had even enlisted Murray's son, David Japanangka Woods, to dig a few shallow trenches in soil which covered radioactive areas at anomaly № 8. Breaking open a small 'white ant' mound, at what became anomaly № 6, we found a high and visible content of bright yellow carnotite. Carnotite is a uranium mineral. Let me put your mind at ease, we did not find double headed termites that glowed in the dark. Anomaly № 1 was near Yurnmaji soakage, where some decades earlier the indomitable and famous Miss Olive Pink had camped with a Warlpiri family. The water hole now watered a herd of cattle which was evidenced by a strong smell of cow shit and a quagmire of muddy hoof prints. The water was undrinkable. A couple of kilometres further east CPM's exploration camp was set up near anomaly № 4 at Wanalyurrpa, just south of the next gap in the Treuer Range. An airstrip was cleared just north of this gap.

On a subsequent occasion as we were once again heading home around sunset Murray pointed to some light blue shrubs four hundred metres south of our track: *"Those are the same bushes as there are at anomaly № 3."* We made a quick detour and found the easternmost anomaly № 15, which had been faulted away from the main mineralized trend.

In a former life Murray had worked as a stockman on Mt. Doreen Station on which Bigrlyi prospect is located. Murray knew this country like the back of his hand and during our prospecting work, without hesitation, took me straight to and showed me a place at anomaly № 5 where as he put it, *"some Kardiya had cracked a rock."* I worked out that that would have been the Bureau of Mineral Resources geologists who more than a decade earlier had geologically mapped the Mount Doreen 1:250,000 map sheet. The government geologists quite clearly hadn't been armed with geiger counters! Later when I headed to some outcrops east of anomaly № 15, Murray told me not to bother "*Me and Mahdeo already checked there.*" That had been Agip's representative Amadeo Muraro two years earlier.

Then there was the time when I was driving on a bush track and Murray sang out, ''*slow down, there is a big hole in the road around the corner.*" There sure was. It took me a while to work out that Murray hadn't been on that track in years. Following our discoveries, a low level airborne radiometric survey failed to find any additional near surface radioactivity. Murray and I hadn't missed a thing.

Back in those days many Yuendumu men carried a *karli* which is one of those hefty non-returning, almost a metre long, Central Australian boomerangs. Occasionally I would carry one myself, it was the thing to do and felt kinda nice.

Murray and I were looking for a lead mineral occurrence, mentioned in a Mines Department publication. This was west of Wanipi, and east of a uranium prospect that CPM had named Dingo's Rest. We went on foot through light scrub. Suddenly, with a whooosh, a bush turkey took off and Murray's boomerang swished through the air on the turkey's tail. The turkey got away, only just. It all happened in a millisecond. I never spotted the turkey until it took off a mere few metres from where we were walking. I had been looking out through different eyes.

Whereas Murray gave me the first inkling of the relationship of Yapa memory to place, I was to learn that this relationship is phenomenal and almost beyond Kardiya imagination. You might be travelling to Alice Springs with a Yapa friend, and as you zip past a certain area on the side of the road, you'll be reminded that that is where you had a flat tyre, or had hit a kangaroo or stopped for a lunch break on a previous mutual trip, and when you say you didn't remember, which is fair enough, because that was at least ten years ago, you'd be told who else was in the car at the time and how they were seated and what they spoke about, in case that jogs your memory, (no chance!)

My apprenticeship with Murray soon led me to the conclusion that the biggest difference in how Yapa and Kardiya see the world, is that we Kardiya have a temporal worldview and Yapa have a spatial worldview. Time and space. These are not mutually exclusive. Both Kardiya and Yapa have east, west, north and south, yesterday, today and tomorrow. But it is the emphasis, the frequency and contexts in which these are used which greatly differentiates both worlds.

These different ways of seeing the world find expression in countless ways and can lead to much mutual misunderstanding, but can also be a source of wonderment for those prepared to open their minds and eyes and glance from either side, across this cross-cultural canyon.

La persistencia de la memoria: (The persistence of memory)

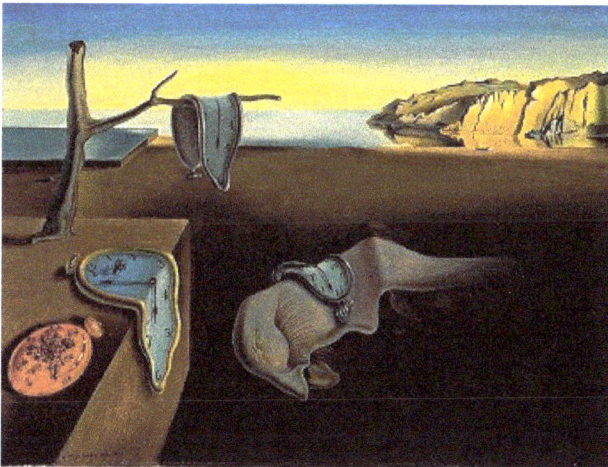

A 1931 painting by Salvador Dali - (Wikipedia)

Role clarity…

When we first arrived in Yuendumu in the early 1970's it was in effect a colonial outpost. Yuendumu was referred to as Yuendumu settlement. Almost imperceptibly over time it came to be called Yuendumu community, which is what it is now known as.

Yuendumu had a core of buildings and houses fringed by camps consisting of humpies known as *yujuku,* and windbreaks known as *yunta.* Kardiya lived in the houses and Yapa lived in the humpies which they had constructed out of corrugated iron sheets, earth, timber, tree branches and canvas. Notwithstanding Ted Egan's earlier efforts at preventing such, between the town centre and the camps there were now rows of Kingstrands. The Kingstrands also called stage one transitional houses, quickly became known as 'donkey houses'. Some bright spark had come up with the idea that Yapa should get accustomed, in stages, to live in houses. The idea had some merit, but there was a significant flaw in the execution of the plan. Stage one houses had no electricity, running water, cooling or heating or anything much to coax Yapa away from their humpies. The donkey houses ended up being used for storage and to shelter from rain or storm. Outside, humpy life with its open fires and congenial, communal social interaction continued.

In between the rows of donkey houses there were ablution blocks which clearly had not been designed to cater for the number of people who used them. To enter these facilities one had to step from stone to stone as one crossed a moat like pool of foul fetid water. It wasn't very nice. Those Kardiya who scoffed at and blamed Yapa for the conditions at the ablution blocks, when making their disparaging value judgements, would not be aware of nor take into consideration the fact that the modern London sewerage system wasn't much older than a century.

Not until after the donkey houses had their own showers and toilets installed were the ablution blocks bulldozed out of existence.

Another feature of the earlier part of our stay in Yuendumu was the effect on Aboriginal Affairs of the ex-New Guinea 'hands'. Papua New

Guinea became self governing on 1st December 1973 and gained its independence soon thereafter on 16th September 1975. These events resulted in a large number of Australian expatriate bureaucrats and public servants, including patrol officers, the so-called *kiaps*, becoming surplus to requirement. ASOPA- the Australian School of Pacific Administration, which trained officers destined to work in New Guinea and the Pacific Islands, had in anticipation of New Guinea independence expanded its brief to encompass the Northern Territory. All Natives are the same after all! The influence of the significant number of these New Guinea 'hands' and ASOPA graduates who ended up placed at that other colonial frontier, namely the NT, was very noticeable, not least by the ubiquitous wearing of long white socks.

Another way this influence manifested itself was the way some Kardiya addressed Yapa in pseudo New Guinea Pidgin. Usually in a patronising tone of voice one would hear such phrases as: *"Him proper good one hey?"* or *"You bin go langa Papunya?"*

Myself, I was once asked in all earnestness by a campaigning politician: *"How do you talk to these people?"* Using one's voice perhaps? Certainly not in a watered down mockery of Tok Pisin!

Harry Nelson recalled being addressed by † Ralph Hunt, the Minister for the Interior, with: *"You bin live here longa longa time?"* to which Harry had replied, *"All my fucking life mate!"*

In 1973 stockmen still plied their trade on horseback and a Yapa 'housegirl' and a Yapa gardener were appointed to every Kardiya household. The Department of Aboriginal Affairs had large numbers of Yapa on a training allowance, carrying out many diverse tasks which are now outsourced to outside contractors. There was a communal kitchen where Yapa men cooked a variety of stews with locally slaughtered animals and locally grown vegetables. Minor housing, plumbing and mechanical repairs were carried out by Yapa. Fences were erected by Yapa. Clothes were washed by Yapa. Yuendumu had a farm which included a piggery, a citrus grove, and a veggie garden. Yapa had role clarity, even if they were subservient roles.

Monday to Friday, four unregistered tractors towing trailers and driven by four unlicensed drivers, would set off in the four cardinal directions from Yuendumu. A group of uninsured volunteers would jump onto each trailer. Late in the afternoon the trailers returned with the volunteers triumphantly and perilously perched on top of huge piles of firewood which were then distributed to all the camps. Robin Japanangka Granites recalls one occasion, when Barney Brown's trailer got detached from his tractor. Barney was hard of hearing and didn't realise what was happening until he noticed lumps of wood flying past his ears. Peggy Brown was launching these projectiles at the rapidly receding tractor to draw Barney's attention as her loud shouts had not been heeded.

Such was the demand for firewood that a group of blind, elderly ladies headed out each morning to gather firewood. They were attached to each other by holding onto digging sticks. They'd head out in single file *pakuru-junpurrpa-piya* (like processionary caterpillars) led by a sighted lady. Late in the afternoon they'd return again in single file attached to each other, however this time balancing large bundles of firewood on their heads.

Their day's work having been done, they'd amuse themselves by playing blind man's bluff but without the need for blindfolds. "*Yanta karlarra*" (go to the west), the sighted lady would sing out to one of the blind ladies, who would promptly stumble over a recently placed pile of firewood, which hadn't been there in the morning. This would be cause for much mirth and hilarity. They all joined in and took it in turns to be tricked and stumble. When sandy blight (trachoma) or cataracts had extinguished their eyes, it had not snuffed out their sense of direction, nor their joie de vivre. Nor were they denied role clarity. They were nobody's clients.

These days many old people spend the winters indoors in bed. New tenancy rules forbid the lighting of fires and sleeping on verandahs, so unless they break the rules, households make do without firewood and keep warm by electric heaters. Kangaroos or purchased frozen kangaroo tails are cooked in ashes or coals outside front fences where restrictions don't yet apply.

After Wendy and the kids moved from the Health Flats into an Education Department house, a friendly old man used to call in early in the morning, wanting to know if we were okay. Wendy, thinking how nice it was of the community that they'd sent an old man to check on our welfare, would invite him in and offer him some biscuits and a cup of tea and have a chat with him, until abruptly he would stand up and leave.

This went on for months. Without warning the old man stopped coming. Neat piles of chopped firewood for our wood heaters miraculously appeared at our backdoor, and †Shorty Jampijinpa came instead of the friendly old man. Shorty immediately got stuck into pruning our lemon tree and the oleanders, pulling out weeds and prickles, watering the lawn and so on. It wasn't until we were informed there had been a reshuffle of training allowance positions that we realised our friendly visitor of the tea and biscuits had been our appointed gardener.

Every morning our "house girl" would appear at our Education Department house. The "house girls" who, like the gardeners, were occasionally reshuffled, were mostly older women not girls. Sometimes they'd be covered in red ochre, having taken part in a ceremony the night before. They'd have a bath before getting to work, leaving the bath coated in ochre, before sweeping, mopping, washing the dishes and anything else we asked them to do. They also minded our two younger children while Wendy was at school. When the chores were done the house girl would go walking all around the community. We would see her carrying little Jenny, with little Joe trailing behind at a distance. She would stop in a shady place and wait for him to catch up. While we were out of the house the house girls' family would come and wash their clothes and bedding in our overworked Education Department washing machine. The Education Department wasn't impressed with Wendy as she applied for more than her expected quota of replacement washing machines.

I recently had my attention drawn to a photograph, unobtrusively placed on the rear wall of the Yuendumu clinic reception room. The photo was taken during the 'training allowance days'. Smiling at the camera there were twenty three Yapa health workers, including a young man who had been trained by a visiting dentist to extract teeth. That young man was Francis Jupurrurla Kelly, who tells me, that at the time he did a six month stint in Darwin. Dr. Dee-dee (Devanesan) had sent him there for further training under Dr. Hargreaves. In Darwin Francis helped to perform autopsies and he spent time at the East Arm leprosarium. These days Francis wouldn't be allowed in the clinic unless he was sick. It is beyond the imagination of most current Kardiya clinic staff, that once there were Yapa in Yuendumu who would give injections, hand out antibiotics, splint broken bones, clean and bandage wounds and cuts, and pull teeth. Today there are four Yapa working at the clinic as part time receptionists.

Yuendumu clinic - Aboriginal Health Workers, 1970s

Just as remote Aboriginal Australia was about to be enmeshed into the so-called 'social safety net', being social security payments to individuals from government, such as the aged pension and unemployment benefits, a cataclysm of sorts befell Yuendumu society when suddenly most people had their roles taken away. No more training allowance, no more raking of rubbish or painting of rocks in the park, or cleaning Kardiya houses, or washing the dishes and clothes, or tending Kardiya gardens, or helping on the farm, or looking after Kardiya children or unloading supplies trucks, or gathering firewood, or slaughtering bullocks for the kitchen, no more sewing or mending of dresses, no more helping the mechanic or the plumber, no more bandaging, no more anything. Soon the farm and kitchen and other communal endeavours would be discontinued. When it was suggested local meat and vegetables could supply the Social Club store this was dismissed. That was not the original purpose of setting up these operations, we were told.

That's the problem with many reforms or revolutions, if you're serious, you have to have something to follow up with; you have to have a 'plan-B'. The fewer retained employees now were paid three times as much as they had under the training allowance, and the others were pushed onto welfare payments which were also substantially more than the training allowance. The increase in cash circulating in the community as a result of these higher payments was inversely proportional to local participation and directly proportional to marginalisation, irrelevance and boredom. The illusion was that Yapa had more when in fact they had less.

That is the trade-off, there is no such thing as a free lunch. If you are forced to accept beads and mirrors, there is a price to pay. As Kimberley musician Patrick Davies warned in his song 'Rocky old Road':

♫ ♫ ♫

And no you can't take all that you're given,
Oft times it means selling your soul.

The situation would improve in due course as self-determination took hold, but never again would Yapa regain universal role clarity in what is, in effect, a Kardiya controlled world.

Serendipity…

As the new policy of incorporating Yapa society into the mainstream economy was gradually being rolled out, the authorities thought up new ideas of how best to implement this. Yuendumu Mining Company No Liability (YMC) and the Yuendumu Housing Association Inc. were two such ideas.

YMC was incorporated on the 20th February 1969. It was set up by the then Welfare Branch, as a social experiment. A group of approximately 30 older men were made shareholders and issued with hard hats and work boots. There was an ethnocentric notion that these older men would hand down their "newly" acquired enthusiasm for mining to the younger generations, not unlike Lee Falk's 'The Phantom', which had given the authorities their initial impetus. It wasn't to be. Sociopolitical imperatives would, together with the rapid changes in mainstream society, ensure that the Warlpiri generation gap would grow to Grand Canyon dimensions.

One of Nugget Coombs' visionary ideas was to use the funds that would be required to pay unemployment benefits to instead, and at no additional cost to the taxpayers, create a large number of small economic initiatives that would employ Yapa. At the time we did not yet perceive the large elephant in the room obscuring Coombs' vision. The new stream of Canberra welfare money was a welcome addition to Northern Territory coffers. Employing Aborigines was not in Darwin's best interests. To turn remote Aborigines, with their welfare money, into clients and consumers on the other hand would boost the services industry, and that is what they did.

I had befriended geologists † Tony Turner and Dave Seymour during the nickel boom. Tony and Dave ran Aminco, a geological consulting firm, which was a beneficiary of Nugget Coombs' vision. Aminco won a government contract to identify and implement mining opportunities for Aborigines.

I ran into my two friends, whom I hadn't seen since our return from Canada, in Yuendumu on one of my breaks from Central Pacific

Minerals (CPM). Serendipity. Aminco had secured a $271,000 government grant to Yuendumu Mining Company (YMC). Our chance meeting led to my leaving CPM and, at the request of the YMC old men, I was recruited to manage the spending of the grant. This was the first time in my career I was able to stay at home with my family.

Before I took over managing YMC, my predecessor Bill Blacker and his crew had carried out small scale copper mining at Mt. Hardy just outside Yuendumu Native Reserve's western boundary. YMC's Land Rover had been used to great effect to explore the greenschist metamorphic rocks north of Yuendumu. That belt of metamorphic rocks runs due west all the way to distant Mt. Singleton, known as Wapurtali to Yapa. It is no coincidence that much of this geologically mapped unit closely follows a *Ngapa Jukurrpa,* a water dreaming. Both Yapa and Kardiya recognise the same rocks, it is just that they have a different way of expressing what they see.

The YMC crew located many barely visible near surface copper carbonate occurrences. They noticed that every time they found an occurrence of blue or green copper carbonate in the rocks, a particular type of plant flourished nearby. It was far easier to find the plants than the copper carbonates. Kardiya geologists call these 'geobotanical indicator plants' or at least the English speaking ones do.

This exploration was carried out with great enthusiasm.

At the time there weren't many vehicles in Yuendumu. Concurrent with the detection of over one hundred copper carbonate occurrences, over one hundred kangaroos were shot. Yapa priorities in action!

Much later, YMC was to carry out geochemical soil sampling in the area targetting gold. Every time we got elevated copper values in the soil, we'd discover, on inspection, the scratchings of our predecessors. We didn't find anything which they hadn't found already.

By the time I joined YMC, its copper mining and exploration activities had ceased. Electricity used to be free in remote communities. YMC as advised by Aminco had considered the possibility of replacing its closed down uneconomic sulphuric acid based copper leaching process with an ammonia based electrolytic winning process. Copper prices had crashed. Soon after, in 1975, Peko-Wallsend Ltd. was to cut its losses and close its Tennant Creek copper smelter, so what hope of economic success would little old Yuendumu Mining Company have, even with free electricity? Screening of gravel products was decided on as having far greater potential.

My brief was to create employment which I embraced with an enthusiasm that was more than matched by the local workforce. Initially YMC workers, including Yapa twice my age, addressed me as 'boss'. I found this to be annoying as I couldn't work out if they were grovelling or being sarcastic. It didn't take long for this habit to stop as Yapa sensed my discomfort. We peaked at 26 employees. We got busy painting, gardening, setting up and working a gravel screening operation and bulldozing seismic survey lines. You name it, we did it. Twenty six Yapa had their role clarity reinstated. All without high-viz vests, white cards, workshops or certificates. I never got to calculate how much unemployment benefits we saved the Australian taxpayer, but even if it was less than the $271,000 investment we ended up with a functioning gravel quarry, some earth moving equipment, a keen local, increasingly skilled workforce, gradually improved cash turnover and a large chunk of Mineral Exploration tenements. We had purpose and a bright future.

1970s - Yuendumu Mining Company's Powerscreen

2021- Some of the equipment being used by an Adelaide based contractor at what used to be Yuendumu Mining Company's quarry.

Passing the baton…

These were exciting and optimistic times. Bilingual education was introduced to Yuendumu School in 1974, imminent Land Rights legislation was being anticipated and the assimilation policy of the so-called 'welfare days' was morphing into self-determination.

Many of us Kardiya took on our tasks with the aim of doing ourselves out of a job by training and passing the baton to Yapa. This didn't happen, and there are many reasons why it didn't, but at the time nothing seemed impossible.

Many programmes and initiatives were started during this self-determination era. A good example was Skillshare in the late 1990s. Yapa aged around 16 to 25 took part in varied activities which included cooking, gardening, making things like barbeques, sewing, literacy courses, landcare, and landscaping. Ed and Amanda Williams were two Kardiya who ran Skillshare for two years together with a capable Yapa man who was destined to take over after Ed and Amanda left. He successfully did so until soon thereafter, Skillshare ceased to be funded. Sudden and unexplained funding cuts befell many programs, especially if they were self-determining and didn't tow the line. Success and independence were prone to be punished.

A significant factor in the failure of the handing over to Yapa was the reluctance of those in power, those holding the cheque books, to cede control and their unwillingness or inability to recognise Yapa capabilities or appreciate and respect Warlpiri alternative ways of implementation. They demand that Yapa become completely the same as Kardiya, in motivation and behaviour, before they can be trusted to take over a Kardiya job. The greatest impediment to a handover leading to self-determination, is the Kardiya inability to accept the radically different priorities and imperatives which govern Yapa and Kardiya lives.

The number of Kardiya would for the time being remain limited but as already mentioned, by stealth, the policy of limiting the number of Kardiya was abandoned. It ceased to be an aim.

Kardiya more than ever rule the roost and virtually none have had their jobs taken over by Yapa. The number of Kardiya keeps rising as does the number of disempowered marginalised Yapa drifting into larger towns. The Kardiya to Yapa ratio is rapidly increasing so that the 'remote Aboriginal Community with no Aborigines' is not entirely impossible to imagine. Remember the hospital with no patients episode in the 'Yes Minister' TV series? It was the most efficient hospital in all of Britain!

Recruits to the cause of tackling Yapa disadvantage

The deluge...

Central Australia is in a meteorological doldrums. Too far south to be predictably affected by the monsoon season, too far from the coast to be affected by sea breezes, too far north to be affected by the roaring forties, too far south to be affected by the trade winds, too far inland to forecast the intensity of the vestigial effect of cyclones (called hurricanes or typhoons in other parts of the world). Yet the mining and construction industries and bureaucrats and politicians alike persist in referring to our 'wet-season' as an excuse or to explain deferrals, delays or inaction or of expenditure of large amounts of money on flood mitigation measures to protect assets. They reckon they know everything and very rarely think of asking locals. I myself have often asked locals if they think it's going to rain. Invariably the answer is 'might be', which is very true. I once asked old † Darby Jampijinpa Ross if it was going to rain, his answer:

"Mighta-be, I nebber see that Imparja yesterday." He was referring to Imparja TV's weather forecast.

Before I switched jobs from Central Pacific Minerals to Yuendumu Mining, we experienced what was to be the wettest year in Yuendumu in living memory. Such a very wet year hasn't been repeated to the present day.

At the start of the downpour a bus load of older Japanese tourists got stranded in Yuendumu. They were the vanguard of Japanese tourism in Central Australia. The tourists were accommodated in a long curved corrugated iron roofed building which belonged to the Baptist church. Termites were eventually responsible for the building's collapse. The building is but a fading memory. In those days visitors were scarce and out of curiosity many Yapa went and talked to the tourists. The tourists had no English, and the Yapa had no Japanese. Communication was by smile and gesture.

The tourists were stuck for a few days during which time the Yapa and the Japanese discovered a common tradition, *ayatori* the Japanese art of cat's cradle, a game in which a loop of string is put around and between the fingers and complex patterns are formed. A brisk exchange of non verbal storytelling sprang up. Yapa ladies on hair string known as *wirriji* told many a story and were rewarded by *ayatori* stories. Some of these graphic stories both *wirriji* and *ayatori* are quite rude and suggestive. Ah! the joys of mutual erotic entertainment and cultural exchange. Check out *ayatori* on Youtube.

After the Japanese visit, Yuendumu became completely isolated. The Yuendumu Social Club store had nothing left. At the time Yuendumu had a communal kitchen. During the deluge the dining hall was opened to Kardiya and all of us, Yapa and Kardiya, were rationed to two meals a day. The kitchen and hall were supervised by Bill Blacker's wife but all preparation, cooking and the dishes were done by Yapa. †Roy Jangala Fry was the chief cook when we arrived in Yuendumu. That is how †Paddy Japaljarri Stewart got his nickname; Cookie Stewart was to become one of Yuendumu's most successful and famous artists.

During the deluge a four engined Connair plane flew over. Air flight regulations required that many engines, because of the low cloud cover. A briefcase was dropped onto our muddy airstrip. Where was our mail we asked. We were told that Post Office regulations forbade the dropping of mail from a plane. Just imagine, our letters might have got bruised!

The briefcase dropped from the plane however was a blessing. It contained the community's cash payroll. With nowhere else to spend it Monopoly-like card games sprung up. You'd check it out and one of the players might have a two thousand dollar stack of bills, enough to buy a very good second hand vehicle at the time. Half an hour later that person had nothing, the stack having been shifted to another player. All the time †Jimija Jungarrayi would be chanting incantations and frantically waving at the clouds to make them go away. It didn't work.

Hunting for kangaroos and bullocks and gathering bush foods was rather tricky in the rain soaked inaccessible boggy ground, so emergency supplies from the Government store were raided and made available to all. The camaraderie was palpable. Indeed in times of need you find out who your friends are. In Yuendumu that was all of us. Last year's bushfires throughout Australia attest to this. As social glue I can recommend a flood or famine or bushfire or a plague of locusts, or a pandemic for that matter.

Our daughter Jenny came home and announced that *"The boys caught a billy can."* It was to be the only pelican seen in Yuendumu since our arrival and since then.

Finally when the wet broke and the country started to drain and dry out, a vehicle loomed over the horizon. A gang of youths had pushed the vehicle a ten kilometre distance through metre deep water at the flooded Hamilton Downs plains. When it arrived it was beset with cries of, *"Any tea?" "Any sugar?" "Any jam?" "Any flour?" "Any chewing tobacco?"* We were all disappointed to learn that the vehicle was a 'flagon wagon' bringing only grog.

Pure arse…

The Whitlam Government's Minister for Aboriginal Affairs, Senator Cavanagh, came to Yuendumu to hold a meeting to discuss the proposed handover of Yuendumu Native Reserve which would become the Yuendumu Aboriginal Land Trust Area. The meeting started with a welcoming speech by † Jimija Jungarrayi. With his usual flair and panache, roly-poly Jimija launched into a lengthy speech. Senator Cavanagh responded with, "*Thank you Mr. Chairman. Unfortunately I don't speak your language...*". Jimija's speech had been in Aboriginal English! We all stared at the floor in awkward silent embarrassment.

Before the handover the area would be de-stocked. We wouldn't get to see the cattle sale proceeds which would go into the Crown's 'consolidated revenue'. Thus the handover would be of a cattle station with no cattle. Magnanimous they were, and so have remained.

As mentioned, Yuendumu after a long dry spell, had been subjected to a deluge. †Bill McKell had resigned from neighbouring Mt. Doreen Station and had become the Department of Aboriginal Affairs (DAA) Yuendumu cattle manager. When Bill took over, the bores and fences were run down, but with the Yapa stockmen he had quickly repaired windmills, fences etc. Nick Browning had been tasked with de-stocking. A batch of Yuendumu cattle had previously been trucked under Nick's supervision and Nick had written a scathing report on the then dire water, feed and fences situation.

The day before the meeting Hans Voight, the Superintendent, had sent Bill McKell and head stockman †Sandy Jangala Tilmouth to Alice Springs on some pretext. Bill was notorious for getting on the piss, and him and Sandy weren't expected back for several days or longer.

The meeting was held in the since demolished reading room, part of the Social Club building. There was Jim Cavanagh, flanked by his minders, sitting on chairs and facing us. All the stockmen were there appropriately dressed in checkered shirts, moleskin trousers, cowboy boots and hats. The meeting was proceeding to the satisfaction of the visitors, as they explained the rationale of the de-stocking, based to a significant extent on Nick's ominous report.

Inebriated Bill and Sandy suddenly staggered in, and interrupted the meeting: *"What the fuck do youse think meaning to de-stock the place. The windmills have all been fixed, you're a fucking bunch of mean bastards..."* Unstoppable Bill was, and all of us who'd sat stumm whilst Yuendumu was once again being screwed, silently cheered. It was very entertaining to see the officials and the Minister squirm. One of them dared to speak up: *"In Nick Browning's report ..."* Bill wasn't having it, *"That fucking Nick Browning, what does he know?"* and then from an NT cattleman's perspective, the ultimate insult: *"He's a sheep man from down south!"*

Bill received a 'Private and Confidential' letter on official DAA paper. He'd breached section something or other of the Public Service regulations. He was accused of, 'belittling a fellow officer' and could he please explain himself. It was signed Hans Voight- Superintendent.

Bill did the rounds with the Private and Confidential letter.

"What do you reckon about this? ",

"'Well I reckon....."

"Can you write that down please?"

Thus he collected a batch of 'I reckons' and Bill's wife Sam cobbled them all together into an irrefutable typed response. It was impossible to tell who'd written the letter as the writing style changed with each new paragraph. I derive some pride, in that there was at least one well camouflaged paragraph, written by yours truly in that letter. When Hans Voight read the letter that Bill had just handed him he asked: *''Who helped you write this letter?"* Bill retorted:

"I wrote the fuckin' thing myself. You think I'm literate or somethin'?"

Some time later Bill ran into DAA's Alan Barker at the Alice Springs Rodeo:

"You know that letter?" a pause, and: *"We think you could have done better!"*

Nothing came of the incident. A lesson learnt in how to deal with the bureaucracy. What can they do apart from sending you to Guantanamo Bay or to give you a hard time, which they were doing already anyway?

The authorities were still intent on de-stocking. Several times they sent out officers to Yuendumu to assess the stock numbers to see if mustering and trucking was warranted. Bill would show them around and when it came to the area near Yuendumu's most sacred site Ngama (Snake Cave) he'd tell the visitors: *"Sorry we can't go near there, that is a sacred site."*

Yuendumu cattle had been covertly shifted to the Snake Cave area. Thus it came to pass that whilst at Haasts Bluff more than ten thousand head of cattle were trucked with a princely return to the Crown of only $12 per head (and who said there was little corruption in Australia?), no further pre-handover trucking took place from Yuendumu.

The Ngalikirlangu Pastoral Company Pty. Ltd. (NPCo) was set up to be the recipient of the remaining cattle after the handover and manager Bill McKell seamlessly moved from DAA to NPCo as did the stockmen.

After the handover, the cattle were once again free to roam beyond the immediate vicinity of Snake Cave. It had been a good season and the cattle had multiplied and thrived. By the time NPCo was ready to muster and truck, some of the bulls were monstrous. The trucking was from the cattle yards at 4-Mile. A nice little earner for Yuendumu Mining (YMC) was when large bulls were getting stuck in the loading ramp and the ramp had to be urgently widened which YMC's welder John Meyers expertly did.

This first yarding of bulls was consigned to several southern sale-yards including Warrnambool, Gepps Cross and Murray Bridge. The bulls topped all these markets and yielded from $700 to $800 per head, a lot of money back then. When the telegram with the cattle prices was read out on the Royal Flying Doctor Service radio network, an anony-mous interjection was heard:

"You're pure arse McKell, pure arse!"

Branding at 4-mile stockyards (photo - BRDU)

Styrofoam...

North of Yuendumu, on the other side of Rock Hill (Wakurlpa) at a place called Ngalikirlangu, NPCo (the Ngalikirlangu Pastoral Company Pty.Ltd.) set up a demountable homestead, drilled a water bore and installed cattle yards. NPCo became one of a number of Aboriginal owned enterprises that aspired to take part in the NT's expanding beef industry.

At Ngalikirlangu, NPCo built an abattoir, and for a brief period, reasonably low priced, locally produced beef slaughtered and processed by locals, became available in Yuendumu shops. Until then all beef in Yuendumu's shops arrived sliced and frozen, shrouded in clingwrap on rectangular styrofoam trays, and in no way could be described as low priced.

I don't think I'm being paranoid when I assert that there was a concerted, behind the scenes effort, by the Kardiya establishment, to undermine the Aboriginal beef industry. No matter what hoops NPCo jumped through, it was unable to secure a licence and the abattoir was made to close down. No more low priced unfrozen five kilo bags of beef.

Yuendumu cattle once again finished their happy free range life, with a miserable arduous journey to a slaughterhouse half a continent away before being converted into neat rectangular shaped portions, shrouded in clingwrap, on styrofoam trays, to make a half a continent return journey in freezer trucks.

The clingwrap and styrofoam industries let out a sigh of relief

In due course NPCo became yet another victim of industrial infanticide.

A wise word is not a substitute for a piece of herring.

Sholem Aleichem (1859-1916)

Just as it is disputed as to whether the Pavlova is an Australian or New Zealand invention, so too it is disputed whether Dutchman Willem Beukelszoon invented *haring kaken* in the 14th Century. Belgians and Scandinavians also lay claim to this invention. *Haring kaken* is a procedure whereby freshly caught herring have their throat slit and their innards swiftly removed and by the copious application of salt the herring's deterioration is significantly delayed. This enabled the fishing fleet to stay out for much longer. *Haring kaken* was to North Sea fishermen as significant an invention as the invention of the printing press, a century later, was to the rest of us.

Growing up in a Dutch household I can recall my father removing a few herrings from a small wooden barrel, cutting off their heads, peeling off their spines, scaling and cleaning them and soaking them overnight in water or milk to draw out the salt. In the morning he would drag the herring fillets through finely chopped raw onion and we would then hold them by the tail above our open mouths and slide them down the hatch, yummy! The separated herring roe and milt was then fried and was a delicious bonus. This ritual was akin to Australian children savouring Vegemite on toast. Raw salted herring is still one of my favourite foods, Vegemite isn't. Very un-Australian of me some would say.

The closest thing to herrings in Central Australia are bony bream. Napperby Creek runs into a salt lake not far south of the Tanami road. The creek flows, not very often, sometimes closing the road at the causeway when water reaches a depth of a metre or so for a few days. Even more rarely, subsequent significant flows happen within a few weeks. Such happened during those initial wet years after our arrival. Countless fish swam upstream. The fish collected in the downstream concrete ditch and then wriggled their way up onto and across the causeway. Most were fingerlings but there were some larger specimens up to 20 cm long crossing the road. Our fishing tackle consisted of wet shirts with which we bashed at the wriggling larger fish. They were bony bream and despite the bones were absolutely delicious, especially so because fresh fish was unknown in Yuendumu. Locals had not seen this in their lifetimes. No one could remember the Warlpiri word for fish. Someone told me it is *warrarna* which I now know is a species of skink lizard. Someone else, that the word is *yawu*, which indeed turns out to be the Gurindji word for fish.

Much remarked on by the locals was the Maori fellow who lived in Yuendumu at the time. He had eaten some of the fish raw after biting off and spitting out the heads, either because that was a custom in the land of the long white cloud or to freak out the locals, I don't know which.

Our guess is that as water flows into the dry salt lake, fish eggs spring to life, phoenix like, and hatch, even after having been buried in salty mud for half a century or more. By the second flow the fish have grown big enough to fight their way upstream. As to why they do this, you'd have to ask the fish.

When the bony bream swam up Napperby Creek a few desert gobies came along for the swim and were caught and placed in the aquarium in the Yuendumu school library. The desert gobie is a small speckled harmless looking fish. It spent nearly all of its time lying quietly on the sand at the bottom of the tank. Only one night when the lights were turned off, did the gobies spring into frenzied activity. Next morning some of the goldfish had disappeared and a few sorry looking goldfish missing big chunks were dejectedly swimming or floating about. Lying quietly on the sand at the bottom of the tank, were a few very fat speckled harmless looking desert gobies.

When first cobbling my Yuendumu story together my brother suggested it be titled 'Red Herrings in the Red Centre'. It could be said that the whole Kardiya intrusion into the Warlpiri Nation is to Yapa one almighty red herring as they continue doing their own Warlpiri thing. A lot of shit they put up with and ignore whenever they can. A resilient bunch they are.

Yuendumu's First Football team 1959 - Photo provided by Coach Ted Egan - (inset)

The Tower of Babel…

I'm so glad my parents insisted on us speaking Dutch at home and encouraged us to adopt the Spanish and later English-speaking cultures that surrounded us. Having grown up multilingual and being conscious of how this has opened my mind, as well as giving me immense satisfaction, I consider that denying children the opportunity to grow up multilingual, when that is attainable, is nothing short of a crime, especially when such denial is deliberate. A language colours your way of seeing and being.

The colours of Dutch are earthy with pretty shapes and patterns.

The colours of Spanish are strikingly contrasting, poetic, vivid and emotionally intense.

The colours of English are subdued but numerous, carefully graded and contained, like the colours on a commercial paint chart where you can choose the colours to paint your walls.

The colours of Warlpiri are rooted in the earth and sky, vibrant and fluid, boundlessly merging into each other.

Warlpiri is the most different from English.

In pre-colonial times the Southern Continent, which was to become Australia, was covered by a brilliant mosaic tapestry of languages. A veritable coat of many colours. That linguistic crown of thorns, the English language, has consumed much of the patchwork and many of the bright colours have been bleached by colonial warming. Don't get me wrong, the crown of thorns is a magnificent creature, so is the cobra.

I consider myself extremely fortunate to have landed on one of the far too few remaining brightly coloured linguistic patches-Warlpiri!

Australian politicians who fully grasp the situation re the Yapa/ Kardiya linguistic schism are as rare as the proverbial hen's teeth. One such was Kim Beazley Sr. In 1999 he declared:

"To deny a people an education in their own language where that is possible, is to treat them as a conquered people and to deny them respect."

Before becoming a politician, Kim had been a teacher and school inspector in Western Australia. His experience in 1961, as a member of the Select Parliamentary Committee on the Voting Rights for Aborigines, which travelled 21,000 miles to hold hearings all around the country, had a profound impact on his views. When he became the Whitlam Government's Minister of Education, one of his first initiatives was to arrange for Aboriginal children to be taught in their own language with English as a second language.

Sadly, even ardent supporters of Indigenous rights often fail to fully understand what bilingual education is supposed to be about. For instance, in Prof. Larissa Behrendt's excellent book 'Indigenous Australia for Dummies', an entry on bilingual education (p.44) includes:

"...some communities, particularly in the Northern Territory, have developed bilingual education models. They run on a proven, effective model, where teachers learn the local languages and then use those languages to teach English..."

Sorry Larissa, you got that wrong. It isn't a matter of teachers (Kardiya) learning the local language, but of vernacular speakers (Yapa) learning to teach. This is much easier to achieve.

So called bi-lingual education was of necessity closely interlinked with self-determination; it was both cause and effect. Bilingual education was introduced in Yuendumu School in 1974, the year after Wendy started to teach there. What better way to introduce the Yuendumu School bi-lingual programme than to show you the induction letter presented to new Kardiya teachers?

Hello Kardiya
Kardiya is our name for white people.
Yapa is our name for Aboriginal people.
My name is Barbara Martin Napanangka.
I am Warlpiri. This is Warlpiri country.
It is our grandfather's and our great grandfather's country
    through Warlpiri Law.
Please respect our country and our community.
I would like to invite you to my Warlpiri country and teach
    you about our culture and language.
Have respect, just sit back and listen and learn.
You are visitors here.
This community Yuendumu is named after the hills east and
    south of here.
Another Warlpiri name for this place is Yurrampi.
It means honey ants. This is a honey ant dreaming place.
Yurrampi children are our Warlpiri children.
They speak Warlpiri, our language.
We want them to stay strong in our language and culture.
They are our future.
We are happy to have 2-way language in our school.
We respect your language and culture, when we speak to you.
Teachers must respect our language and remember it's our
    kids first language.
They are not dumb when they don't know much English.
They are young and still learning.
We love our community and we hope you like it here.
We are proud Warlpiri people.

The first time I became conscious of the politics of language, the denial and derision of mother tongue as a tool of assimilation in action, was in Canada. I was working for Panarctic Oils as a well site geologist in the Canadian Arctic Archipelago. When Panarctic Oils drilled the Hoodoo Dome №1 well on Ellef Ringnes Island, a newspaper had reported that we were drilling 300 miles north of the North Pole. The newspaper article failed to specify that we were north of the magnetic North Pole! At the drilling site the radio room was next to and within earshot of the dining mess. A French-Canadian helicopter engineer was overheard by us speaking to his wife on the radio telephone. *"Why is he tarkin thet language? This is an English speakin' country."* So there you have it folks, the virtually uninhabited Canadian Arctic Archipelago is English speaking! I told them, *"He's talking to his wife, maybe he doesn't want you guys to know what he's saying."*

No Yuendumu story is complete without a mention of Massachusetts Institute of Technology Professor †Kenneth Hale.

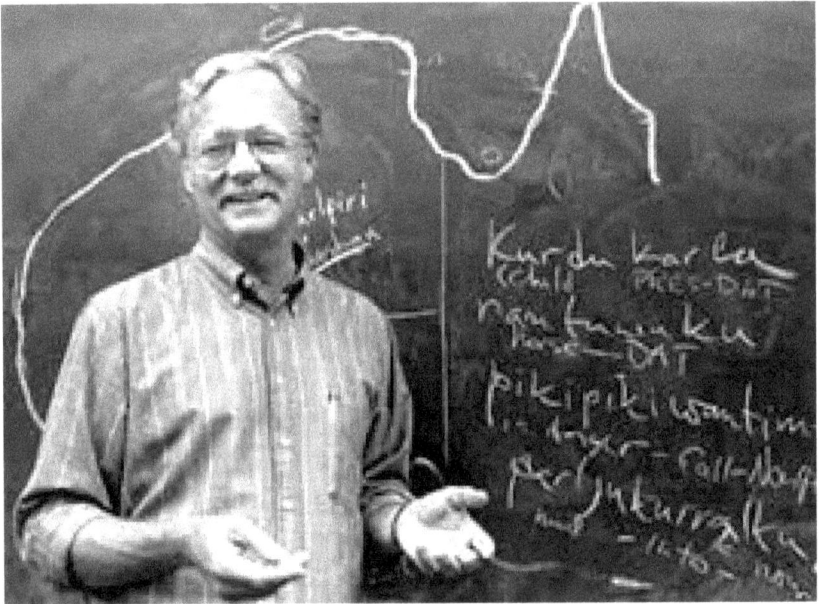

Ken Hale Japanangka teaching Warlpiri literacy

Ken is credited by his former colleagues to have been proficient in over sixty languages. Ken would never have counted these himself.

He was a soft spoken modest man, who changed the lives of many whom he interacted with, me and Wendy included. He was the most intelligent person I've ever met, a true genius and a nice guy to boot. Many now old or middle aged Yapa remember Japanangka Hale with fondness and admiration. Ken was the only Kardiya I'm aware of who had learnt Warlpiri as an adult and, Yapa who didn't know him, when speaking to him on the phone, would assume they were talking to a Warlpiri Yapa. Ken had learned Warlpiri long before we arrived in Yuendumu and had so impressed many Yapa that when bilingual education was introduced they asked the Yuendumu Social Club to pay for Ken's airfares for him to come and assist with the integration of the Warlpiri language into the Yuendumu school curriculum. In June 1974, Ken gave a two week crash course in Warlpiri literacy and elementary linguistics to Yapa school staff including †Jeannie Egan, †June Walker, Robin Granites, †Perry Langdon, Tess Ross, †Rex Granites, †Helen Nelson, †George Robertson, †Miriam Napaljarri, Valerie Martin and †Connie Rice. He delivered the course in the Warlpiri language. He also gave compulsory Warlpiri lessons to the Kardiya school staff.

Ken Hale used to post tape recordings in the mail to his friends in Yuendumu. They were in the style of Alistair Cook's Letters from America but were in impeccable Warlpiri. I recall listening to one of these recordings in which Ken described going skiing with his family. There were these *watiya kirrirdimpayi* - very long timbers, stuck on their *wirliya* - feet on this slippery cold surface of frozen water. Not a word of English.

These tape cassettes ended up in the school's small language room. These would be played to Yapa and their replies would be recorded.

Ken's missives were full of questions, in Warlpiri of course, such as *"How would you say this? Would you say it like this, or would you say it like that?"* He was forever polishing his Warlpiri. One of his correspondents was †Darby Ross. Darby would listen intently and then have his reply recorded. After listening to his reply he'd say *"Nangala, that is maju. I've got to do it again."* *"What's wrong with it?"* Wendy would ask. *"Too much English,"* Darby explained. Nothing but pure Warlpiri would do. It was the least Ken Hale deserved.

Ken's command of Dutch and Spanish, my other languages, was faultless. He spoke both languages beautifully and without a trace of a foreign accent. When Ken spoke Dutch he sounded like a Dutch university professor, when he spoke Spanish he sounded like a Mexican.

Ken mailed the novel 'El Otoño del Patriarca' by Gabriel García Márquez to me. Ken wrote me a note in Spanish explaining that the book was rather hard to read, not so much for the vocabulary but for the style whereby whole pages were written without punctuation. He signed the note Canuto Japanangka which is actually quite funny! Spanish and Warlpiri were Ken's favourite languages. They are my favourite languages too.

Ken told us he was teaching Warlpiri to his sons in America. We found this a bit hard to believe, but at Ken's funeral in 2001 Ezra Hale gave his eulogy for his father in Warlpiri.

† George Jampijinpa Robertson would become one of the first fully Warlpiri/English bi-literate Yapa. Before settling in Yuendumu he had been a stockman. George had done a stint at Billiluna Station. Brothers Bob and Joe Elliott were trying to set up a cattle operation at the Black Hills, near the abandoned Tanami gold mine. Some Yapa were living and working at the Black Hills; these included Clifford Jungarrayi, Harry Jupurrurla Walker, George's father Major Jangala, Barney Japanangka and George himself. George, aged fifteen years old at the time, which I calculate to have been in 1965, was given the task of shifting a herd of cattle from near Hooker Creek due south to the proposed station, a distance of more than 200 km. There was one stretch with no surface water. George shot a *kanyarla* (a euro or rock kangaroo) and noticed mud on its feet. He tracked the animal back a considerable distance and came to a claypan which had filled with water after a cloud burst. Using consummate skill at finding water and keeping the herd moving, George arrived at the Black Hills without having lost a single beast, only to be met by Roy 'Bluey' Harvey who ran the Police Station at Wave Hill. George was arrested and imprisoned. The Elliott brothers absconded over the hills and far away never to return. The Black Hills cattle duffing operation came to an abrupt

halt. It was in prison that George had become literate and as he told Wendy, when he learned to read, it was as if a blanket had been lifted off his head. At George's funeral in 2013, held in the Baptist Church in Yuendumu, nearly all the eulogies were in Warlpiri. George would have liked that.

The most effective way of implementing a bilingual programme is by what is known as 'team teaching'. A Kardiya teacher and a Yapa teacher working together as a team can, if they have mutual respect and understanding, reach dizzying heights of achievement.

A boy owned a shiny new bicycle, way back when there were very few bicycles in Yuendumu. The boy was allowed to keep his bike in the classroom. Another non school attending boy, who was a close relative of the bike owner, came into the class and asked to borrow the bike. A conversation took place in Warlpiri amongst the children and the Yapa teacher. Because the bike wasn't being used, the Yapa teacher then gave permission for the bike to be lent. The Kardiya teacher, much enraged by the impertinence of the school wagging child, hadn't understood a word that had transpired but nonetheless put a stop to the bike being lent and the bike stayed put.

Think about this. It illustrates much that is different about Kardiya values. These values include attitudes to possessions, family obligations, school attendance for its own sake, discipline, and rewards and punishment. But foremost this example illustrates who was ultimately in charge- the Kardiya teacher.

The Tower of Babel - painting by Pieter Bruegel the Elder - 1563

FRANK BAARDA

Gimme shelter - Jagger/Richards - 1969

In hindsight, Yuendumu Housing Association (YHA) was one of the more meaningful endeavours under the policy of self-determination. Qualified Kardiya staff members (a carpenter, a plumber, a bricklayer, a builder, a tinker, a tailor and a candlestick maker) each had two or three local offsiders. Again, no high-viz vests, no white cards and no certificates, but they could fix a tap or lay a brick and mix concrete. Admittedly, even back then, on occasions Yuendumu people travelled to Darwin to take part in such as a bricklaying course to return with certificates of attendance, which as you might imagine made all the difference (there really ought to be an 'ironic' font!).

The Housing team made slow steady progress and had a lot of laughs whilst doing so. I believe that with the possible exception of the School, YHA was the first Yuendumu organisation (that is what we called them-nowadays they have evolved into 'agencies' and even 'service delivery agencies' and 'job providers') to have Warlpiri workers entitled to long service leave. In Australia to be entitled to long service leave requires ten years of continuous service to a single employer, an increasingly rare eventuality even in mainstream society.

Those intellectual giants at the Department of Aboriginal Affairs bestowed a brick making machine upon YHA. The machine was surplus to requirements and shipped from Amoongana near Alice Springs. To the best of my knowledge not a single Besser block was ever produced in Yuendumu using that machine. It remained surplus to requirements. The machine was not long ago retrieved from the rubbish dump and is now at Yapa-kurlangu Ngurrara Aboriginal Corporation (YKNAC), our fairly recently incorporated outstation resource organisation. Not sure if YKNAC has any intention of firing it up, or plans to keep it as a museum piece.

YHA did 'Stage 3 conversions'. A 'donkey house' from the welfare era would have three rooms added, a large living room, a kitchen, a verandah and a 'wet' room which combined toilet, bathroom and laundry. These houses would be connected to water reticulation and the power grid and a septic pit would be dug. A covered breezeway connected the three new rooms to the original single room. Solar hot water, an electric stove, a refrigerator, a washing machine and an evaporative air cooler would be installed to wrap up the conversion.

In 1984 YHA employed three Kardiya and ten Yapa and up to then as well as carrying out routine maintenance on all the houses had completed forty two such conversions with an annual budget equivalent to less than the price of a single one of the houses subsequently built by outside contractors.

It is worth noting that for a long time these Stage 3 houses suffered much less vandalism and neglect than subsequent edifices. Yapa felt a greater sense of ownership: "*We built these ourselves*". Only a few of the original converted 'donkey houses' survive.

One year during the annual school holidays, to overcome boredom, the activity of choice with some children was to vandalise the school. YHA unilaterally decided to do something about it. They secured all the classrooms and placed a person to guard the premises at night. When school resumed, YHA presented the Department of Education with a modest bill. The Department refused to pay the piper on the grounds that no Purchase Order had been raised.

I won't elaborate on what happened during the following annual school holidays. Suffice it to say I first read about what happened, years earlier, in a little children's book titled, '*El flautista de Hamelin*'.

Then there was the time that †George Moore, the then manager of YHA decided houses should be visibly numbered. Yuendumu houses are allotted lot numbers. Not much pre-planning went into this and the lot numbers are literally all over the place. Inside the external fuse box would be written "LOT 57". George thought it would be convenient for the lot numbers to be clearly visible on the outside cover of the fuse boxes. He showed a lad working for YHA what to do. He opened the cover, said "*See, LOT 13*", then painted 'LOT 13' in large letters on the outside cover. He told the lad to do the same for all the houses. When George came to check on progress, he found 'LOT 13', 'LOT 13' , 'LOT 13', 'LOT 13', clearly visible on a row of houses. Shows you how much these lot numbers mean to Yapa who know where everybody lives anyway.

Yuendumu Housing Association was under pressure to collect rents and become self funding. †George Moore, was less than successful in this as he'd rather spend his time building houses with his crew than with administrative matters. All was breezing along quite nicely until suddenly, effective 1st July 1996, the Darwin run Northern Territory Department of Local Government had its way with its so-called 'Umbrella Concept'. YHA was placed under the Yuendumu Community Government Council's umbrella and ceased to exist. A first step towards the eventual appropriation of Yuendumu's houses. All our dealings in relation to housing such as repairs and rent henceforth were with the Yuendumu Council.

When YHA was at its height, the mentoring, facilitating, advising, organising, workshops, courses, consulting, pathways to employment, role modelling, meetings, forums and conferences industry was still at an embryonic stage but would within decades flourish like an introduced weed or toad. The participants in this growth industry, the so-called 'Aboriginal Industry', seem to be more intent on riding this gravy train than in arriving at its destination.

They have a vested interest in prolonging the journey.

In November 2012, Indigenous Advancement Minister (Papunya's Alison Anderson)'s maiden speech to the Northern Territory Legislative Assembly included:

"...my dream is to see the day that housing in these places are built, occupied and maintained by their owners..."

As often repeated in that iconic Australian film- The Castle:
"Tell her she's dreamin'!"

Donkey houses - (Stage 1 housing)

Have a drink on me…

Buchanan/Donegan 1961

One of the consequences of the sudden increase in money floating around in Yuendumu combined with the marginalising role denial resulting from the early 1970's reforms, was a drinking binge of epic proportions. Every time I went to West Camp, I would see surreal scenes of zombie-like drunks staggering around in slow motion trying to hit each other.

It was around this time that Wendy wrote Yuendumu Flagon Wagon, a song recorded by Bloodwood an Alice Springs folk group:

Engine roaring, tailpipe draggin'
Drunken shoutin', hear them bragging,
Yuendumu flagon wagon,
Made it home again.
Every time, rain or shine,
Cops are waiting far behind,
Kids clear out and the women are crying,
Daddy come home with a load of wine.

Over time the superintendents were replaced by community advisers by administrators by town clerks and so on. In my mind I don't have a clear picture of when and in which sequence these title changes took place, possibly because there was no immediate notice-able change at all.

The Yuendumu Council had taken over running the community but were answerable to the Department of Aboriginal Affairs (DAA) in Alice Springs. Initially the Council was run under the authoritarian leadership of a hulking strong Yapa man who wasn't a Yuendumu local and who'd been thrown in at the deep end by DAA. Without DAA support this Yapa man had to resort to his own bullying personality to control matters. After a year or so the community became aware that without external backing this man was vulnerable and that they had the power to get rid of him, which they did.

The Council then recruited Knobby and Noddy. Knobby Salter's sole qualification to run Yuendumu was that he'd been the secretary of the Westies Football Club in Alice Springs. He was a drinking buddy of several Yapa from Yuendumu who had occasion to play football in Alice Springs. Noddy (Sam Brown), was an alleged plumber. Knobby and Noddy had no inkling as to what they would be in for when they accepted their positions.

Early in the morning, in front of the council office, armed with a clipboard, Knobby would read out the names of council workers and mark eight hours and a tick beside those present on a list. This list formed the basis of the Council payroll. Council workers then either went home to play cards or drink or went to work depending on what they felt like doing that day. Self-determination in action. After the roll call, Knobby and Noddy would retreat to their flat and spend the rest of the day drinking and swearing, shouting abuse at each other and arguing and fighting. On one occasion a prominent Yapa man, who was to become a well respected elder later in life, broke down the door to the flat because Knobby and Noddy wouldn't let him come in and join their social milieu.

This state of affairs went on for a long time and illustrates what I mean when I assert self-determination was set up to fail. The people in charge of funding, those who handled the payroll, did nothing to rectify the obviously derelict situation. I've already told you how Sam's stellar Yuendumu plumbing stint was cut short. It took some

Yapa, after a lot of damage to Yuendumu society and to council assets had been done, to finally send Knobby packing. This is but one example of bureaucratic sabotage by inaction. Much more such sabotage was to follow.

The alcohol situation took a long time to sort itself out. The serious drinkers drifted into Alice Springs, many forever. Drinking sessions started to self-regulate such as when drinking at Kirrirdi Creek, people who insisted on returning to Yuendumu were made to walk back the twenty or so kilometres, thus arriving sober and exhausted.

Mud sticks, decades after this period of out of control drinking, the stereotype of the dysfunctional communities with their "rivers of grog" and endemic domestic violence, sexual abuse and traumatised children, persists. Only yesterday (12th June 2020) Scott Morrison, our current Prime Minister, who works hard at giving the impression of being a fair and reasonable sort of a bloke, when discussing Indigenous matters, opined that the 'Gap' could not be closed without first dealing with "...*the abuse, sexual violence, alcoholism and drug abuse in Indigenous communities.*" He quickly snuck this sentence in as a self evident fact and if you'd blinked you would have missed it. Yet another Australian politician who is an accomplished member of a dog-whistling ensemble.

I despair when no matter what I say to refute this stereotype, there are those who cannot be convinced that the circumstances in these communities have changed dramatically and that in those deleterious aspects are vastly improved. They cannot see they're being deceived by political opportunists and a sensationalist press that thrive on perpetuating these lies. These all too easily conned people also believe Elvis is still alive, and that Harold Holt was abducted in a Chinese submarine, and they would also have believed that in 1943 the railway yards in Haarlem had been totally destroyed by an Allied bombing raid.

As for those drunk, unwashed and unemployed Yapa one sees roaming the streets of Alice Springs, or occasionally drinking in the dry Todd

River, those who fit the stereotype, I've come across a saying which is well worth thinking about:

"Don't judge people for the choices they make when you don't know the options they had to choose from."

Song by Patrick Davies, 'Bought and Sold'

Just the other night on the river sand,
I was in conversation with an old black man,
and here is the question that he asked of me,
my boy, how come all my land's been sold
without asking me?
No don't have enough time in my day,
to be messed around or led astray,
a drunk out on the street, I would rather be,
at least I wouldn't have half the pain and the misery.

Birds of a feather…

Despite 'Knobby and Noddy' style setbacks, in Yuendumu, self-determination had a significant influence on which way the wind blew. In Alexis Wright's book, 'Tracker', Forrest Holder wrote that whitefellas needed to decolonise their minds. In Yuendumu, step by small step, we were doing just that.

Yapa became more confident and assertive and Kardiya began to shed their colonial superiority and be more respectful of and open to Yapa society. Self-determination was never fully realised and indeed later was totally reversed, but nonetheless in Yuendumu we became increasingly more equal while not sacrificing our differences. As both Kardiya and Yapa progressively discarded some of their ethnocentricity, we became colleagues, friends and neighbours and colour blind.

Yuendumu became a great place to be. A great place to raise your children, be they Kardiya or Yapa. That birds of a feather flock together proved to be fundamentally true in Yuendumu, and Yapa and Kardiya chose to continue to effectively live in their separate worlds. Nonetheless a spirit of intended equality and mutual respect prevailed. An additional bonus for us Kardiya was that we could, whenever it suited us, take refuge in white privilege. This white privilege meant that we Kardiya would virtually be guaranteed employment, role clarity and job security and housing, higher wages, prompter housing repairs, access to better vehicles and less harassment by the authorities. We had bank accounts with worthwhile credit balances, accumulating superannuation benefits and often investment in property. We had a much lesser chance of being locked up or have our children taken off us and the list is endless.

Only very occasionally would Yapa rail against some unequal treatment. There was the time when a Yapa teacher was very angry when all the Kardiya teachers got new curtains. *"They already have curtains. We have only rags and blankets for our windows. Why can't they give us curtains?"* Yapa teachers, with a few exceptions, aren't provided with Education Department houses, let alone curtains! White privilege would manifest itself in both overt and subtle ways. White privilege also meant that at any time we could open the cage and fly away to our nest eggs, and most of us did.

There is no denying that some Yapa in true hunter-gatherer style saw Kardiya as a resource to be harvested, which some cynics label as "intelligent parasitism." Myself I consider Yapa dignified generosity in welcoming us as friends and family in their midst on their lands to be magnanimous symbiosis.

Ceremonial object...

When I first started to manage Yuendumu Mining Company I 'inherited' the 'Flatstone Quarry'. In Yuendumu we've always referred to 'flatstone', the correct term is 'flagstone'. We often refuse to be corrected.

A few kilometres south of Yuendumu there is a ridge that consists of thinly bedded sandstone and siltstone. The rocks belong to the 400 million years old Cambrian Yuendumu Sandstone Formation. The stone has its origins in a shallow lacustrine environment, that is a shallow slowly sinking lake bed, to which thin layers of sediment were added over time. Occasional fossil worm tracks and tubes and other sedimentary features attest to this origin. Mica contained in the sediment washed into the lake and settled as flat lying flakes. Because of this the rock splits easily into thin slabs resulting in beautiful paving stones.

Before my arrival, Yuendumu Mining used air powered rockdrills and dynamite to mine the flatstone; dynamite is also known as 'fracture'. Back then Wikipedia didn't exist, otherwise the following might have raised alarm:

> *"Higher velocity explosives are used for relatively hard rock in order to shatter and break the rock, while low velocity explosives are used in soft rocks to generate more gas pressure and a greater heaving effect. For instance, an early 20th-century blasting manual compared the effects of black powder to that of a wedge, and dynamite to that of a hammer."*

I didn't need the internet to work out what had happened. Often I'd utter, *"If only they'd used gunpowder."*

Back then charcoal, sulphur and saltpetre (potassium nitrate) would have been readily available, but these days, subsequent to the various politically motivated fear campaigns, a visit from the police is a likely consequence of harbouring supplies of these three ingredients of gunpowder.

At the quarry, slabs of sandstone had been recovered from huge piles of shattered debris. The deposit had been ruined and not much usable material remained. I later found out that a self-service of public servants had plundered almost the entire production. Delving into the previous half a decade of administrative data I could not find a single dollar of flatstone revenue.

Yuendumu Mining proceeded to salvage what flatstone we could. †Dick Japangardi Marshall did a 'dot painting' on one of the flatstone slabs, and quick as a flash a group of men produced around two dozen or so flatstone paintings. This we perceived as a wonderful opportunity to vertically integrate our quarry and to add value to its production.

I duly filled a suitcase with rock paintings and like a vacuum cleaner salesman dragged the heavy suitcase around Sydney and Melbourne to various galleries.

The consensus from the commercial art world was that the paintings were very beautiful but that overseas tourists couldn't take the heavy paintings back in their handbags, blah, blah, blah…No one pulled out their cheque book. In desperation I'd leave a painted rock at each gallery visited and I asked them to sell it for whatever price they could get, take off what they considered a fair commission and send us a cheque in the mail and to let us know how many more they thought they could sell. A trusting soul I was. Yuendumu Mining did not receive a single response, not one cheque.

Years later Yuendumu's art centre received a phone call from someone in Darwin. They'd found a painted rock in a shed. The caller asked if anyone knew anything about it, and was it valuable?

When Cecilia Alfonso the Yuendumu art centre co-manager rang me to ask if I knew anything about this, I told her the story of the heavy suitcase. As for the value, I told her that stolen goods had no value. Subsequently one of the painted slabs turned up on eBay. I was glad to be informed that the South Australian Museum acquired it at the bargain price of $600. Mind you, by now Yuendumu Mining Co. could have done with that money and so could have Harry Nelson, the artist who painted it.

More recently, anthropologist Melinda Hinkson found another of the long lost painted slabs of flatstone. It is stored in the restricted section of the National Museum in Canberra and is labelled 'Aboriginal Ceremonial Object'. I guess my lugging of the heavy suitcase could be regarded as a ceremony of sorts.

Photo of ceremonial object, (S.A. Museum)

Smoke signals…

Another important aspect of community life in the 1970s was communication with the 'outside' world. Communication was by letters in the post or by short wave radio or in person by what was then a six hour trip each way and which invariable involved an overnight stay in Alice Springs. The Royal Flying Doctor Service (RFDS) radio network was used for medical consultations and emergencies and telegrams. Later this was upgraded to include 'radphone' contacts whereby the RFDS radio operator would 'patch' you to talk to someone talking on the phone. The latter was great for debt collection, you'd call someone who owed you money and the whole of Central Australia would be listening in. They soon paid up!

Geoff Whiting, nicknamed 'Fish', manned the DAA radio which was linked to the RFDS network. Confidentiality and discretion weren't Fish's forte. For example passersby would congratulate you on your birthday long before you received the telegrams to that effect.

Once upon a time Fish received a very lengthy telegram which was all in Warlpiri. The telegram was spelled out using the NATO phonetic alphabet. Thus Fish would hear and transcribe *"November, yankee, alpha, mike, papa, uniform, romeo, lima, alpha,"* spelling out *nyampurla* which in English is 'here'. He'd hear and transcribe *"November, golf, uniform, romeo, romeo, juliet, uniform,"* spelling out *ngurrju*, which in English is 'good'. *"Could you repeat that please?"* More followed, but after three minutes or so the RFDS radio base in Alice Springs would relegate Fish to the end of the queue forcing Fish again and again to wait until his turn came around. The telegram droned on and on and Fish had no idea what the telegram was about, which he found most frustrating. Some hours later Fish took the carefully transcribed message to the recipient who was Mary Laughren (Napaljarri), the school linguist.

Taking her time Mary read it. When she finished reading it she looked up at Fish, who was standing by in anticipation, and said *"Thank you,"* leaving Fish floundering. †Rex Japanangka Granites, a qualified Warlpiri school teacher at Yuendumu School, was in Western

Australia on Yapa ceremonial business and had conspired with Mary to have a go at Fish. Rex had sent the long telegram to Mary knowing how Fish would react and that undoubtedly this would give us all a good laugh. Their conspiracy worked and we did get a good laugh. Fish was never told what was in the telegram.

Soon thereafter many Yuendumu organisations got their own Codan transceivers and joined the RFDS network. Fish's services were no longer needed.

Long before the advent of reliable telephones and the internet I operated an amateur radio station. It enabled me to keep in touch with the rest of the world, practice my languages and make some friends. From time to time Wendy would issue a reality check, *"Why do you bother to speak with someone on the other side of the world when there are plenty of people you could be speaking with right here."* My lame unsatisfactory answer, *"Because it's not the same."* A bit like emails and Zoom I suppose.

Amateur radio can be quite addictive; there is something akin to fishing about it. The rarest fish can be caught in the early hours of the morning, when it is daylight at those exotic locations half a world away. Wendy's limit of tolerance was exceeded when I tried to move the transceiver into the bedroom. She put her foot down with a firm hand. The transceiver was moved to my workplace instead. Tony Juttner installed a twenty-metre high rotatable antenna, at the time Yuendumu's tallest structure, and I enjoyed many years of obsessive radio telecommunication. That was until the Yuendumu Housing Association backhoe when excavating a septic tank, snagged one of the guy-wires and the antenna tower came crashing down onto the power lines and I had to go cold turkey.

A QSL card is a contact verification card which radio amateurs exchange by post. George Robertson did me a black and white possum dreaming which I used as the front of my QSL card. It was probably the world's first and only QSL card with a Central Australian Jukurrpa design.

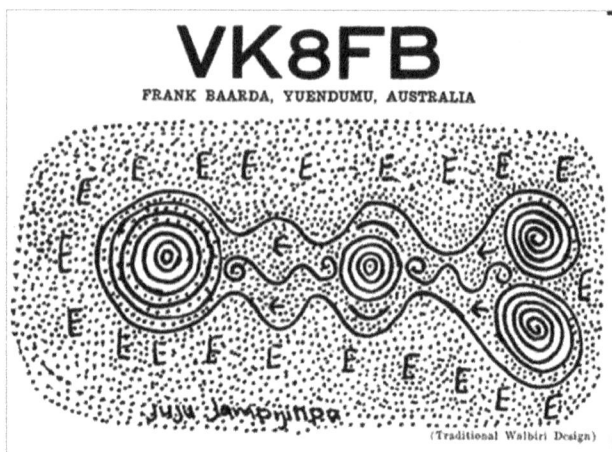

VK8FB
FRANK BAARDA, YUENDUMU, AUSTRALIA

Juju Jampijinpa

(Traditional Walbiri Design)

There were over 300,000 licensed amateur radio operators in Japan. Many Japan/Yuendumu conversations took place, *"Konnichi wa Katsu-san. Watashi-no QTH-wa Yuendumu-desu, anata-no signal reporto..."*. QTH is amateur radio Q-code for 'location'. Back would come *"Arrigato Frank-san I cannot find Yuendumu on the map!"* Thus arose my humble contribution to putting Yuendumu on the map.

Parallel to Kardiya radio communications there is the bush telegraph. Whenever Yapa bump into other Yapa they tell each other where they are going, where they came from, who they saw on the way, what happened and to whom and on and on. Some outsiders assume this is idle gossip, but they'd be wrong. It doesn't take an anthropology degree to work out what is happening.

Not all that long ago, less than a century in fact, small groups of Yapa would range across the desert, their traditional lands. It was important to know where others were likely to be, where bush foods were available or crops had failed, what condition the water holes were in, when and where ceremonies would take place and where potential marriage partners were growing up. It was a matter of survival and of social glue. Such a habit or custom lingers on long after its survival imperative has faded into the mists of time.

One of the Kardiya teachers at Yuendumu school had a younger wife whom he jealously guarded. She followed him like a doggy. The Warlpiri masters of metaphor named them 'Truck and Trailer'. But, and this is important, never to their face. The bush telegraph had ensured that everyone knew who 'Truck and Trailer' were except for 'Truck and Trailer' themselves. The same with 'Groper' our then town clerk, may he rest in peace.

The imperative to keep harmonious relations within Yapa society had resulted in the evolution of an etiquette which required people to be very aware of the consequences of what they said, and to whom they said it, and when to keep their mouth shut. Many diplomats could learn from Warlpiri society. With the arrival of the modern day bush telegraph namely mobile phones- cell phones if you live outside Australia- and social media such as Facebook, this etiquette flew out the window resulting all too often in social conflict. 'Truck and Trailer' would these days definitely find out that they were, and so would have 'Groper'.

The weather...

A number of remote localities were contracted by the Bureau of Meteorology (BOM) to act as weather stations. The weather report consisting of a string of digits would be read out via the RFDS radio network. For many years Sam McKell did the Yuendumu weather report.

Another such weather station was at Rabbit Flat. Rabbit Flat was a road house that used to advertise itself as 'The Remotest Roadhouse in Australia'. It is approximately 300 km northwest from Yuendumu on the Tanami road. Rabbit Flat Roadhouse has since closed. Bruce and Jaquie Farrands were the owner operators of the roadhouse. Jacquie in her delightful French accent, not unlike that of the Belgian TV detective Poirot, could be heard each morning reading out the Rabbit Flat weather report. Not for me to try and render her accent on paper, suffice it to say that the most common digit in the weather reports was 'zero'. Try it yourself, block your nose and gargle your 'R's *"Rabbit Flat weather... zero zero zero zero four... zero zero zero zero seven... one five zero zero zero... zero five zero zero zero..."*

BOM has since installed an unmanned automatic weather station at Rabbit Flat. Occasionally Rabbit Flat features on the ABC TV weather map. Not all that long ago Rabbit Flat at 42 degrees celsius, topped all temperatures featuring on the map and that was in April! The TV announcer said, *"Spare a thought for the residents of Rabbit Flat."* What residents?

An eye for an eye…

On our way back to Australia in 1971 we called in on the National Museum in Mexico City. We tagged along with a group of Americans being guided by a feisty English speaking Mexican young lady. When one of the 'gringos' smugly broached the subject of Aztec human sacrifices, the guide retorted by pointing out that the number of people sacrificed during the Aztec Empire period was minuscule compared to the number of people being sacrificed in Vietnam.

Not long after we arrived in Yuendumu, I witnessed so-called "payback". A man had killed another man in a grog fuelled murder. Slowly walking eastward on Yuendumu's main road was the guilty man. He was barefoot and bare chested, and was followed by a large crowd. From the opposite direction came another man, also barefoot and bare chested and followed by a large crowd. When they met, they silently embraced. Holding the embrace, the man representing the aggrieved family, slowly and deliberately ran a sharp knife from shoulder to shoulder across the other man's upper back. No wincing no sound. From the cut there trickled countless rivulets of blood all across the guilty man's back. Although the cut had not been very deep, the effect was rather spectacular and gruesome. Not a pretty sight. The aggrieved family had got what these days is called 'closure'. The Warlpiri word *nyurru* says it all. *Nyurru* means 'finished'. The matter is closed. The guilty man suffered but he got to have a life. That man was found guilty of manslaughter in a subsequent Kardiya trial, spent a few years in prison and on his release became a model citizen, both from a Kardiya and a Yapa perspective.

Many Kardiya freely criticise "payback". They consider it barbaric and uncivilised. These same Kardiya would also look down their noses at the ancient Aztec civilisation with its amazing calendars, irrigation systems and pyramids, a civilisation which flourished when Europe had barely come out of the Dark Ages.

Such self righteous condemnation of Aztec human sacrifices and Australian Aboriginal "payback" is a bit rich coming from a society which when it, not all that long ago, first set foot on this continent regularly savagely flogged its miscreants often for relatively minor misdemeanours. And that is not to mention the numerous public hangings. A society whose Government thinks dropping bombs on foreign lands and selling arms to war criminals can be justified. A Government that is complicit in communications from Pine Gap near Alice Springs, on Arrernte land in our very own Northern Territory, which help guide extrajudicial killings by unmanned drones

Nyirawu is Horsfield's bronze cuckoo. *Nyirawu ngulaju jurlpu kuuku-kurlangu* – the *nyirawu* bird belongs to the *kurdaitcha man*. *Kurdaitcha* men are known in Warlpiri as *jarnpa* or *kuuku*, pronounced, you guessed it: cuckoo.

The *kurdaitcha* men traditionally used to wear emu-feather boots so as to leave no tracks when sneaking up on their enemies to exact tribal punishment.

When Yuendumu first got a police station, a *kuuku* on a mission got drunk and was arrested. Virtually the whole population of Yuendumu excitedly gathered outside the police station wanting to get a look at the *kuuku*. Our curiosity wasn't satisfied. Police snuck the *kuuku* out the back of the station and took him to Alice Springs on alcohol related charges. The *kuuku* had come to Yuendumu to execute Yapa justice, but ended up facing Kardiya justice instead.

The times they are a changin'.

♫ ♫ ♫

The long arm of the law…

Before our first police station was built, the local constabulary consisted of one Kardiya policeman and one Yapa police tracker. The policeman lived next door to us and jail was a small caravan in his back yard. Often we'd hear drunken traditional chanting emanating from that caravan. Whenever a crime had been committed, first call was to the tracker who resided in a humpy in west-camp.

I had a Valiant car stolen by a gang of youths. It didn't take long for the sergeant and the tracker assisted by a group of volunteers to track the vehicle to the six-mile cattle grid on the Tanami Road west of Yuendumu and thence northward up the wire fence track. The vehicle had run out of fuel at a relatively short distance from Yuendumu. One of the volunteers picked up a jerrycan of petrol and drove me to the Valiant.

There they were, hanging their heads, the assembled gang of car thieves. Also the triumphant crowd of volunteers who had tracked my car. The Kardiya policeman turned his back and mumbled *"I see nothing."* The police tracker then handed me a sturdy boomerang and I delivered a hard whack on the arse to each of the culprits. No court case with overworked lawyers talking in incomprehensible legal jargon, no pile of paperwork, no pompous magistrate admonishing the lads a few months after the event. The Valiant was never stolen again.

A fresh addition to the local police contingent was Ben Gollidge. Ben was young and keen. He was very popular in Yuendumu where he had started a youth boxing club and set up a BMX bicycle track at the rear of the police station. Ben really liked it here. Against his wishes he was transferred to Borroloola in the Gulf country. He was a single bloke occupying a 'married house', so to make better use of available housing stock, NT Police moved Ben out and a married officer in.

In 1977, anti-drug campaigner Donald Mackay was murdered near Griffith, in the Riverina district of New South Wales. Mackay's murder had repercussions all around Australia. Criminal syndicates shifted marijuana growing to more remote regions. The NT was a 'beneficiary' of this shift.

Not long after Ben left, we read in the papers about the corrupt young policeman who had accepted a $50,000 bribe and turned a blind eye to a large marijuana plantation controlled by Bela Csidei, a major Sydney crime figure. That corrupt young policeman was our Ben.

I've often pondered how different Yuendumu's youth development would have progressed had the NT Police had a more flexible housing policy.

Nulla-nullas

I received a message that my uncle and aunt from Victoria were on a bus tour and would be arriving in Alice Springs on the weekend. We set off early on Saturday morning to meet them. When we arrived in Alice Springs their bus had just left the hotel. To catch them up we had to travel an extra 80 km to Ross River where we were directed to the "Dutch couple's" cabin. There, once again, we had it driven home to us that we now lived in a different world. Uncle Henk and Auntie Co had been greatly impressed by the bus driver who in their estimation was a super hero because he'd changed one of the bus tyres and as a bonus had a great singing voice with which he'd impressed the passengers with bush ballads whilst driving the bus. We didn't let on we didn't think changing a tyre was such a big deal. Auntie Co was very disappointed as, on the television, she had seen countless kangaroos and emus and other wildlife, yet on this trip, the total tally so far was two dead kangaroos.

As we had come such a long way we were given permission to stay and joined a circle of tourists who were being enthralled with outback tales around a campfire by an old Kardiya with a bushy beard and a bush hat. We all got to taste a bit of damper cooked in a bush oven and had a drink of billy tea. At one stage the old feller produced a hefty nulla-nulla which we got to handle and pass on. He then demonstrated how two 'lubras', as he referred to them, would have a fight. They would sit cross-legged opposite each other and one would smash the other on the head with the nulla-nulla. She would then hand the nulla-nulla to the other one, who would in turn smash the other one on the head. Back and forth this went on for a long time. They have very thick skulls, explained the old bushie. I can still picture our younger son Joseph's little grin as he gave us knowing looks and silently giggled throughout the performance.

When finally one of the lubras was unconscious, the other one had won. The 'clash of the lubras' story was followed by some more 'believe it or not' tall tales about the 'natives', including the tale that during the war, when timber railway sleepers were cut with a two man crosscut saw, they'd put a Warlpiri man on one end of the saw and an Arrernte man on the other, as this would result in greater output as the two natives would expend extra effort so as not to be the weaker one and be the first to give in. A likely story!

Back in the cabin auntie Co asked me *"Frenk, is dut all troo?"* We weren't about to steal the old codger's thunder. *"Sort of,"* I answered and changed the subject.

A *kuturu* is a hefty, straight, cylindrical shaved mulga-wood stick with tapered ends. It is as much as a metre in length and 6 cm in diameter. It is better known as a nulla-nulla.

Nulla-nullas used to be commonly carried by Yapa women. Occasionally a fight would break out. A couple of ladies would discard their tops and bare breasted face up to each other, brandishing *kuturu,* and shouting loud abuse. One of the swear words used was *jinti-maraylpi,* which I was told means, 'cunt like a full moon', rather poetic don't you think?

The adversaries would be backed by a cackle of *kuturu* flourishing lady friends and relatives. Whilst a *kuturu* can cause serious damage, this rarely was the case. A ritualistic to and fro clashing of *kuturu,* not unlike traditional Japanese stickfighting, would ensue. Once one of the protagonists succeeded in clocking her opponent, the fight would usually stop or peter out. Some more shouting, the tops put back on, and the two parties would retreat in opposite directions, turning around from time to time, waving their *kuturu* and yelling abuse which eventually would fade into the distance. The grievance had been publicly aired. *Nyurru,* finished

Bruce Johnson, the council superintendent lived next door to us. Emanating from the school oval a loud cacophony drifted towards us. As we looked across we saw a scene reminiscent of a Jolliffe Witchetty's Tribe cartoon. A fight had broken out to which it seemed the whole population of Yuendumu had been drawn. A few boomerangs could be seen flying and there was much shouting, running and milling about. *"Geez, that's the biggest fight I've ever seen!"* said Bruce. Our police Toyota, with its rattly cage, entered the fray and it was reminiscent of the biblical parting of the waters. The crowd slowly dispersed and emerging unscathed from the centre of the maelstrom, in amongst a group of children there were Bruce's daughter Kathy, and little Donovan and Joey and Jenny Baarda.

An Education Department psychologist recently told the school staff that Yuendumu children are all traumatised because they have witnessed fights. If she'd attended one of these fights she would see that no-one is traumatised. The children witness these fights with excitement and even enjoyment. Most such disturbances in Yuendumu are a spectator sport, foil fencing at the Olympics comes to mind.

The psychologist lady was told that these fights are part of the culture, a way of dealing with conflict. The psychologist lady wasn't having it. As far as she was concerned, teachers at Yuendumu school needed to have strategies in place to deal with all the traumatised children.

Children are no more traumatised than they would be at a football match, yet the authorities keep sending paid trauma counsellors and conflict resolution experts to Yuendumu to teach Yapa how to suck eggs.

The Night Patrol

† Lucy Napaljarri Kennedy was the first Yuendumu resident to be conferred the Order of Australia. That was in 1994. The investiture booklet states that amongst other important roles she played, she was *"... one of the instigators of a group of grandmothers and mothers who regularly undertake night patrols of the Yuendumu Community to keep the peace..."*

Night Patrols are now widespread in the Northern Territory, but it was in 1986 that the Julalikari Council in Tennant Creek established the first indigenous voluntary night patrol in Australia. It was in Yuendumu however that the first specifically women's Aboriginal night patrol was started. That was in April 1991.

Volunteer elderly ladies, armed with *kuturu* would patrol Yuendumu on foot at night, until the early hours of the morning. The ladies would tip out any grog they'd encounter, and send wandering kids scurrying home to their families. They'd take no lip from drunks and wouldn't hesitate to report them to the police. The police were happy with this co-operation as every call-out would earn them two hours of overtime and would usually result in charges being laid of introducing, consuming, possessing and/or distributing alcohol in a restricted area. We were all surprised and impressed that these ladies had so much authority.

These days older ladies have no accreditation nor ochre cards (a government issued 'working with children' authorisation) thus the Night Patrols of old cannot happen. The ladies would be liable to be accused of taking the law into their own hands and be charged with being armed with an offensive weapon.

Years later, when I had a stay in Alice Springs Hospital, Lucy Kennedy was down the corridor from where I was. She regularly complained screeching loudly in incomprehensible language. The nurses who treated her like the cantankerous demented old crone she'd become, had no idea that they were dealing with what had been a dignified lady who'd been honoured by the Queen.

A couple of years ago the Mining shop suffered a series of break-ins. On one such occasion I emailed the coordinator of the Night Patrol: "*...there are some distinctive shoe prints at the front of the shop. Suggest night patrollers come and have a look at the prints, as I'm fairly confident sooner or later they'll recognise the wearer*". The response included "*...we cannot as you suggest go and look at foot-prints nor are we able to investigate to find the persons responsible... Any investigation is a police matter and you would need to follow this up with them...*" Yes indeed.

Night patrols have substantially deviated from their modest but effective Yapa origins, and have become a significant industry run by well paid Kardiya unable and unwilling to look at footprints. Night patrols are now carried out by part time paid licensed drivers in flash Hiluxes and wearing high-viz vests. Night patrols (men's and women's) cruise around Monday to Friday evening and sign off at midnight. You can hear or see the Hiluxes coming from a great distance. Most break-ins and other anti-social behaviour occurs after midnight or on week-ends. The Night Patrols did however until recently fulfil a useful role by giving night time roaming children a lift home, but even this doesn't happen anymore. Children are no longer allowed in government vehicles. It is against regulations.

Full time salaried night patrol co-ordinators have become de facto vehicle fleet managers, they manage a few vehicles that serve hardly any purpose. You've heard of the novelty box which has a button at the front which when you press it the lid pops open, a hand emerges and reaches out to press the button and then retracts into the box and then the lid snaps shut? Night patrol vehicles are a bit like that.

Rivers of Grog

† Banjo Jungarrayi Tex was a regular visitor to our home. Banjo appeared to be able to smell beer through a sealed can or wine through a sealed glass flagon. It was uncanny how every time we'd acquire alcoholic drinks Banjo would soon pay us a friendly visit. As a trained geologist I could not accept there was anything supernatural about Banjo's extraordinary olfactory sense. I gave it some deep thought and came to the conclusion that Banjo divined the likely availability of grog at any one place at any one time by applying a mental algorithm to his observations of the movement of all vehicles in and out of and within Yuendumu. No different to tracking and anticipating the movements of a mob of kangaroos and not unlike how Google Maps functions, when telling you how to avoid heavy traffic. Elementary my dear Watson.

It became customary for Banjo and his gang to turn up with their boomerangs at my Sports Weekend birthday party. They would click their boomerangs in time to the music emanating from the record player or later in the evening from a live band. One year, unbeknownst to me, Banjo and his gang formed a human conveyor belt and quick-smart removed all the cans of beer that were cooling in the freezer. They didn't even stick around to click the rhythm for the rest of the evening. Bastards! That was the last time I supplied beer at my birthday party.

The NT Liquor Act (1978) introduced the drinking Permit System. Soon after the Act was passed, several well attended government instigated community meetings were held to discuss application of the new laws. Yapa were offered a choice. At these meetings, the majority argued for prohibition, but there were also those who argued for equal drinking rights.

As with most communities, Yuendumu chose to become a compromise 'Restricted Community'. In restricted communities grog was forbidden except for permit holders.

A 'Drinking Permit' authorised the holder to bring alcohol into the community and to consume it at home. There continued to be heavy penalties for supplying grog to non-permit holders, or for possession or drinking grog on Aboriginal land without a permit. Vehicles bringing in unauthorised grog, if caught, would be impounded; as little as one can of beer was legally enough to justify seizure. The legal threat of confiscation oddly applied only to vehicles bringing in grog and not to vehicles bringing in marijuana.

Initially a significant number of Yapa applied for drinking permits, but over time Yapa did not reapply for these permits. Under the Warlpiri obligations system, the compulsion to share, Yapa permit holders were under tremendous pressure to run grog into Yuendumu for non-permit holders. Kardiya also came under this pressure but for us Kardiya it was much easier to say no. Subsequently Yapa preferred to occasionally drink illegally rather than reapply for a burdensome permit.

As already mentioned, serious drinkers drifted into Alice Springs. The Arrernte people and Kardiya of Alice Springs weren't too happy about this and occasional moves were made and continue to be made to persuade Yuendumu to open a wet canteen. Yuendumu successfully resisted these pressures and our drunks have remained predominantly an Alice Springs problem. Not entirely unlike Pontius Pilate washing his hands. Not entirely unlike the present Australian Government's policy of deporting criminals to New Zealand thereby making them a NZ problem.

During this self-determination period, applications for Liquor Permits were received at the Yuendumu Council office. The applications would be mailed to the Liquor Commission in Darwin, together with comments and recommendations from the local police and the council. The Liquor Commission would then issue or refuse to issue the permits. Refusal was rare.

With minor exceptions, the Liquor Permit System generally worked quite well. I can recall one occasion when a 'permitted' Kardiya couple openly drank beer in their front yard, not exactly a sensitive display in a community with many rather thirsty 'restricted' people, but such aberrations were rare and soon dealt with, usually by a quiet word from a Yapa council member.

This is the way the Liquor Permit System worked. For example, if a new policeman went to the council office and lodged a drinking permit application, he would receive a visit from a Yapa council member and he'd be advised that there was a rule that liquor permits could only be approved if the applicant had lived a minimum of three months in Yuendumu. Reapply in three months time, he'd be told.

This would send a message to the policeman, *"Yuendumu is ours, we run the show, you are here to work for us."* I'm not aware of any Kardiya who had their permit refused after the three month wait.

Wendy and I stopped having alcohol at home after a few midnight visits from piss-pots who'd run out of grog. We decided it wasn't worth the hassle and haven't applied for a permit ever since. I recall a Yapa man confronting me about this. Did we think ourselves to be above the need to apply for a permit like all the other Kardiya? The thought that some Kardiya might prefer to abstain, didn't occur to this person. All Kardiya drank in this person's mind. Stereotypes are a two way street.

These days we don't have a locally run Council and drinking permit applications are mostly dealt with at the police station.

Ten kilometres from Yuendumu, on the Tanami road to Alice Springs, there was a cattle grid at the Yuendumu Land Trust Area's (YLTA) boundary fence. When the Liquor Act came into effect, a large narrow tall sign detailing the restrictions imposed by this new legislation was erected at this grid known as 'rumsgate'. Diagonally across the face of the sign, the bright red word BULLSHIT, had been spray painted. An identical sign had been erected on the Tanami Road at the YLTA's western boundary. The twin sign had also been adorned with a large red spray painted 'BULLSHIT'.

Before neighbouring Mt. Allan pastoral lease became Aboriginal land, drinking parties would sit in the shade of the eastern bullshit sign on the legal Alice Springs side of the grid where middens of empty beer cans arose. Near the sign was also where stashes of grog were hidden in a holding pattern prior to being smuggled into Yuendumu. Not sure when the sign disappeared. After the Intervention, the grid itself was removed and one of those notorious 'no alcohol, no pornography' signs was installed. Why was the grid removed? Because they can! Yet another sneaky way of erasing history, tightening control and disregarding Warlpiri land ownership.

Most people are unaware the grid and sign ever existed. Only us old timers miss our boundary grid and our passive resistance bullshit signs.

The liquor laws had a sobering effect on Yuendumu society, as had the Night Patrols of old, which together with the mentioned evolving self-regulation eventually resulted in Yuendumu's 'river of grog' being reduced to a mere trickle, long before the Intervention festooned the countryside with signs.

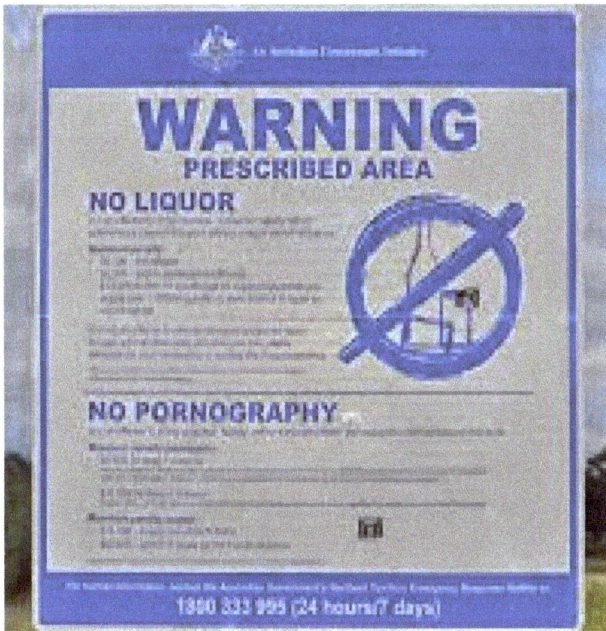

*The almost illegible fine print was written in legal jargon,
incomprehensible even to most people whose mother tongue is English,
let alone Warlpiri speakers.
It surely must have been erected for the benefit and edification of
visiting law students and lawyers.*

All together now...

Lennon/McCartney - 1969

Warlpiri has both inclusive and exclusive personal pronouns. As one would expect 'inclusive' means the person or persons you are talking to is included, and 'exclusive' means the opposite. *Ngalipa* means 'you and me and everyone else', *nganimpa* also means 'all of us' but not 'you to whom I'm speaking', nor 'your mob'.

Once you get used to it, this distinction is quite useful.

Both *ngalipa* and *nganimpa* translate into English as 'we' or 'us', but in English the distinction isn't always evident. For example if I say to you: *"Right now we have to go to a meeting,"* you don't know for sure if you're meant to go with us. In Warlpiri such ambiguity doesn't arise.

When we first arrived in Yuendumu, it was definitely not *ngalipa* in that colonial setting. As mentioned it was most definitely 'them and us' – us Kardiya and them Yapa or vice versa. The 'them and us' paradigm mercifully rapidly faded. The *ngalipa* social glue was driven by self-determination and its partner, bilingual education.

The authorities were, and continue to be, disconcerted whenever their power grip on Aboriginal Australia is loosened and because of this, both self-determination and bilingual education have been unfairly blamed for policy failings and subjected to political and bureaucratic sabotage.

It isn't easy to control something you don't understand, something guided by a different set of priorities than your own or something implemented in a language other than your own.

But for a period of time Yuendumu social coherence and resilience triumphed over the authorities, a time when we were *ngalipa*, all of us united together.

Before Yuendumu airstrip was sealed and before runway lighting had been installed, two year old Sascha McKell fell into a sewer pit. Before Yuendumu had sewerage pipes, every building and residence had a septic tank. The lid had been left off one of these and Sascha fell in. Sascha's older sister Carrie raised the alarm. Sascha's mother Sam jumped in but couldn't get out. She started mouth to mouth on her daughter alternating resuscitation with screaming for help. It was †Rex Granites who, having heard the screams, galvanised Tony Juttner and Rod McGee into action. Tony and Rod hauled Sam and Sascha out and took over resuscitation whilst racing Sascha to the clinic. Sascha had turned blue and had swallowed a fair bit of the toxic brew. The inevitable infection would be fatal if not urgently dealt with. It was already getting dark and the Flying Doctor plane would not be able to land.

That is when Yuendumu rallied to the call. Every available vehicle that had lights was lined up along the runway. † Garth Japaljarri Spencer, one of Yuendumu's bush mechanics, had pulled an engine out of a car. The engine-less car did however have a battery and lights, so Garth and his mates pushed it 1,500 metres all the way from North Camp to the airstrip and lined it up next to the other cars.

The RFDS plane landed safely and the still unconscious Sascha was airlifted to Alice Springs. By the next morning Sascha was sitting up in her intensive care hospital bed.

Years later someone got lost near Mt. Theo outstation. At our diesel pump, a Warlpiri Youth Development Aboriginal Corporation (WYDAC) Kardiya volunteer was on the phone to the Kardiya police organising a Kardiya search party. It was then I realised how things had changed over the years. It had reverted to 'them' and 'us'.

When Sascha was being saved, the thought that Yuendumu society consisted of Yapa and Kardiya didn't cross our minds, it made no difference. It was not part of the equation. It was *ngalipa,* all of us Yuendumu mob, who had sprang into action.

Back then we attended the same meetings, the same community

barbecues, the same volley ball matches, the same movie nights, and the same events such as community concerts. There were many Yapa and Kardiya friendships. We knew each other. We went hunting together on weekends and were shown amazing Jukurrpa sites. We went on holidays together. We went to the same parties. We danced to the same music. We played music together. We went to the same funerals. We had plenty to share with each other in conversation. We were *ngalipa.*

In 2015, A. Miravitchi was on his way to Wirliyajarrayi (Willowra) in a small truck towing a trailer with three tonne of steel on board. He was going to do a job for YKNAC the Yuendumu Outstation resources organisation. A.M. took a wrong turn and ended up near Banana Bore where because of recent rains, he became thoroughly bogged.

Sascha, who was in charge of the Yuendumu office of the Central Desert Regional Council, decided that the council workforce should get involved in the search for A.M. Brian Jakamarra Wilson and his wife Wendy Napaljarri Kitson followed his car tyre tracks and found A. M. who had come close to perishing after having gone missing for four days. Brian was the council grader driver and very familiar with bush tracks in the area. In a neat twist of fate, the Sascha who had instigated the successful search and rescue of A.M. was one and the same as the Sascha, who almost four decades earlier had been saved by a united Yuendumu community effort.

Meanwhile in a parallel universe the NT Police had been searching by aircraft in the Willowra area which was over 100 kilometres further northeast of where A.M. was found.

A search and rescue expert, arrived from the big smoke and met with a group of locals who'd been involved in the successful search. The expert praised the local team effort which had only narrowly avoided a tragedy. The meeting then went on to discuss and work out what had been learned from the incident and the expert generously contributed his expertise. All are now better equipped to in future deal with such an emergency.

Subsequently Sergeant Plod, in charge of search and rescue in the Southern Region arrived and met with the rescue team. Sergeant Plod chastised the locals. They should have contacted his unit in the first place. None of the search party had accreditation to embark on such an enterprise, and what is more if this had ended in a tragedy, they would have had tampered with the evidence (heaven forbid!). I've since found out what this Sergeant Plod's real name is, but for legal reasons I'll refrain from here naming him. What I'm also sure of is that Sergeant Plod is not included in *ngalipa*.

I spy with my little eye...

I have already mentioned the different ways in which Yapa and Kardiya see the world. The perceptions of time and space, the different priorities, different value judgements. It is all these, that make living in Yuendumu so interesting and worthwhile to me, and which are best illustrated by examples:

Yuendumu School had a small swimming pool. English Miss Twigg was teaching our older son Donovan's class. She called me over to show me the drawings her pupils had done of a session in the pool and asked me to pick the one Don had drawn. I didn't hesitate. Don had drawn a full page of blue water and a number of brown circles and a pink circle representing his classmates and him. All of Don's Yapa classmates had drawn a detailed map of the school yard- a small blue square for the pool, a number of buildings, paths and accurately placed trees and tanks.

I gave † Paddy Jupurrurla Nelson a lift into town. A kangaroo suddenly emerged from the bushes and jumped in front of my car. I swerved simultaneously braking and tooting the horn. The kangaroo only narrowly escaped. I had saved its life.

Paddy saw me as a typical not too bright Kardiya who needed to be educated. A while later Paddy said with some strained patience: *"Next one, you hittem."* That was a lesson in Warlpiri priorities well taught and as it turned out well learned.

Months later, suddenly a bush turkey flew out of the scrub in front of my car. I pushed the accelerator and aimed for the turkey and I *bin hittem*. That was the most expensive turkey we ever ate because the windscreen of the Hilux had to be replaced.

Wendy and some Yapa ladies on a hunting trip had meandered through the scrub a long way from Wendy's car. The ladies asked Wendy to go and get some water from the car but Wendy, after looking around at the mulga, which to her was identical in every direction, asked, *"Which way is the car?"* The Yapa ladies handed her a two year old child to carry with her. The child without speaking a word, pointed in the direction of the vehicle. It was like handing her a compass.

One time Wendy was asked to take some women out hunting in her car but she said she had too much work to do. *"That's alright,"* they said *"You can just drop us off and pick us up when the sun goes down."* But she forgot and it was after nine o'clock, the sun well and truly down, before she remembered. She was very upset and sure that the women would be very angry with her. She was not even sure she would find them in the dark, but there they were. They had walked back to the Nyirrpi road and were sitting around quite happily by their fire with many cooked goannas. *"Oh I'm so sorry, I forgot you."* Far from being angry they felt sorry for Wendy. *"Wiyarrpa Nangala, you poor thing, you forgot."* They gave her a nice big fat goanna tail to take home for Jungarrayi. Incidentally, they taste delicious, a bit like chicken with a crayfish texture.

On one of her trips down South, when her mother was still alive, Wendy got into conversation with one of her mother's friends:

"So whatever do you do out there?"

  "Well, we go hunting."

  "Hunting! My George loves hunting! And what do you hunt for?"

  "Goannas."

  "Goannas!?? And what do you do with them?"

  "We eat them."

Then in an incredulous tone of voice:

  "How do you eat them? With vegetables?"

Only at this late stage of the conversation did a mental picture suddenly spring to Wendy's mind. She could suddenly imagine how her mother's friend visualised life in Yuendumu: A merry band of Yapa on horseback wearing hunting caps, crimson jackets and jodhpurs. A blast on the bugle, a pack of hounds, *"Tally Ho, Tally Ho!"* chasing down a goanna through the scrub. Subsequently a roast goanna on a platter encircled by roast potatoes and pumpkin, carrots and a generous serving of peas, and a small apple in its snout, and on the table a little brown jug of gravy. Bon appetit!

In 1987, the then Manager of the Yuendumu Social Club, in a

blatant act of nepotism and without consultation, awarded a contract to his brother-in-law's firm to demolish our community hall. Yuendumu Mining Company's bulldozer was subsequently used to build an amphitheatre on a large vacant block and at which we erected a billboard screen. Movie shows were henceforth to be after-dark open air affairs. The audience brought some deck chairs but mostly just blankets and would then happily settle down on the ground to watch a film. The site of the amphitheatre and screen has since been taken over by the Central Land Council's Yuendumu office and by the residence of the local Warlpiri Rangers' manager. Community film nights are a thing of the past. Satellite television, DVDs, pay TV and now Netflix have put paid to that.

A highlight of Yuendumu film nights was when the film 'Eliza Fraser' was shown. Not long ago I read the Wikipedia entry on the 'Eliza Fraser' film and it was again driven home to me, how differently from us Kardiya, Yapa see the world. Here in Yuendumu the highlight of the film was to see Lindsay Roughsey and his Mornington Island 'gang' in action. We rolled with laughter on our blankets when the hapless Captain Fraser, played by Noel Ferrier, walked along the beach and struggled through the scrub followed by a group of Yapa who subtly, but brilliantly mimicked Noel Ferrier's awkward stumbling through the bush. When Noel attempted to throw a spear and the woomera went flying instead, the understated on screen mocking enjoyment of the Mornington Islanders was contagious. The scene when the Mornington Islander women went hunting and dumped all the infants on the unsuspecting Kardiya lady, Eliza Fraser played by Susannah York, was a particular source of enjoyment to the women in the Yuendumu audience.

Eliza Fraser was at the time the highest budget Australian film ever. None of what we saw is mentioned in the Wikipedia entry which notes that 120 Aborigines from Mornington Island had been flown to take part in the filming, and which has a brief mention of Lindsay Roughsey amongst a large number of other Kardiya actors listed. I suspect Kardiya audiences missed much of what we saw, and undoubtedly Yapa audiences missed much of what Kardiya audiences saw.

In Wendy's English-as-a-second language class, students were tasked with writing English captions on a set of drawings. A girl had labelled a picture of a hopping kangaroo, "*A meat running away.*"

Mrs. Ramakushna was an Indian lady who taught cooking to post-primary girls. In Warlpiri, *jurru* is head, *jurru-rama* means dizzy or confused. Crazy people are called *rama-rama*. When Mrs. Ramakushna tried and failed to convince her rather carnivorous pupils to use meat frugally, she inevitably became known as Mrs. Rama-rama.

A visiting primary school teacher from Sydney, came to an 'exchange' arrangement with a Yuendumu teacher. The Yuendumu class would send writing and drawings to Sydney and the Sydney class would reciprocate with work of their own. Back then it was all done by mail. The Yuendumu class were asked to draw and write about what they'd done on the week-end:

"*I went hunting with my father and uncles and we shot four kangaroos.*"

"*I went hunting with my grandmothers and aunties and we got seven goannas and some bush potatoes.*"

"*My older brother shot an emu.*"

"*My mother got a pussy cat and three rabbits .*"

"*We got a big lot of bush onions and bush bananas,*" and so on.

The Yuendumu kids had taken part in botanical devastation on a large scale and a veritable wildlife massacre. Back came the response from Sydney: "*It is wrong to kill native animals.*"

"*It is against the law to pick native plants.*"

"*The emu and kangaroo are on our national coat of arms and shouldn't be harmed,*" and so on.

The Sydney children were clearly well versed in the rules and regulations regarding native flora in Sydney's parks and reserves and saw meat as having no fur or skin and coming on styrofoam trays. They believed that the killing of animals and the breaking of rules is wrong and should be punished.

Some of these Sydney children may have grown up to become bureaucrats involved in Aboriginal affairs or may even have ended up joining the NT police or judiciary.

Before Helen Juttner (Napanangka) did a stint at the Mining shop and then became Yuendumu's postmistress, she had been a teacher at Yuendumu School. She was looking for her little boy Juan and searched for him all over the school yard.

"He was here. He was probably looking for you. Look, he went that way," said the Yapa teachers.

"How do you know that?"

"Look, here are his footprints."

"Where?"

"Look, right here." They touched a very clear print

"Oh, is that my little boy's footprint?"

"Don't you even know your own son's footprints?!" the incredulous Yapa teachers exclaimed. Fancy that! What a mother!

Kardiya travelling with Yapa never cease to be amazed when Yapa spot a kangaroo in the distance, the presence of which they'd been oblivious to. Our suspicion that Yapa have better eyesight is soon invalidated by the knowledge of the inroads made by trachoma. So what is it? One possible explanation is that whereas, generally speaking Kardiya scan, Yapa stare into space and see the big picture. This theory is supported by the fact that when Nissans, Landrovers and Landcruisers first became available to older Yapa they'd be forever damaging or destroying the side mirrors of their vehicles as they ploughed through the scrub on hunting or wood gathering trips. To what extent this scanning habit of ours has been inculcated by our ability to read, I can't tell. Wendy thought this ability might have something to do with movement, but that wouldn't explain how motionless kangaroos are equally well spotted by Yapa. A Kardiya friend who also noted this uncanny Yapa ability to spot kangaroos thinks Yapa "pare back" the landscape leaving a kangaroo's shape blatantly obvious.

When telling a Yapa friend what I'd written, he offered a straight-forward explanation, *"We adults teach children to look at shapes of plants and animals right from when they are babies. We point out kangaroos every chance we get. They grow up looking out for kangaroos."*

As always the best way to learn is to listen to those who know.

All over the NT, billboards had been erected by the Bushfires Council. The billboard featured a frilled-neck lizard and the slogan:

"We like our lizards frilled not grilled."

†Robert Hoogenraad, a linguist friend of ours, was working at the Institute of Aboriginal Development in Alice Springs and was given the task of translating the slogan into Aboriginal languages.

Robert found the task near impossible because the phrase was utterly nonsensical to Yapa. He was however given a Warlpiri translation: *Jamankurla ngurrju ngarninjaku wanka,* which translates as 'Frill-necked lizards are good to eat raw.' The Warlpiri translator was not happy with this. They must be cooked before eating she insisted. Yapa like their lizards grilled.

Another Bushfires Council slogan that Robert found problematic to render in Yapa languages was, *"We love an unburnt country."*

The lion sleeps tonight - Linda/Weiss - 1961

♫ ♫ ♫

Just before the era of traveling circuses ended, we were lucky to have a circus visit us in Yuendumu. I'm talking about a full blown circus, with a big tent, musicians, clowns, acrobats and animals. The owner of the circus was interviewed by Junga Yimi, (True story) the Yuendumu School magazine. In his interview, the circus owner declared that he was in the transportation business. He explained that transporting his circus required far greater effort and resourcefulness than putting on a show.

On the night of the show, when the lions entered the arena, Yuendumu dogs went berserk and the lion tamer refused to do his act in the cage with the agitated lions. The public co-operated and there was complete bedlam, as people rushed about hitting and chasing and ejecting the dogs skulking under the tiered seats, only for the dogs to find an unmanned section of the tent and sneak back under. It took a long time for the tent to be cleared of dogs and for the lions to calm down sufficiently for the lion tamer to timidly coax them back into their carriage, so the show could resume. We never got to see the lion taming act, but the dog hunt was probably just as entertaining.

One of the circus performers was Miss Cindy, an acrobat who, dressed in a tutu, gracefully climbed up a rope and performed acrobatic stunts high up in the tent canopy. Every time Miss Cindy did the splits the men let out a mighty roar. Miss Jinti was the talk of the town long afterwards. Female genitalia are called *jinti* in Warlpiri.

We didn't go to the circus on the second night but we knew when Miss Cindy was on. We could hear the roar of the crowd, on the other side of town, from inside our house.

Miss Cindy was most likely chuffed by her enthusiastic reception and Yuendumu men were pretty chuffed too. A win-win situation!

Music to my ears...

Before babies can walk and talk they will bob to music. No matter what their skin colour, or the language spoken by their families. They dance to music, any music, before they can speak and sing. Music and dancing transcends race, culture and identity. Even if not a single word is understood, music can speak to you. It can make you cry tears of joy, it can awaken your libido, it can make you get up and dance. I'm sure that as a baby I bobbed. I'm blessed in that Wendy and our children and grandchildren share my love of music. Our great grandchildren bob and dance. It is yet another reason for us to have so enthusiastically embraced life in Yuendumu which has a lively and accessible music scene.

Music has had a seminal influence on my life. This is not a coincidence, just another instance of destiny being kind to me. Dad told me that his mother had joined choirs all her life. She knew countless songs, had a beautiful voice and was a soprano. Apparently whilst she never learned to speak proper German, she had no problem learning and singing German songs.

Dad himself joined the *Ruhrtaler Mandolinen Truppe* when he was barely seven years old. When in old age he told me this, he could still hum *Heinzelmännchens Wachtparade* the song with which his mandolin marching band had won third prize in a competition held in Oberhausen. Dad also remarked that only fifteen years later the members of his marching band had replaced their musical instruments with weapons.

Dad wooed my mother with his banjo-mandolin. During the war he swapped his much loved banjo-mandolin for some cooking oil.

In Argentina we would listen to my mother and her two sisters singing Dutch songs in triple harmony in our garden. By the time we left Argentina, my then almost eleven year old brother, Ted ,was an accomplished guitarist, and we revelled in traditional Argentine songs which we sang in harmony.

When I first arrived in Yuendumu, a group of men used to gather everyday around dusk at the northern periphery of Yuendumu. The men would sit cross legged on the ground in a circle and sing Kurdiji, (a Warlpiri ceremony) songs accompanied by the clicking of boomerangs. I was invited and joined the circle of singers. Despite having no idea of the meaning of the lyrics, which in any case were in a secret archaic form of Warlpiri, I was able to join in singing and boomerang clicking. It was then I noticed, or imagined, that the rhythm lagged a fraction of a beat behind the song, not an offbeat like in Dave Brubeck's Take Five, but a consistent small fraction rendered in unison with uncanny precision. I have since theorised that this may be part of the reason why traditional Aboriginal music has, for want of a better word, an 'eerie' sound to 'western' ears. I much enjoyed joining the group of men and got quite fond of the sound. I never learned anything about the Kurdiji ceremonies, the music was enough for me. It is disappointing, but these days there isn't much live accessible traditional Warlpiri music to be heard. Kurdiji ceremony still goes on, as does sorry business (mourning rituals), but the more light hearted increase ceremonies for the bush tucker dreamings, rarely happen. No chance for young people to learn the songs.

Country and Western music was pervasive in Yuendumu on our arrival. Charley Pride's 'The Snakes Crawl at Night', Willy Nelson's 'On the Road Again' and many a Slim Dusty number could be heard at all hours emanating from countless transistor radios. The Brian Young and Buddy Williams country and western travelling shows regularly performed in Yuendumu. These shows were very popular. Invariably local musicians would be invited on stage to join the travelling muzos. Notably among these were Harry Japangardi Jones and Jimmy Japanangka Langdon. Jimmy was to enjoy some success at the Tamworth Country Music Festival.

The Brian Young Show travelled by air until 1981 when in a plane crash one of his musicians was killed and another suffered severe burns. Brian Young was not physically big but his promotional caps and T-shirts proclaimed in large print 'Brian Young - The Big One, Second to none'. With his trailers and caravans he certainly made a big showing.

Yet another illustration of the richness of the Warlpiri language is the verb *muyiny-muyiny,* pronounced like the colloquial German 'good morning' - *Moin Moin.*

Muyiny-muyiny describes the pelvic thrusting a man makes when copulating. Buddy Williams thrust his hips when playing the guitar, so naturally this earned him the nickname *Muyiny-muyiny* which gave everyone a chuckle.

The Poor Boys was one of several bands that had sprung up in Yuendumu. They regularly rehearsed in our open garage with power supplied by extension lead. Many other, mostly male, young musicians also got a crack at practising and learning to play and sing, all made somewhat easier because microphone hogging is not the Warlpiri way. Everyone got to have a go. Wendy at school staff meetings was often urged to tell the musicians to turn down the volume, or to turn off the power. She suggested they should ask them themselves. *"But it is your power!"* she would be told. Schoolkids would surround our garage and dance. The volume remained undiminished. Wendy did not feel the urge to abuse her position of power. The garage is no more because the Department of Education replaced it with a security cage to lock a vehicle in; we were powerless to prevent that.

Over the decades we witnessed a shift in popularity of music genres from Country and Western to Blues, Soul and Rock and Roll, Gospel, Reggae, Disco and more lately to Hip-Hop and Rap. Along the way we enjoyed many hybrid forms of music. Amazing Grace played in a fierce rock beat is an example of Yuendumu musical creativity. The adoption of new genres did not entirely displace the old and all of these genres can be heard in Yuendumu today, albeit not as frequently or loudly as before. A pity.

Currently, the loudest music of all, is Christian music emanating from strong amplifiers at night enveloping Yuendumu's residential area. Sometimes pleasant but not always, the music is, on occasions, punctuated with hell and damnation preaching in an American accent. A fair bit of the Christian singing is in Warlpiri.

Guitarist Micah Hudson (Photo - Neil Murray)

'Gladly' the cross-eyed bear...

Less than a year after the Yuendumu ration depot was established, the Native Affairs Branch of the Department of the Interior granted permission to the Reverend Phillip Steer and the Reverend Laurie Reece to carry out missionary and welfare work in Yuendumu. The Baptist church commenced operations in Yuendumu in February 1947. In April 1950 the Reverend Tom Fleming and his wife Pat took over running of the church, which they did for the next twenty five years. Tom (Jungarrayi) and Pat (Nangala) were still here when we arrived.

We are all familiar with the proverb, 'The road to hell is paved with good intentions' attributed to Saint Bernard of Clairvaux (1090 - 1153). Missionaries to Aboriginal Australia have come to be much maligned by some people of good standing, some in academia, as well as employees of Aboriginal organisations, a smattering of others and some Indigenous people themselves. One common criticism arises from their involvement in the Assimilation Policies and the Stolen Generations which are both examples of good intentions gone dreadfully wrong. There is something inherently unfair in judging historical events by current mores and standards, just as it is inherently unfair to history's victims to pretend these historical events never happened. Then of course there is the other side of that coin whereby missions provided some refuge and protection against the ravages of frontier conquest.

The Baptist Church could be criticised for not having promoted Warlpiri literacy when it first came to Yuendumu. In contrast the Lutherans in Central Australia did encourage literacy in the local languages and much of their missionary work was and is carried out using the vernacular. I've attended two funerals at the Alice Springs Lutheran Church in which all the hymns and much of the service were in the Luritja language.

In Papunya most church attending adults are literate in Luritja and the well attended church services are conducted using Luritja prayer books and hymn books. Not long ago Wendy and I attended a funeral at Karinyarra outstation 60 km south of Yuendumu. Many friends and relatives had travelled from as far as South Australia. A Yapa pastor from Papunya presided over the open air service and burial which were entirely in Luritja. At the Yuendumu Baptist church, on the other hand, adult Warlpiri literacy has never really taken off.

✝Lothar Jagst a linguist with SIL (Summer Institute of Linguistics) arrived in Lajamanu in 1967. SIL is an international faith based organisation. In 1978 Steve Swartz took over Lothar's work and this culminated in 2001 with the publication of *Yimi-Nyayirni-wangu Kaatukurlangu*, the Warlpiri Bible.

It is worth noting that ✝ Connie Nungarrayi, Theresa Napurrula Ross and Christine Nungarrayi Spencer, were some of Steve Swartz's main collaborators. They all became Warlpiri literate as a consequence of Yuendumu Schools' bilingual programme.

At first the Warlpiri bible was rarely read in Yuendumu's Baptist Church. It was mostly used to place a hand on it while praying to God to heal a sick relative, but as gradually more people are becoming literate in Warlpiri, so too is the Warlpiri bible increasingly used in worship.

Yuendumu was nonetheless extremely fortunate because from the very start of their missionary presence the Baptists did not preach, support or practice assimilation and neither were they complicit in the Stolen Generations. I can still picture the Reverend Fleming with his white hair matching his long sleeved white shirt, his lanyard suspended glasses and his highly visible old fashioned hearing aid.

Father Tom and his wife Pat Fleming would be sitting on deck chairs they'd brought along to watch a corroboree ceremony. Whilst Rosie or Jilly or someone would be explaining the dance and the Jukurrpa to them, Mrs.Fleming would be doing a running commentary for the benefit of her husband. There was no hint of disapproval whatsoever by them, nor any animosity towards them from the ceremony participants and the general audience.

Harry Nelson recalled Father Tom asking a young lad of the appropriate age: "*Shouldn't you be in the (initiation) business?*"

The Yuendumu Baptist Church has coexisted with, and indeed complemented Yuendumu Warlpiri Society and continues to do so. The publication of Laurie Reece's Grammar of the Wailbri (sic) Language of Central Australia in 1970 as well as the annual Easter Purlapa held at alternating Warlpiri communities further attest to this mutually respectful coexistence.

† Mosquito Jungarrayi Morris dreamt the Easter corroboree. In Mosquito's dream the old corroborees were associated with darkness and the new Purlapa with bright light. Mosquito remained an active participant in both church and ceremony.

Darby Ross was one of the most active Christians in Yuendumu as well as being one of the most important ceremony men. On separate occasions I've seen Darby duly festooned with *wamulu* and painted up being both Jesus and an Emu. Darby's performance was fabulous in both instances. Anthropologists refer to the behaviour of blending two unrelated different belief systems as syncretism, fusion and replacement, trust them to try and define such a complex and nuanced relationship.

Darby didn't confine his Christianity to his role as Jesus in the Easter Purlapa and other church matters. For many years he used to dress up as Father Christmas and make an appearance as a not all that convincing Santa Claus at the Yuendumu School Christmas party. For reasons best known to himself Darby had replaced Santa's sonorous Ho Ho Ho with a high pitched Hee Hee Hee whilst vigorously ringing a bell.

Inspiration struck the Yuendumu School one year when the post primary boys and their teacher assembled Santa's sleigh out of plywood and metal tubing. Mary, the linguist, very kindly made her Holden ute available to tow it. Darby settled into the sleigh, the ute set off and all augured well as Darby started ringing the bell whilst Hee Hee Hee-ing. When the driver got up a bit of speed bits started falling off the sleigh and Darby stopped ringing the bell. He also stopped his Hee Hee Hee-ing. He sat in the sleigh gritting his teeth and holding on for dear life whilst the oblivious driver sallied forth leaving a trail of debris in his wake. Darby arrived in the sleigh's tangled iron pipe skeleton which he struggled out of very awkwardly as fast as he could, which wasn't very fast at all.

That was Darby's last appearance as Santa Claus. The baton was taken up by younger, even less convincing successors. These latter-day Santas believed that frightening small children was part of their brief, much to everyone's great amusement except for the children.

Never again was a Holden ute drawn open sleigh to make an appearance in Yuendumu.

'Oh what fun it is to ride ….'.

♫ ♫ ♫

Today, Sunday 17th May 2020, a crowd of over 100 people attended the Yuendumu Baptist Church when twenty babies were dedicated to God and two middle aged men were baptised. The minister and his wife and Wendy were the only Kardiya present and didn't utter a word. The proceedings were entirely in Warlpiri. It was a joyous occasion.

It had all been organised by Yuendumu Christians without input from the Commonwealth Government, the NT Government, the Central Desert Regional Council, the NT Police nor the Central Land Council. No outsiders attended. I don't think it occurred to anyone to invite them.

At the Yuendumu Baptist church there is a song they sing, *'Ngaju kapurna purami Jijaji'* which translated is 'I will follow Jesus'. Some Kardiya have been heard to sing *'Ngaju kapurna purrami Jijaji'*, which translated is, 'I will cook Jesus'. Ha, the perils of unfamiliar language.

Wendy regularly attends the Baptist Church. I do so only at weddings and funerals, and I do that as a matter of respect, not out of religious conviction. Just as well, because after 48 years in Yuendumu I still can't hear or pronounce the subtle difference between *purami* and *purrami*. I too would run the risk of cooking Jesus.

Most, if not all, Warlpiri people who regularly attend the Baptist church, are also heavily involved in Warlpiri spiritual matters. To be a good Warlpiri is synonymous with being a good Christian. As a sceptic non-believer, I struggle with such concepts as the Holy Trinity. To Yapa the Holy Trinity is a cinch. Their cosmology, their Jukurrpa, is chock a block full of sacred multiplicities.

Santa's Sleigh 1978- (Photo-Mary Laughren)

The inroads of Christianity into Warlpiri quotidian existence aren't confined to the Baptist Church. By October 1977, a group of around fifty people had been living at Waite Creek, 160km west of Yuendumu, for a couple of years. They were taken there in council trucks, left with many drums of flour and other supplies and then apparently forgotten, until a year or more later they walked into Vaughan Springs station with a child in pain with ear ache. Then council staff did go out to check on them and found many drums of flour unopened. It was a good year for bush potatoes.

They had been living off soakage water in Waite creek at a known soakage place called Nyirrpi. Eventually the soakage water ran out. Tiger Japaljarri had befriended John Henwood, a redeemed Pentecostal who had been told by God to go into the desert, and was camped on a sand dune about 5 km away. Brother John had a vehicle and a rifle. He was obliging and useful. When drilling for water at Waite creek was unsuccessful, Tiger then suggested Brother John's sand dune. In 1976 drilling struck water at a depth of 140 metres at Jitilparnta. Halleluja! 'Old' Nyirrpi was just within the Mt. Doreen Pastoral lease and the group moved to Jitilparnta but the Nyirrpi name stuck with the new location.

The group needed a Kardiya to deal with the dominant outside world and invited the United Pentecostal church in Alice Springs to set up a Mission at 'new' Nyirrpi. It is no exaggeration to say that if it wasn't for Brother John, Nyirrpi would probably not exist. Broter John took on the bulk of interaction with that other planet, the outside world of funding submissions, welfare, and bureaucratic rules and control. John dealt with the beads, mirrors and blankets with energetic initiative and prayer. Nyirrpi has since grown into a sizeable community with a population of several hundred people. Brother John would spend the rest of his life in Nyirrpi. He was to become a good husband and step-father when he married Pintubi George's widow Alice. Brother John died prematurely from cancer and lies buried in Nyirrpi cemetery. Nyirrpi residents remember him with fondness. The Pentecostal church remains an influential part of Nyirrpi society.

From its inception Nyirrpi community has maintained close ties to Yuendumu. Most of its original population came from Yuendumu's west camp and many were of Pintubi descent. The relations between Yuendumu Baptists and Nyirrpi Pentecostals however weren't always cordial. The Pentecostals tend to be less tolerant and more evangelical than the Baptists. From time to time they hold meetings in Yuendumu aimed at converting Yuendumu-*wardingki* to their faith. They do so with varying degrees of success. In 1987, at the Sports Weekend, Baptist/Pentecostal animosity came to the boil. The Baptist Minister wrote a five page open letter to the people of Yuendumu and Nyirrpi, in that letter he wrote, "*It is my belief that all the United Pentecostal teachers should be asked to leave because their teaching is wrong and they are dividing communities. ... John Henwood himself has told me that I am not a Christian.*" The letter was in effect a declaration of war. The God Wars as we non church goers would dub subsequent events.

The way this confrontation first manifested itself was by the playing of louder and louder Christian hymns as the competing church groups attempted to drown each other out. Some skirmishes had already occurred in this Battle of the Sounds, but at the Sports Weekend the music grew to an ear piercing crescendo. †Andrea Martin told me that her father † Sampson Martin, whose home had been converted into a Pentecostal bastillion, couldn't sleep so he prayed to God, begging the divinity. He pleaded, "*Wapirra please make them stop!*" Andrea thought it all very amusing and told me that because the music was so loud, Wapirra had not heard her father's prayers and as a result, the noise didn't abate. Either that or Sampson had been praying to the Lord God the Utterly Indifferent; the god in Kurt Vonnegut's, 'Sirens of Titan'. When I told this anecdote to Harry Nelson he traded it in for an anecdote from the flagon wagon era in which a drunk had had a fight with †Dennis Williams, and after staggering to his camp the drunk was heard to pray '*Wapirra you punish-im that Dinnish!*' I find it interesting that these unanswered prayers are always in English.

Since 1989 the Little Sisters of Jesus have had a presence in Yuendumu. They have made many friends in Yuendumu, with their natural charm and low key non bible-bashing Catholic mission of leading by example. Periodically a priest from Balgo Mission across the West Australian border would hold mass in Yuendumu or even perform a Catholic funeral service as some families whose elders had spent time on Catholic Missions have stayed Catholic. Sometime ago the last remaining Sisters, Claire and Magali left Yuendumu and now live in an often visited flat in Alice Springs. The God Wars are in the past. The truce is holding.

N. Poulson and his Easter story painting, Baptist Church

Enclaves...

Harry Nelson recounted, that when he was Council president at a time when the Yuendumu Council still had some decision making power, as more housing became available, they decided that Yuendumu would not have ghettos or enclaves. This was a deliberate Yapa instigated policy as they astutely realised that Apartheid would result in Yapa being treated differently and getting the raw end of the deal, as they always had. This policy had a long lasting profound effect and made Yuendumu rather unique in this region, and in my opinion a better place. Gone was the siege mentality we encountered on arrival, and as people got to know their neighbours, Yuendumu became a truly integrated community.

Many other communities have separate Yapa and Kardiya areas. Nyirrpi was one such community. The old people's camp and the Kardiya houses were on the north side of the longitudinal sand dune that runs through the middle of Nyirrpi. Here they were close to firewood and away from noisy children. The government authorities alleged that Yapa living near the windmill were polluting the water supply, which is nonsense, as the water was pumped from a deep groundwater aquifer. At a community meeting the Yapa were told they had to vacate their camp and move South of the dune. Some of the older men, including † Charlie Jampijinpa Gallagher, brought their spears and boomerangs to the meeting to express their objections, but this proved futile. After the old Yapa were moved south, a compound was built for them at the southern edge of Nyirrpi away from the other houses. The compound has tiny little separate bedrooms, a bathroom and a laundry, and was never occupied by the old people, who thought it was haunted. Now it is used as visitors quarters by Kardiya who like having a little room for themselves. For many years all Kardiya houses in Nyirrpi were on the North side of the dune but later a couple of Kardiya houses popped up near the visitors' compound.

In Yuendumu decades of building and house allocation decisions with little or no local input have unfortunately much eroded our unique social patchwork. There are now rows of Yapa houses and rows of

Kardiya houses with only a vestigial sprinkling of fully integrated residential patches remaining.

Not long ago the Education and Health Departments, at great expense and with very little consultation, had perfectly good cyclone fences removed from their staff houses. The see through chainwire fences were replaced with high Colorbond fences which supposedly would prevent break-ins by youths and children. They also prevented residents talking to their neighbours or to passers by.

When it turned out that the Colorbond fences proved to be perfect cover for the nefarious activities of the youths and children when the residents were at work or absent, school staff complained about the fences they hadn't asked for.

At great expense the Education Department had their front Colorbond fences removed and replaced by high cyclone chainwire fences. Back to the future.

'Blue Poles', Yuendumu School dog proof fence.

Out of our league...

In the meantime Yuendumu Mining Co (YMC) had spent most of the initial 1974 two year $271,000 grant creating employment as was our brief. Having had it driven home to us that we weren't going to get further funding, we battened down the hatches. We cut employment and took several other austerity measures. It was as if we'd come under the thumb of the IMF, only in our case it was the Department of Aboriginal Affairs. In a desperate move to improve our cash flow, myself and YMC Directors attended a two day auction at Hatches Creek. A large mining operation had been placed under liquidation. Hatches Creek is east of the Stuart Highway, a fifteen hour drive of more than five hundred kilometres on the back-roads from Yuendumu. We hoped to purchase a grader. A maximum of $13,000 was all we could spend. Our eye was caught by a magnificent Caterpillar D6B bulldozer. The market value of the bulldozer was in excess of $20,000, thus it was way out of our league.

†Roy Japangardi Kunoth was the main plant operator at our gravel quarry at the time. His Kardiya uncle Ted Kunoth from Mt. Ebenezer, who owned a similar D6 bulldozer was at the auction as was Roy himself. † Paul Sitzler, who we'd befriended in Yuendumu where construction firm Sitzler Bros. had been active for years, was there.

A common myth, which is still current, is that Aborigines and Aboriginal organisations can tap into a bottomless pit of money. Normally I rail against that myth, especially as in my experience that bottomless pit is often non existent or evanescent at best. But this was not the time to tilt at the windmills. On this occasion we took advantage of the myth.

On day one of the auction I made myself very loud and conspicuous.

I bid on everything, always being very careful not to 'win' too much. Paul Sitzler meanwhile at my request was telling all and sundry that the Yuendumu mob had lots of money and that they had their eye on the bulldozer. Our Yapa contingent were the only black faces at the auction and strutted around as if money was no object. Once again I was to witness superb Warlpiri acting as they oozed wealth and dignity. At the end of day one we had around $12,000 left to spend and had made our mark.

That evening, by a campfire our Directors befriended the auctioneer, who was a Kardiya from Sydney, who, like so many urban Australians, had "never met an Aborigine" or were unaware of having done so.

The next morning before the auction started, our new friend the auctioneer gave us permission to "fire up" the bulldozer. Roy hopped on the machine and put it through its paces. The YMC contingent behaved as if we already owned the machine. That is when Roy's uncle Ted sprang into action. Ted was well known, but no one at the auction, except us, knew that he was Roy's uncle. Ted quickly spread a rumour that he could hear a rattle in the D6 engine, he should know, as he owned a similar machine. The engine was on its last legs and would cost a fortune to repair, Ted told anyone who cared to listen. That is when our Sydney auctioneer friend started day two of the auction. The bulldozer was the first item.

All eyes turned to us as I placed the first bid: "*$5,000 dollars*," then in quick succession, someone "*$6,000,*" me "*$7,000,*" someone "*$8,000,*" me "*$9,000'*" someone "*$10,000,*" me "*eleven thousand,*" pretending to be poised to go to $13,000 (which I couldn't), a brief silence... and then very quickly our friend the auctioneer without pausing: "*going, going, gone.*"

Roy and YMC directors did a little jig, and then it was time for the next item, a set of recently replaced second hand bulldozer track chains. "*Ten dollars*" I shouted, the crowd burst out laughing but there were no further bids. These used chains were complete with grouser plates and represented thousands of dollars worth of spare parts.

The thousand odd dollars we had left over, we spent on paying for the transportation of our newly acquired assets to Yuendumu.

The D6B transformed the operations at our gravel quarry and was to save YMC from going broke on many occasions by carrying out small scale but profitable earth-moving contracts.

Seismic Lines

One of the most profitable tasks performed by our bulldozer was the clearing of seismic lines for the oil and gas exploration industry.

In seismic surveys, signals are fed into the ground and the returning reflections and refractions recorded. These measurements are then analysed and converted into images. Just like ultrasound scans in modern medicine.

Lines are cleared so that 'thumper' trucks, which lower a hydraulically vibrated pad onto the surface, can quickly and efficiently cover the survey area. A string of 'geophones' which is moved along as the survey progresses record the returning signals which are fed into a recording truck.

The cleared lines are effectively only used once and exploration companies make an effort to ensure these lines have minimal environmental impact. For example, creation of windrows is avoided so as to prevent future erosion.

In 2D-seismic surveys usually a series of parallel straight lines covers the area being surveyed. In 3D-seismic surveys the area is usually covered by a crosshatch pattern of straight lines.

I was peeved when I found out that the Central Land Council charged more for Sacred Site Line Clearance than Yuendumu Mining did for Bulldozer Line Clearance!

During one of these surveys, I was approached by Thomas Rice. *"These tracks are useless,"* he told me. *"Too straight. Should be bendy."*

On these straight tracks the kangaroos and emus could see you coming for miles.

Land Rights...

> **'We will legislate to give Aborigines land rights – not just because**
> **their case is beyond argument, but because all of us as Australians**
> **are diminished while the Aborigines are denied their rightful place**
> **in this nation'**
>   *(Whitlam-1972)*

It is ironic that the Whitlam Government is widely believed to have passed land rights legislation. It was actually the subsequent Fraser Government that, after watering it down somewhat, passed the legislation.

Such events as the 1963 Yirrkala Bark Petition, the 1966 Wave Hill Walk-off and the 1967 Referendum had engendered a new mood which was given much impetus by the Whitlam Government and had finally led to the passing of the Aboriginal Land Rights (Northern Territory) Act 1976.

Another irony is that Aborigines were "given" land rights, whereas in fact they never ceded the land in the first place and it had been stolen from them. It was as if someone who'd burgled your house returned some of his loot as presents on your birthday.

Wendy hoped at the time, that the legislation would mean, *"The invasion stops here. Everything they still own, can't be taken."*

She and many of us were to be bitterly disappointed on that score, as by stealth, Kardiya society regained effective total control of the land. Only a Treaty or Treaties could rectify this fraud, but for a while land rights were received with much acclaim and were a cause of hope and celebration. Much of Australia erroneously believes Land Rights are a fait accompli.

The Warlpiri were fortunate in that large areas of their traditional land was 'unalienated' and thus claimable under the new legislation.

Neighbouring tribes were not so lucky.

For example the Warumungu people who had first asked for their land back in 1975 were to be frustrated by such ruses as the town boundaries of Tennant Creek being expanded in 1978 to encompass 750 square kilometres, the size of a major city. Alienated land such as towns and pastoral leases could not be claimed. The NT Government fought the Warumungu Land Claim tooth and nail in the courts and it wasn't until the 1990s that the Warumungu got some little piece of their land back.

From the 1870's when the Warumungu were a thriving tribe with a strong culture, the appropriation of their lands had reduced them to a dispersed and dispossessed nation with only around 200 Warumungu speakers in the 1980s in contrast to an estimated three thousand Warlpiri speakers.

The Warlpiri Land Claim hearings were presided over by Justice Toohey. Hearings were held in Yuendumu from 18th to 21st March 1978. Justice Toohey witnessed traditional dancing and heard testimony from numerous Yapa as to how they were related to the land and he was presented with genealogies prepared by anthropologists. These proceedings in the main public hall were witnessed by a large number of Yapa and a large number of dogs.

When George Robertson saw what the genealogies looked like, he prepared one for his own family and when George presented his genealogy, it was evident from the very impressed reaction by Justice Toohey, that Yuendumu had achieved a first.

Whilst in Yuendumu Justice Toohey attended and enjoyed himself at a party at which Yapa and Kardiya danced to loud rock and roll music. I recall the judge remarking that such hadn't happened at any other settlement he'd attended. Yet another first for Yuendumu.

The hit list...

The pastoral and mining industries were very paranoid as to how Land Rights might negatively impact their interests. This paranoia was to be repeated in relation to the 1993 Native Title Act.

During the Warlpiri Land Claim hearings, Bruce Farrands at Rabbit Flat had also been infected with this paranoia. He was quoted as having declared that if he'd lose his road house, he would dynamite it. I was also told that Geoff Eames, a lawyer involved in the Warlpiri Land Claim, and a certain Yuendumu based geologist, were prominent on the well-armed Bruce's hit list! As it turned out the Warlpiri generously, had a square kilometre excised from their claim, partly on the basis of Bruce and Jackie's twin Jampijinpa sons, having been born in Rabbit Flat, (Jarntu-jarra, a two dog dreaming). Bruce had famously delivered the twins whilst receiving instructions on the RFDS radio. The abandoned Rabbit Flat Roadhouse is now covered by a unique non-Aboriginal freehold title, a small island in the Warlpiri Land Claim sea.

Paranoia is nothing new in relation to remote Aborigines. During WWII, a theory was floated that German Lutheran missionaries and Australian Aborigines were conspiring as fifth columnists against the Allies fighting Nazism. The Lutherans at Hermannsburg Mission (now renamed Ntaria) copped the same prejudice as did the Barossa Valley Germans of South Australia and the Cape York Germans, only in the latter case this paranoia and prejudice was motivated by the perceived potential of Yapa cooperation with a feared Japanese invasion. Japanese pearl divers in Broome also were in for a rough trot.

In 1982, Geoff MacDonald's 'Red Over Black - Behind the Aboriginal Land Rights' was published. I was told a certain communist geologist made a cameo appearance in this book, in which it is alleged Aboriginal Land Rights are a communist plot. Just as for the WW II Lutheran plot, the allegation was subsequently found to be unfounded and gratuitous, as well as which was the implied allegation, that a certain geologist was a communist. I suspect that geologist was the same one as on Bruce's hit list.

On Anzac Day, Tony Juttner would do the predawn rounds and

assemble a group of Yuendumu residents at the flagpole outside the Council office. As was usual those days this included both Yapa and Kardiya. As well as the many Yapa men who'd worked on the Stuart Highway and the railway or mines during the war, there were some who'd actually enlisted in the army. Tim Langdon wearing long white socks was a regular at our dawn service.

I had had nothing to do with Australia's wartime efforts, but I played the trumpet. Tony would drag me out of bed. Tony's father † Wally Juttner would drive across from Papunya where he worked. †Leo Martin from nearby Mt. Denison Station and †Bill Waudby from Mt. Wedge Station were also regular attendees. Very traditional was Wally Juttner, he would bring a "wriggly" or "corrugated" as Bundaberg Rum bottles were known because of the ribbed glass they were made from. After the service the Kardiya old timers would retire to the police station for a game of two-up and a piss up.

Thus there we were a small enthusiastic group shivering early in the morning doing the dawn service...

> *"At the going down of the sun and in the morning*
> *We will remember them*
> *Lest we forget"*

Followed by an inaccurate but passable rendition of the Last Post.

Wally Juttner was of the last generation of Barossa-Deutsch speakers. Lutheran Germans from Prussia and Silesia had settled in the Barossa Valley of South Australia in the 1840s. Wally speaking what had evolved from 1840s German and me speaking 1950s Dutch could understand each other.

Keith Hicks, Yuendumu's community adviser, was a survivor of the 1964 HMAS Voyager disaster. He was a regular participant in the Yuendumu dawn services but on one Anzac Day had decided to visit Bruce Farrands at Rabbit Flat instead. Bruce, a military enthusiast, told Keith that he rued not being able to take part in Anzac Day commemorations.

"You should have gone to Yuendumu where they have a dawn service and Frank Baarda plays the Last Post!" Bruce was told.

"I'll have to change my mind about that Frank Baarda," Bruce told Keith.

It was then that Bruce removed that communist geologist from his hit list.

The good oil…

The seventh chapter of anthropologist Yasmine Musharbash's book 'Yuendumu Everyday' (published in 2008) is titled 'Hithering and Thithering'. In it Yasmine shows that the apparently random "take me here, take me there" that us Kardiya have often been subjected to, actually has structure and purpose. It is Yapa fulfilling their social obligations, no different to us visiting an old aunt in an Old Folks Home and her asking you to call into her neighbour to pick up her knitting book. The neighbour then asks you to ask your aunt to return the novel she borrowed. Hither and thither you go.

When hippyish Peter Bartlett and fully fledged hippy Al Oshlack (both Japaljarri) arrived in an old army truck, they were soon 'Hithered and Thithered'. Their truck was commandeered to go hither and thither for days and weeks and months on end.

On one memorable trip, †Jimija Jungarrayi and the Spencer family were ferried cross-country to their homeland at Yarripirlangu. Not far from Yarripirlangu is Newhaven Station. Alex Coppock, the station owner, caught up with Jimija and told him that he was on station land. No, no, said Jimija, this is my country. *"I have a piece of paper from the government that says I own this land,"* asserted Alex. *"This is my country,"* countered Jimija and as proof clapped his hands in time, as he chanted the relevant Jukurrpa song. Back and forth this went, this is my land, this is my country, this is my land, this is my country like a Monty Python argument. Finally Jimija came up with a recipe for co-existence: *"This is your land, but it is my country."* The authorities could have saved themselves millions of dollars on lawyers and anthropologists. Jimija had anticipated the Native Title Act by almost two decades.

You might recall the vanished sheep, that were teleported *'Langa Liveringa'*. Another Station which we pin-cushioned with drill holes looking for coal back then, was neighbouring Noonkanbah Station. In 1966, neither the multinational company we'd been hired out to, nor our exploration team, gave consideration to the possibility that the original inhabitants of the land we were drilling on (*them there*

Niggras'), might have a spiritual link to that land, that the land might be sacred. Not an inkling. Not a single thought. Zippo.

In 1980 a convoy of trucks loaded with oil drilling equipment and escorted by hundreds of police, drove up from Perth which led to violent confrontations between police and Noonkanbah anti-drilling protesters. The trucks forced their way through community picket lines onto sacred land. The oil company backed down from its proposal to drill for oil on Noonkanbah, but the Western Australian Government for bloody minded political reasons persisted and drilled a well in its own name. The well was dry, what in the oil exploration industry is known as a 'duster'.

This was a duster in more ways than one.

Less than a year after the highly publicised Noonkanbah confrontation, Jack Mulready who had worked for the same firm of geological consultants I had worked for on graduation, popped his head into Yuendumu Mining Company (YMC)'s office. He now worked for the Moonie Oil Company which was proposing to drill in the Ngalia Basin. Jack knew I had done well-site work in both Australia and Canada. This resulted in YMC, as well as being contracted to prepare the drill site, being awarded the contract for well-site geological supervision.

Davis №1 was the first ever deep oil exploration well drilled in the Ngalia Basin and wasn't far from Central Pacific Minerals' Bigrlyi uranium discovery. The Yapa name for Davis Gap is Palkura.

Following the Noonkanbah protests, the oil and gas exploration industry had developed a new sensitivity to Yapa spiritual connection to land and was eager to be seen to be doing the right thing.

† Jack Jampijinpa Gallagher and I walked the proposed access track. *Wajarnpi* trees (*Acacia estrophiolata*- desert ironwood) were part of a Jukurrpa, and hence needed protection.

Many stands of a particular type of tree are part of a jukurrpa dreaming track. Tree types are not uniformly distributed, so when travelling through country, the species of trees and the associated 'stories' would confirm where you were, especially when there were few other landmarks.

As Jack spotted each *wajarnpi* tree, he would point, *"Dat one, leebim,"* and I would tie a bright orange piece of plastic flagging tape on its trunk. Jack would then make a wide arc with his arm and say: *"Dat one, knockim."* The track needed only to be wide enough for drilling equipment laden trucks to pass, but Jack seemed to have envisioned and approved of a huge field of clear-felled mulga scrub with only a few scattered *wajarnpi* trees remaining upright.

Alex Coppock, the same Alex who'd confronted Jimija at his Newhaven Station some years earlier had grown up amongst Warlpiri children and whilst I don't think he spoke Warlpiri he certainly could understand it. YMC subcontracted him to grade the track and drill site at Davis № 1 after YMC's D6B bulldozer had cleared them. At the site itself, there was a stand of juvenile ghost gums. These were also part of a Jukurrpa. Alex said: *"Frank, them gum suckers is younger than youanmee."*

Despite his childhood background, Alex showed that he subscribed to the Kardiya concept of Jukurrpa: "A long time ago in the Dreamtime". As Alex saw it, these gum suckers were way too young to be part of a Jukurrpa. Alex seemed convinced that only old trees could be sacred. Timelessness is not an easy to grasp concept for us 'time's arrow' people.

A well site geologist is on 24-hour call. As each sample is taken the geologist washes and dries the sample, looks at it through a binocular microscope, describes it, and importantly, places it under ultraviolet light to see if there is any visible oil staining. The bright yellow-green fluorescence of crude oil under UV light is a seldom seen sight, but I can assure you, it is a thing of beauty. Just like the Northern Lights. At Davis №1 neither fluorescing oil staining nor the Northern Lights were seen.

On a visit to the rig, Wendy thought she could smell the odour of kerosene coming from the hot plate on which I was drying a sample. Davis № 1 encountered a thick section of shale which modern analytical techniques showed to be hydrocarbon 'source rocks'. On completion of the well, a bottom-hole core was cut and before setting cement plugs to protect encountered aquifers, natural gas saturated formation water was blown out of the hole. A tiny flame erupted at the end of the flare line.

"*Fraaank, I got more gas in mah stummack,*" the Canadian drilling supervisor declared.

Like the Western Australian Government's Noonkanbah well, so too the Moonie Oil Company's Davis № 1 well was a duster.

GPS

Old †Alex Jupurrurla Wilson, when he was Central Pacific Minerals' camp caretaker, had shown me a worn path in the saddle between two low lying hills east of the camp (Wanalyurrpa) and west of Anomaly №15 (Rapalpa). Alex told me that this was the route taken a long time ago by laden camels travelling from Old Mt. Doreen Station to the Pikilyi (Vaughan Springs) region and that Wijinpa rock-hole was close by, a bit further south.

On oil exploration wells some reprieve in the round the clock sample logging routine results from such as drilling bit changes or running and cementing intermediate casing. That is when the geologist can catch up on sleep, or wander around the drilling site. It was during one such break that I set off in search of Wijinpa. The Davis anticline, the exploration target at Davis №1 and which is clearly visible on air photos, lies east of Wijinpa. I walked westward through the scrub and in the distance, as I escaped the noise of rig operations, I could vaguely hear a choir of birds. That is what I headed for. Eventually I disturbed a flock of zebra-finches (*jiyiki*) that suddenly took to the air. There hidden in thick scrub at the base of a sandstone outcrop was the water filled Wijinpa rock-hole. In a grassy clearing nearby I found several seed grinding stones, which I assume are still there.

To the north-east of Wijinpa, just north of the uranium bearing sandstone formation, there is a small black conical hill. This hill consists of an arkose (a feldspar rich sandstone) with a dolomitic matrix. Weathering of this dolomite (calcium/magnesium carbonate) content has resulted in a coating of black pyrolusite (Manganese dioxide).

It is here that Katirli-katirli the giant *Kinki* (cannibal) woman, who came from Kanaji, the 'Giant's Hole' south-west of Yuendumu, defecated which she is doing for eternity. I have not been able to disassociate the little black hill with the image of a giant woman having a shit ever since. Thus, the landscape is crisscrossed with stories, songs, ground paintings, experiences, observations, metaphors and memories.

When Yapa approached the pile of shit on foot, they knew that

Wijinpa wasn't very far away. They would soon be able to quench their thirst. So too, Kardiya driving North on the Stuart Highway, when reaching a sign that says "Tennant Creek" would know that the nearest pub wasn't very far away. They would soon be able to quench their thirst. Thus the country is festooned with sign posts.

As they reached the Giant's turd it would speak to them: *"Go west, when you reach a saddle in the hill, turn south,"* and as they disturbed the zebra finches, the latter would take to the air and exclaim: *"You have almost reached your destination."*

Yapa invented the GPS long before we did.

Mining their own business...

The Warlpiri have a long history of being involved in mining. The most notable and spectacular evidence of ancient Yapa mining activity in the region is the ochre mine at Karrku (Mount Stanley) south of Nyirrpi. Karrku is a prominent mesa tabletop hill capped by Vaughan Springs Quartzite. A layer of blood red specular haematite occurs below the quartzite. Haematite is an oxide of iron, as is rust. A long horizontal tunnel has been excavated near the top of Karrku, undoubtedly over millennia. I was told that this is the oldest continuously worked mine in the world. The ochre is called *karrku*, the same name as the site. It has been widely traded and was used in countless rituals and ceremonies, and continues to be so used.

Then there is the *kanti* quarry north of Vaughan Springs Homestead. A *kanti* is a stone knife. It is flaked out of silcrete, a hard white weathering product consisting of cryptocrystalline silica, and has a moulded black *palya* (spinifex-wax) handle at the blunt end. When † A.Winwood-Smith, (AWS) was Yuendumu Mining's exploration coordinator, he'd been shown the site of the *kanti* quarry. One of AWS's tools of trade was a GPS.

AWS, myself, Harry Nelson and † Paddy Nelson set off to the quarry which I hadn't yet seen. We took the station track from the homestead which goes past Yintaramurru, a significant permanent water hole in a creek bed. When the track reaches a gap in the east-west aligned Wapurtarli range near Singleton Bore, it swings eastward. From this north-west corner of the track, the *kanti* quarry is due north west according to the GPS coordinates AWS had previously recorded. Paddy had been sitting quietly on the back seat of the Landcruiser, but became agitated when we set off in a north-westerly direction. He insisted we should proceed due west to Janyingki, (the western limb of the range). Don't worry AWS told him, we've got a GPS and it tells us where to go (the shortest distance between two points is a straight line after all). Being the arrogant, controlling Kardiya who knew best, we ignored Paddy and continued cross country due north-west. After bouncing a considerable distance in rough terrain, almost by magic, we accurately in a straight line had reached the *kanti* quarry. Very smug, we were.

The quarry itself is astonishing. Hundreds of metres long there stretches a wide thinly vegetated field covered with densely strewn silcrete flakes, the obvious detritus from centuries of *kanti* manufacture from a large flat silcrete exposure, the bright white shards and flakes in sharp contrast to the dark brown soil.

During the final bouncing leg of our journey Paddy remained taciturnly silent. He was sulking and had clearly lost his enthusiasm for the trip. So I had a quiet word with Harry: *"What's bugging your old man? Why is he jawuru (sulky)?"*

Harry explained: traditionally Yapa used to walk due west to a water hole in the range and go north to the quarry only after having quenched their thirst. Had we walked on that hot day in our straight line short cut with our smart-alec GPS, we would have perished. It would have been as if we'd taken a tollway shortcut and there would be a price to pay.

Karrku (photo - BRDU)

Nyurrupatu, the kanti quarry (photo - R. Graham)

Grasshoppers…

Prior to carrying out exploration activity we would check out the area with Traditional Land Owners (TLOs) to ensure we wouldn't disturb any sacred sites and that we were welcome. Whilst all ground is sacred, TLOs generally would only get upset and object to trespass on specific sites and their surroundings. As we travelled east along a fence line south of Waputarli (Mount Singleton), †Paddy Nelson told me that we were traversing a *Jintilyka-Jukurrpa* (a grasshopper dreaming.) Later with Harry Nelson, Micah Hudson and Ambrose Jupurrurla Wilson, we carried out a soil sampling survey.

The area was subsequently drilled under the Mount Doreen Joint Venture we had with Posgold Ltd. In one hole we struck a layer of coarse perfectly rounded polished sand grains at 20 metres depth, clearly an ancient buried creek bed. Evidence that this now dry land had not always been so.

We found no gold, but I have never seen so many grasshoppers in my life!

Cradle to Grave...

When we first arrived in Yuendumu most women gave birth locally. After a report on infant mortality, official pressure to give birth in Alice Springs was such that soon most births took place there. No effort nor expense was spared when it came to ensuring mothers-to-be arrive in Alice Springs Hospital on time to give birth. The days of birth in the bush or in the community are gone. There have however been a few women who have avoided the clinic and gave birth locally. Their children do not exist and have no, later almost impossible to get, birth certificates. They are destined to grow up as criminal unlicensed drivers.

This birthing in Alice Springs could have had implications when it comes to the traditional social significance of place of birth, including ownership of land. Fortunately it is not the place of birth that determines the child's Jukurrpa, but the place where, after conception the child quickens in the mother's womb, indicating that a child spirit from that place has entered the child. Thus there are many people born in Alice Springs Hospital who came to this world as Yurrampi (Yuendumu honey-ant) children. Hospital births have significantly reduced infant mortality and Yapa society is very flexible and acquiescing when it comes to adjusting to new circumstances and imposed directives.

The much diminished, birthing and post birth role of grandmothers, mothers and aunties was a price Yapa society was prepared to pay. It would be nice however if the authorities would cater for both medical safety as well as the cultural role of families.

Very recently a resident Kardiya midwife has been appointed in Yuendumu, but am told the policy is still to persuade mothers-to-be to give birth in Alice Springs and the midwife's role is mainly confined to providing ante-natal care. Yet another ethnocentric ticking the box and covering their arse exercise.

Early one evening I heard the Royal Flying Doctor Service (RFDS) plane arrive. On the way home I passed a group of people sitting on the ground outside the clinic. "Who is being flown out?" I asked. *"No, Jungarrayi, someone just had a baby!"* I was told with great elation. A mere one hundred metres north of my workplace, a healthy baby was born. A little girl who started life by beating the RFDS to the delight of her family.

On the same day the baby girl who beat the RFDS was born, a service was held at Yuendumu Baptist Church for a great-grandmother. After the service, the cortege drove 90 km north of Yuendumu. The old lady was buried at 'Flood-out' which is the active remnant of an ancient river system. The Warlpiri name of the place is Pirrpirr-pakarnu.

Emanating from 'Flood-out', a fan shaped area of hundreds of square kilometres, is clearly outlined on airborne radiometric survey maps due to the slightly higher radioactivity caused by Potassium-40 weathered out of granite.This radioactive area is part of a palaeochannel. The buried creek bed at the grasshopper dreaming hundreds of kilometres to the south-west of 'Flood-out', attests to the vast extent of this ancient drainage system.

One of the few "privileges" (more like a concession), afforded Northern Territory Aborigines, is the right to choose a bush burial. The right to be buried in your own land, the land that owns you and to which you return. In Yuendumu there is a choice, the cemetery or your homeland.

It was usual for the council or other Yuendumu organisation to send out a backhoe to a homeland to excavate the grave, but this is no longer the case. Either no equipment is available or a large payment is demanded before heading out. Some families dig their graves with shovels or reluctantly choose the cemetery.

One manifestation of authoritarian regimes is the ever increasing proclamation and enforcement of new rules and regulations. The tightening of the screws. The grip of control. The social disruption. The surreptitious use of divide and rule tactics.

During the war my maternal grandfather and one of his young daughters, (my mother), were shot at when they were searching for lumps of coal on the railway tracks. What had been a perfectly normal peacetime activity which harmed no one had been declared to be a punishable crime which justified shooting at the perpetrators. Luckily they missed.

The authorities had also made citizens responsible for the trees on the nature strip in front of their houses, thus much of the population spent sleepless nights listening out for what had been their friends, desperate neighbours, who'd try to steal your tree for firewood. Part of 'us' became 'them', those tree robbers.

I see much the same paradigm playing out in Yuendumu, new rules and increased trepidation amongst friends and neighbours. And the habit of simulation. Thus it came as no surprise to me to hear of moves at tightening the rules on bush burials aimed ultimately at having these suffer the same fate as had bush births. Cradle to Grave Control is what they crave. Bastards!

Whereas hospital births had reduced infant mortality, I can't see any improvements in mortality resulting from cemetery burials!

FRANK BAARDA

Intermission - O Canada

♫ ♫ ♫

Cundill Meyers & Associates the geological consultant firm I'd
worked for in Western Australia transferred me to their newly opened
Canadian office in Calgary. In December 1969 we boarded P&O's SS
Oriana bound for Vancouver.

My first job in Canada was as a well-site geologist on an oil exploration well near Bison Lake in northern Alberta approximately 700 km
north of Calgary. This northern part of Alberta consists of so-called
muskeg country which is covered by a thick water saturated accumula-
tion of vegetation debris, and is only passable when frozen solid during
the coldest part of the year. Drilling rigs can only drill one or two or at
most three wells a year and then get the hell out of the muskeg before,
because of warmer weather, the authorities close the roads to prevent
damage. Stranded rigs are secured and have to sit out the summer
without being able to drill further south.

Alberta has a legislated grid system of 'town' (east-west) and
'range' (north-south) lines. The remote roads follow this system and
are monotonously straight. I prepared myself for this first sortie to the
frozen Canadian outback by reading all about what to do in case of
breakdown. Stay calm, don't panic, don't fall asleep. Make sure that
there is sufficient ventilation to prevent carbon monoxide poisoning if
keeping the engine running to keep warm. Freezing to death, whilst
reputedly being the most painless possible death, is not recommended.
As a last resort a motor vehicle has a lot of flammable components to
keep you warm. Stay calm, don't panic, don't fall asleep.

As I set off with newly studded tyres, I soon found out that driving
on icy roads was very similar to driving on slippery roads in the
Australian outback after rain and thus didn't present an insurmountable
problem. I'd already learned how to handle slippery roads. I made

good progress until eventually as I approached the drill site I was on one of those east-west 'town' roads, when at an unexpected curve I ran off the road and came to rest in a deep snow embankment. Stay calm, don't panic, don't fall asleep.

After a long while I heard the hum of a snowmobile (also known as a ski-doo in Canada) in the distance. I was saved! When the Chinese looking snowmobile rider pulled up beside my car, I asked him for help. He just ignored me and seemed most disinclined to come to my rescue. Whilst fearing for my life I pleaded and pleaded. He finally took pity on me, and without saying a word, attached a chain to my car and pulled me onto the road.

It took me a long while to figure out what had happened. The Chinese looking fellow was actually a Canadian Indian, who had probably suffered too many racist taunts, insults, put downs and unfair treatment. His 'empathy to palefaces bank account' had suffered too many withdrawals. It may well have been my Australian accent which changed his mind. This was to be one of the very few instances in my life in which I bore the brunt of racism. It upset me a great deal, and I can't begin to imagine what it must feel like to be an Aboriginal Australian and cop this sort of shit as a continuous never ending part of your life.

A notable visitor to Yuendumu was †Warren Mitchell whose most famous role was that of Alf Garnet, the cockney bigot in the TV Series 'Till Death do us Part' which had been my father's favourite TV programme. Warren was doing a comedy gig at the Riverside Hotel in Alice Springs. Warren decided to visit a remote community and gravitated to the Yuendumu Mining store. I spent a very enjoyable and interesting few hours showing him around. I told him the story of the Royal Visit to the oil drilling rig I'd worked at in the Canadian Arctic.

Canada's Prime Minister †Pierre Trudeau (Justin's father) invited the British Royal family to tour Manitoba and the Northwestern Territories. Nothing like a Royal visit to unite a nation and to score some electoral brownie points. With military precision the Royal family split up and were sent forth to various locations during their ten day tour.

At our drilling rig on Ellef Ringnes Island a stranger turned up on a crew-change flight. He asked many questions and turned out to be from the Canadian Security Services. Prince Charles and Prince Phillip were to pay us a visit and his brief was to make sure it was safe for them to do so.

Well, as you can imagine, we tough Arctic pioneers were thoroughly underwhelmed. As the cook laid out the dinner plates he'd be addressing the as yet invisible visitors,

"Whatcha reckon Chuck? Is this Good enuff?" "You don't laik it Dook? well ya can take it or leave it!" Or someone would hold up a hand of cards over his shoulder for an invisible royal visitor to see: *"Whatcha reckon Dook, should I raise them?"*

The arctic had suffered a sixty degrees Fahrenheit (15°C) heatwave and our frozen airstrip had turned to mud. All our Royal visit rehearsals had been for nought.

On oil drilling rigs there is a bank of diesel engines that are needed to hold back like a pendulum or to lift a very heavy string of steel drill pipe. These engines set up an almost continuous loud roar. Ears and brains amazingly filter out this noise so that normal conversations can be had and the hum of a distant aircraft can be heard.

As we sat around the dinner bench playing cards, the radio in the next room crackled to life.

"Arctic rig, arctic rig, this is Royal flight two, do you copy?"

As we shrugged our shoulders and continued our card game, the drilling engineer sprung into action and got on the radio.

"Royal flight two, this is arctic rig, roger roger, copying you loud and clear, over!" and then again in that posh Pommy accent,

"Roger, roger, arctic rig, this is Royal flight two, any traffic in your area? Over!"

Which was a bit of a silly question considering where we were. Our drilling engineer was getting into the swing of things. In a strong Canadian accent,

"Roger, roger, Royal flight two, this is arctic rig. Negative, negative, negative, no traffic in our area, over!"

Throughout this Biggles like performance we gave each other knowing amused looks, but did eventually put on our parkas and nonchalantly headed outside. Royal or not, planes were a rare enough sight that they warranted a look. Way off in the distance we could hear a hum and see a dot on the horizon. We waved to the crew on the drilling deck and pointed at the approaching aeroplane. The aircraft got a bit closer and we speculated on whether the Dook himself was flying the plane. He was after all, known to be a pilot. We again waved at the crew on the rig floor and pointed at the approaching plane to make sure they didn't miss out. The low flying plane got closer and was by now clearly visible. We thought it was highly likely Prince Phillip was flying the plane. By now we were getting a bit excited and were sure that Prince Charles was his father's co-pilot. If we'd had little Union Jacks without a doubt we would have vigorously waved them especially when we jumped for joy as the aircraft dipped its wing at us and circled the drilling rig, and how exciting was this? It dipped its wing a second time as it headed to the horizon whence it came from. When it was all over we all stared at the ground and avoided eye contact.

The Royal visit was never mentioned again.

I derive some nostalgic pride in the fact that I had Warren Mitchell, a world famous comedian, in stitches. Warren asked if he could use the story. It almost goes without saying I granted permission, and ever since, I've watched everything he did but no, alas no Arctic Royal visit in his repertoire. May he rest in peace.

If I didn't know it then, I know it now: *"The most effective way to fight racism and prejudice, is to make it ridiculous,"* Warren told me. This isn't hard to do, bigots often suffer from foot in mouth disease and make themselves ridiculous without us having to take the trouble and make much of an effort to do so. You need only look at the White Australia Policy's bizarre and ludicrous 'dictation test' which was in any language the official applying the test chose. If you weren't paying attention, *any* language. A Tamil speaking Sri Lankan could be tested in Polish, or a Mandarin speaking Chinese could be tested in Hungarian.

And how fortunate *you're* not Professor de Breeze who has spent the past thirty-two years, if you pleas trying to teach Irish ducks how to read Jivvanese.

(Dr Seuss - 'Did I ever tell you how lucky you are')

Some of my best friends…

> *You all know those famous platitudes:*
> *"I'm not racist."*
> *"Some of my best friends are… "*
> *"Our cleaning lady is…."*

In Australia from time to time, a debate pops up, "Is Australia a racist country?" a rather disingenuous question when this wonderful nation of ours has never fully come to terms with its racist foundations. We cannot pretend that the Terra Nullius dispossession, the introduction of diseases, the massacres and poisoned damper, the 'smoothing of the dying pillow', the assimilation policies, the Stolen Languages, the Stolen Children, the Stolen Bones and Sacred Artefacts, the Stolen Wages, the Stolen Freedom, the Stolen Dignity and Respect never happened and neither should we ignore the current dog whistling cacophony. It is indeed as in Patrick Davies' song '*A Rocky Old Road that we travel'* and we still have a long way to go as a nation.

Neither should we forget that it was the first parliament of our new nation which passed the Immigration Restriction Act of 1901, the so-called White Australia Policy which wasn't fully dismantled until 1973, the year we arrived in Yuendumu.

It was on the ship which brought my family to Australia that I remember a young man who played a ukulele and who entertained us with Indonesian songs on the deck. The young man told us that his brother had been denied entry into Australia because he was too dark. Later during my studies I was to become familiar with Soil Colour charts. I now think the use of these charts wasn't confined to soil science. I suspect the Australian "populate or perish" apparatchiks in Europe made use of the CSIRO soil colour chart when enforcing the White Australia policy. It was a delicious irony that as we approached the equator, the Dutch East Indian ukulele player moved down the colour chart and by the time he disembarked he was almost as dark as the uniforms worn by NT Police.

Close to the bone

In Yuendumu the self-determination/bilingual education winds of change had caused displays of overt racism to become rare and to be promptly stomped on whenever they surfaced. The same couldn't be said for Alice Springs. The Kardiya population of Alice Springs could simplistically be divided into pro-Yapa and anti-Yapa and still can. You had to choose your friends. You had to choose sides. Sometimes you had to bite your tongue.

At around this time Wendy wrote her song 'Close to the Bone'. Here is the chorus:

Don't talk to me about niggers and boongs,
I don't laugh when you mention gin jockeys and coons,
Coz you're cutting a little too close to the bone,
You're knocking my family, my friends and my home.

Micah Hudson and myself used to drive into Alice Springs to take part in the Monday night jam sessions held at the Riverside Hotel featuring the Booze Brothers. This was the same venue at which Warren Mitchell had performed. We often ran into other Yapa musicians such as Sammy Butcher and Frank Yamma who had travelled long distances to be there. Herman Marcic and his band generously and graciously made room for new talent and visiting musicians. We played and fired up the mostly white audiences and got them up dancing.

On one occasion I walked in and the bouncer made a gesture acknowledging my naked trumpet, I didn't have a trumpet case. When I looked back I saw Micah held up at the door. By 'coincidence' my entry had resulted in a full house. My offer to swap places with Micah, who was a far better musician than me, bounced. Herman saw what was happening and let Micah in, but by then it was too late and our euphoric anticipation had vanished. We didn't play or dance that evening.

This is not an isolated incident. There was the time our son Joe and his friend Japanangka tried to get into the Alice Springs Casino. Japanangka was refused entry allegedly because of the clothes he was wearing. 'Dress Regulations' are an often used euphemism to restrict access to Yapa. Japanangka and Joe retreated to the car park and swapped clothes. On their second attempt to enter the Casino, Japanangka was again refused entry. Seems to be that the well known proverb 'clothes maketh the man' fails to account for skin colour! In Yuendumu we don't have 'Dress Regulations', this is obvious to all who know me.

Wendy recalls an extreme case of this nonsense when she went to a bicycle shop in Alice Springs. Our adopted Yapa daughter, a child at the time, was told by the shop lady to wait outside. When our dog then entered the shop she said, *"It's OK for your dog to stay."* Some people have no idea how stupid they sound.

In Yuendumu, optimism reigned twenty years after the introduction of bilingual education in the NT. This is best illustrated by an excerpt from an article by Wendy: 'The impact of the bilingual program in Yuendumu 1974-1993' in 'Aboriginal Languages in Education' (published by IAD):

"The status of the Warlpiri language has improved greatly in the community, in the eyes of both white people and Warlpiri people. It is not ignored or put down by anyone. Lots of meetings are conducted in Warlpiri these days, with the decisions being related to the white people afterwards. And as the language has gained in respect, so have the people. The bilingual program, together with the much less racist treatment of Aboriginal people, seems to be producing young people who are more sure of their identity and more proud of it." In the year 2000, a quarter of a century after Wendy wrote, 'Close to the Bone' the biggest ever public 'demonstration' in Australia took place. An estimated quarter of a million people walked across the affectionately nicknamed Coathanger, the Sydney Harbour Bridge, in support of

Reconciliation with Australia's First People. This also was to be the high point in anti-racist sentiment in Australian society. Overt racism was at a low ebb. In 2010, a mere decade after the Sydney Harbour Bridge walk, a group of contractors moved into the accommodation facilities Yuendumu Mining Company had set up. I showed them the ablution block and kitchen and their rooms. One of the contractors asked me:

"Do coons walk around here at night?"

I thought I'd misheard so I got him to repeat,

"Do coons walk around here at night?"

"We don't call them that here, maybe they do in Alice Springs, and yes they do walk around here, this happens to be their home."

There have always been and always will be racists, far more than I like to imagine, but at least I thought that multicultural Australia had driven them into the closet. The Intervention has reopened that closet door. The door remains open. Our leaders with their xenophobic dog whistling have much to answer for.

Turkeys...

Like in the Drover's Dream song, Yuendumu is subjected to a very strange procession. Often these visitors gravitated to Harry Nelson who usually referred to them as, 'Turkeys' or sometimes 'Clowns'. I tend to be less kind and refer to them as *kujurlpa* one of the Warlpiri words for 'tosser' or 'wanker'. I would again like to emphasize that we always followed Warlpiri manners and never called them these names to their face.

Danish author and filmmaker, Jens Bjerre, had visited Yuendumu in the 1950s. In 1957 his book 'The Last Cannibals' was published. The book included a section on the Warlpiri tribe. Several decades later he paid a return visit with the Danish ambassador in tow. He was somewhat put out when no one seemed to remember his visit nor volunteered to take him and the ambassador to 'snake rocks'. He wasn't listening when several times it was pointed out to him that Ngama is known as 'Snake Cave' and not the 'Snake Rocks' he kept on mentioning.

After reading a review of Bjerre's book, I came to the conclusion that the Danish pair were tossers.

> *"His first visit was to an aborigine reserve in the desert of central Australia. There he became a member of the tribe, moving with them on their nomadic wanderings, sharing in a kind of life that has not varied for thousands of years from the complicated system of tribal marriage to the gruesome ritual of circumcision..." Kujurlpa!*

On our bookshelves there is a book 'Sentics'. It was given to me by the author, Professor Manfred Clynes, who in an uncharitable moment I described as epitomising that thin line between madman and genius. Professor Clynes was a polymath who died in January last year at the age of 94. As I remember, he graduated in music, computer science, psychology, neurology, engineering and more. He invented Sentics which gave rise to a cult following, the American Sentics Association, based unsurprisingly in California.

The basic premise of Sentics as Manfred explained it to me, is that if for example, you flashed a red card to a Native American, and then to an Italian, and then to a Chinese, the resulting brainwaves from all three would be very similar. This didn't surprise me in the least. The book contains more examples than I needed to discern the self evident truth of the premise.

Manfred came to Yuendumu school where he'd been given permission to test the children. In a class room an instrument had been set up from which different sounds emanated. A high pitching upward sweeping whistle, a low ponderous humming sound, a mid-range pitching tremolo. The children were each given a test sheet with words on a check list and a square in which to put a number. The word list included 'joy,' 'anger,' 'love,' 'reverence,' 'grief',' and 'hate'. They had to match the sounds to the words on the list. The words were read out to them. The children conferred among themselves in Warlpiri and decided communally where to put the numbers. On completing the tests they'd be rewarded with peanuts and dried apricots. These kids are experts at reading faces. When they gave the "right" answer they would detect a hint of pleasure in Manfred's face, a "wrong" answer and there would be a hint of disappointment.

It didn't take long for the children to start sharing the "correct" answers, with others at the subsequent testing at the social club library. Some even came back for a second go if they'd "failed" the first time. All of this unbeknownst to Manfred as it had all transpired in the Warlpiri language. He rewarded the school with a classical piano recital (as well as the individual peanuts and dried apricots). I suspect that the Yuendumu children yielded the highest correlation coefficients of all of Professor Manfred Clyne's global research.

Wendy invited Manfred for dinner. He told us the children had difficulty distinguishing between 'love' and 'sex', a distinction not all that clear in Kardiya society either. A problem with the word 'reverence' had prompted Manfred to ask a girl what 'reverence' was. The girl didn't hesitate in answering: "*That is when someone hits you and you hit them back.*" To the girl 'reverence' meant nothing. 'Revenge' was something she did know about.

Manfred, despite having rather short stubby fingers, was an accomplished concert pianist. After dinner we were privileged to get a piano recital of our own. After he sat down he played a very fast piece of classical music. He told us that at the school he had experienced something that had never happened to him before. He told us that no sooner had he started playing this piece, all the gathered children had burst out in unison in loud uncontrolled laughter. *"Actually Mozart composed it as a humorous piece,"* he said.

To the school children, in those pre-television days, that a short Kardiya with short stubby fingers, a goatee beard and thick glasses should sit down at the piano and with a flourish, start playing a classical piece in an allegro tempo, was something that had never happened to them before. They thought it was very funny. Manfred lost me when during dinner he declared in a 'believe it or not' tone of voice: *"These people are very intelligent, you know!..."*

Kujurlpa!

FRANK BAARDA

Hybridization

A fairly common trait of Kardiya when arriving in remote communities, is that they are intent on reinventing the wheel. *"New fucking brooms with new fucking ideas,"* as † Bill Mckell so eloquently and succinctly once put it. I was to be no exception.

Yapa capacity to let Kardiya carry on with their delusions never ceases to amaze me. There is no *"We already know about that"* or *"That's been tried before"* about it. Why enlighten Kardiya, when they don't listen anyway?

Yuendumu Mining Company became involved in the native seed trade in 1980. I very smugly, just like teenagers who are prone to think they've invented copulation, thought I'd introduced seed trading to Yuendumu. In hindsight, at the time I was surprised and gratified by how little persuasion and encouragement was required for seed collecting to be enthusiastically embraced by Yapa. Turns out that twenty years earlier, superintendent Ted Egan had arranged for the collection of several drums of mulga seeds which were sold to a UN agency.

In 1979 Rod Horner who was then working for the Department of Aboriginal Affairs approached us. Central Australian tree seeds were in demand for de-desertification projects in the Middle East. An exporter needed 1,000 Kg of *Acacia victoriae* (Prickly wattle- *yalupu*) seeds to fill an order which originated in Libya, and was offering $30/ Kilo. In 1979 $30,000 was a lot of money but unfortunately severe thunderstorms had damaged the flowering trees, and almost no seed was available locally that year. Rod told me that about 300kg of the order was filled from Docker River, almost $10,000 worth, not to be sneezed at.

Yapa have been collecting grass and acacia seeds from time immemorial. Baby-carrier coolamons (*parraja*) were used to clean the seeds, and women became very skilled at using a "two-way" rocking motion to very efficiently winnow the seeds. In English this is called 'yandying'.The seeds were ground on grinding stones and the flour cooked into damper or porridge. When wheat flour made in large industrial mills became available, gathering, cleaning and cooking of native seeds gradually ceased. In 2010, what Yuendumu Mining paid for one kilo of seed, could buy almost two 12.5Kg bags of self raising flour.

Yuendumu Mining has had seeds brought to it from as far away as Ti-Tree, Haasts Bluff and Nyirrpi. The Mount Allan (Yuelamu) people were however the champions, not least Ted Briscoe's family at Desert Bore (Pulardi) a short distance from Yuelamu.

Alice Springs based Rod Horner who first introduced us to the seed market, continued to be our sales agent for a modest commission. Supply of seeds has literally dried up. We're enduring a long period of almost no rainfall, as well as which a very lucrative Aboriginal Arts market has acted as a disincentive to time consuming seed gathering.

In forty years of trading we handled twenty five tonne of seeds and bush tucker. Whilst we have dealt in 35 species, mostly Acacia trees, only a few species accounted for most of the trade. The most important species traded by far was the so-called 'bush tomato', *Solanum centrale*, followed by red river gum and mulga.

Peter Latz a Kardiya who grew up in Hermannsburg Mission is the author of 'Bushfires and Bushtucker- Aboriginal plant use in Central Australia' Peter's seminal book was first published by IAD Press in 1995. Latz's book is based on knowledge he gained from Yapa informants, and it is the Aboriginal people of Central Australia to whom he has dedicated his book. A revised and updated second edition was printed in 2018. The illustrated book has names of species in several Aboriginal languages and has proved invaluable to me when communicating with Yapa in relation to the seed trade and other botanical matters. Older Warlpiri people can identify and name countless native plants and trees.

I'd told Yapa to bring in a small quantity of any different variety of seed which we hadn't dealt with before and also to please bring a branch or leaves or flowers, anything to help identify the seeds. I would tell them that I'd let them know if we were interested in larger quantities.

So there we had a small quantity of an unidentified seed and a small tree branch in a flour drum.

"*Niya nyampuju?*" (What is this?,) I asked †Darby Jampijinpa. He frowned, handled the sample, held up the branch, racked his brain, and mumbled "*I come back tomorrow*". He came back the next day and repeated the performance. This went on for several days. It had him worried. I know the feeling, such as when I can't remember someone's name or where I left the keys, or when I don't know what that piece of string tied to my finger is doing there. And then suddenly, with a big grin "*This one kurdurrurdururru!*" I looked it up in Latz' book. It is *Acacia maitlandii*.

Late one afternoon after I'd just closed the shop I was approached by two Yapa ladies,

"*Can we buy some kuyu?*"

"*Lawa we're closed.*"

Just then Steve Midgley from the CSIRO's Australian Tree Seed Centre and a French academic student whose name escapes me pulled up. I'll call him Jean-Pierre. They introduced themselves and Jean-Pierre told me in a very strong French accent he was doing a "*zeezis on muuelga*". The Yapa ladies were sitting down on the ground in the hope I'd change my mind. The Kardiya were starting to tell me why they'd come. They were researching whether the needle leaved variety of mulga hybridised with the broad leaved variety. Did they have samples with them? I asked, and they soon produced some out of their vehicle. I turned to the ladies and told them I would open the shop for them but first they had to help these Kardiya.

Both ladies immediately identified the two varieties of mulga (gave their Warlpiri names) and enthusiastically told the CSIRO bods in great detail the various places where these different varieties could be found and much more. If I'd known the Warlpiri word for hybridisation or at least be able to express the concept in Warlpiri, I'm sure those ladies would have been able to provide the answer Steve and Jean-Pierre were seeking. In another universe these ladies might have written a 'Thesis on Mulga'. There would have been no need for someone to travel from the other side of the world to write it.

The two ladies had this in common: they both wanted to buy meat after the shop had closed. Otherwise they were entirely random. I have no doubt that many more Warlpiri ladies know a thing or two about mulga.

Africa...

♫ ♫ ♫

Nkosi sikelel'i Afrika - (God Bless Africa)

During the 1970s and 1980s the CSIRO introduced Central Australian acacia trees, predominantly *kalkardi* (*Acacia colei)* to villagers near Maradi in Niger. Central Australian acacias are drought resistant and the protein rich seeds mature during the sub-Saharan harvesting off-season and thus supplemented the diet at times when sorghum and millet were in short supply, especially after crop failures.

†Kay Napaljarri Ross, †Rosie Nangala Fleming and Wendy accompanied the CSIRO on a 'cultural exchange' visit to Niger. The villagers had been harvesting *kalkardi* for years but as the seeds were too hard for their traditional pounding, had to pay to get their seeds ground at a mill. Rosie showed how in Australia seed was traditionally cooked until the shells were cracked and could then be easily hand ground. Although *Kalkardi* was successfully introduced to Niger, ironically, the seeds are now exported from sub-Saharan Africa to Europe for the exotic luxury food market as the high price received can buy a greater quantity of lower priced food and goods in Niger. Even these lower prices are normally out of reach for many Niger villagers.

On the way to Niger, Kay Rosie and Wendy called in on Armand's gallery in Paris. Armand used to regularly visit Yuendumu on his Australian Aboriginal art buying sorties. Rosie was overjoyed when she saw some of her own paintings for sale on the other side of the world. While there, Kay and Rosie sold Armand some more paintings.

In Niger, Kay, Rosie and Wendy had their eyes opened to a whole other world. I got to hear how notwithstanding their poverty the people of Niger were very enterprising. I was told about their joie de vivre, their generosity and their friendly charm. Wendy told me that both Kay and Rosie were very impressed with the children working in all the little businesses that lined the streets of Maradi. *"These are proper good worker kids,"* they said, *"We have useless kids in Yuendumu."* Cultural cringe is not confined to Kardiya.

Kay and Rosie gave as much as they got. The Africans much enjoyed their Warlpiri visitors, with their genuine interest in African customs, embracing of African people, and the way they would pick up and cradle Niger babies. They got on like a house on fire.

Rosie in Niger

I was told how the nomadic Fulani would herd their animals through a patchwork of small paddocks delineated by stones on Hausa land but would only do so after harvest and when this did not interfere with Hausa agricultural endeavours. How the Tuareg from the north with their mobile villages were tolerated. How the Christian minority and Muslim majority peacefully coexisted. Sadly, since the Yuendumu visit, the situation in Niger has gone pear shaped.

In Melinda Hinkson's book 'Remembering the Future - Warlpiri Life through the Prism of Drawing' there is a Welfare era photo showing a 'housegirl' hanging up the washing on a Hills Hoist in the backyard of the missionary Fleming household. The very good looking, lively young woman smiling at the camera was †Rosie Fleming. The very same Rosie who'd travelled to Africa with Kay and Wendy. For a time Rosie lived with Kay Smith, the former manager of the Old People's Programme in a so-called 'lolly house'. A couple of the very few remaining 'donkey houses' had received a prize winning refurbishment and dubbed 'lolly houses' because of the bright colours they'd been painted.

After Rosie returned from Niger, Kay Smith tells me that for a while, she became 'African Rosie'. In her bright coloured African clothes, Rosie would tell her friends and anyone who cared to listen, all the things the independent people of Niger did for themselves, such as casting spoons and bowls and car keys out of molten metal salvaged from old car bodies. Rosie would preface her African tales with, *"They are very clever Yapa people."* She'd copied what she'd seen in Niger and planted lots of trees around the perimeter of the lolly houses. She hoped other Yapa would be inspired to do the same. I've just checked out the lolly houses, they're surrounded by lots of native trees.

Interestingly Kay Ross came away from Niger with a very different point of view. She felt sorry for the people of Niger, *"They have no Kardiya to help them."* Kay saw Kardiya as an asset that no one should have to do without.

When news spread of the sudden death of our six weeks old grandchild, it was †Tilo Nangala and Rosie who were the first to arrive at our home to share our grief. *"That little boy is in heaven now,"* they consoled us.

At the first community meeting at which the Federal Government sought long term leases over residences within the Yuendumu 'prescribed area' proclaimed by the Intervention, Wendy recalls Rosie getting up and talking about the jukurrpa in and around Yuendumu.

"This place doesn't belong to you Government people, it has jukurrpa," she asserted. *"My jukurrpa. From my grandfather, and it's the jukurrpa for some other families too."*

She started telling some of the jukurrpa stories. She knew all about the jukurrpa of this place and that it belonged to Yapa, not to *'you government people'* as she repeatedly called them. *"That is not what we are here to talk about"*, Rosie was told. She was silenced and dismissed as a crazy old lady, yet she was more on the ball than all others present. If Kardiya get land handed down from their grandfather, can other people just come and take it over? Kardiya have documents to prove their ownership. Yapa have songs and stories. Rosie was asserting ownership, but no one listened, least of all those 'Government people'.

At the tail end of her life Rosie lived at the granny flat at the rear of the manse where she had been a 'housegirl' all those many years ago. The art centre adjoins the rear of the manse and Rosie would spend her days there, sitting down painting and chatting to the artists, the volunteers and the visitors. She was always willing to spend time with Kardiya, teaching them about her culture and language. Occasionally she would sing Jukurrpa songs.

This was before Rosie got dementia. As her condition deteriorated she was seen wandering around collecting plastic bottles. Had we seen her mother she kept asking. She even started losing her Warlpiri sense of direction and had to be helped to find her way home. She was looking for places and camps where they used to be many years ago, places and camps which no longer existed. Rosie ended up at the Hetti Perkins Home for the Aged in Alice Springs. Away from her dogs, friends and family, away from her home, from country, away from reality, she was unhappy and confused. She didn't last long.

Three days before I wrote this, Rosie passed away. Far from her jukurrpa. Far from the country she belonged to. Far from the land she no longer owned. Her surviving dogs now live at the art centre and are well looked after. Rosie was Jimija's widow. She was Harry Nelson's mother in law. Rosie was 91 years old. Rosie had a long rich and interesting life. A life well lived. For those who believe, Rosie surely would have finally found her mother.

In the early 1970s Rex Connor, the Whitlam Government's Minister for Minerals and Energy, declared that in future all uranium exploration in Australia would be carried out by the Atomic Energy Commission. Large areas of the Ngalia Basin became vacant as potential explorers refrained from applying for Exploration Licences. Yuendumu Mining Company (YMC) built up a significant portfolio of licence applications which when Rex Connor's restrictions were lifted led to a number of joint ventures in which large companies spent large amounts of money (millions) on behalf of YMC. These funds were only repayable if exploration was successful, which didn't happen.

One such joint venture was with Afmeco, a French company. Afmeco bosses came out to negotiate a joint venture and brought with them a folder containing photographs of Afmeco's African operations. Grinning out of glossy photographs were happy Africans carrying out mineral exploration tasks such as bagging samples at a drilling rig. This was to show their good faith and how they had experience working with 'natives'. Fair enough, after all we are often reminded that all 'natives' are the same. Afmeco also sold YMC a good second hand Land Rover for one dollar.

Mary Laughren the Yuendumu School linguist had graduated at the University of Nice, France. She had done her linguistic field work in Cote d'Ivoire. Awa, her friend from the Ivory Coast, came to Yuendumu to visit Mary. I must confess that I wasn't entirely immune to vivacious, French speaking Awa's charm. Proper *yuntardi* (beautiful) she was. Afmeco had set up camp near Cussack Bore around 50 kilometres west of Yuendumu. I enthusiastically offered to show Awa around the bush, including a visit to Afmeco's French speaking geologists. I was taken aback by Awa's reception. The French geologists' body language left a lot to be desired and was in sharp contrast to their keen unfolding of the folder of African photos. I guess Awa was the wrong colour and not conveniently stuck in a glossy photo album.

When in October 2017 a highly publicised ambush occurred in Niger in which four US Army Special Forces soldiers were killed, my curiosity was piqued. Niger after all was the country to which Rosie, Kay and Wendy had travelled. Turns out the US army has 800 personnel in Niger. They are building a drone base in the Agadez region. And guess what else there is in the Agadez region? Yes sir, uranium mines controlled by French companies. Niger was and is the poorest country in Africa despite being responsible for 5% of the world's uranium production.

Most likely Afmeco's glossy photographs had been taken in the Agadez region.

Conflagration...

Spinifex plains and Mulga scrub are the dominant vegetation regimes of Warlpiri country. Spinifex is a hummocky grass which is characterised by its sharp spiky leaves. Central Australian spinifex belongs to two genera (*Triodia* and *Plectrachne*) which, in Peter Latz's book we are told, are very difficult to distinguish. Yapa do make such a distinction and recognise hard ('porcupine') spinifex and resinous soft spinifex.

At Mereenie, a three day workshop on 'Environmentally sound oilfield practices' was held. Grant Japanangka Granites, Douglas Jakamarra Wilson and myself attended. Douglas was Yuendumu Mining's main bulldozer operator at the time. The Mereenie oil and gas field is located approximately 150 kilometres directly south of Yuendumu as the crow flies. To get to Mereenie on the back roads from Yuendumu, one has to skirt Gosse's bluff, a spectacular circular impact crater believed to have been caused when a comet struck earth. Wikipedia tells me that the Arrernte also believe a cosmic impact to have been responsible, they just have a very different way of telling the story.

At the workshop Peter Latz gave a memorable talk. As I recall, Peter had the spinifex army attacking the mulga scrub and slowly winning. Mulga (*Acacia aneura*) in nature requires fire and rain for the seeds to germinate and grow.

From a point of ignition, a spinifex fire fans out until it reaches new short growth on a recently burnt fan shaped patch of ground. The fire then dies out. Subsequent fires fan out in different directions at different times, creating a fascinating mosaic pattern of burning on spinifex plains which is very much evident on air photos or satellite images as well as on some Aboriginal dot paintings. From time to time, patches of spinifex miss out on being burned and grow tall and dry. The higher fuel load leads to intense fires which on reaching a mulga grove, incinerate the trees and seeds instead of germinating them. It could be said that the civilian mulga trees are the collateral damage from the advancing spinifex army. An army with greater firepower.

On the second day of the workshop, the Bushfires Council of the NT delegate gave us a demonstration of back burning. Spinifex burns well. A sudden strong gust of wind and whoosh the back burn got away. All workshop participants spent the rest of the day putting out the fire. Another lesson learned. Very embarrassed was the back burning expert.

When Yuendumu Mining was actively exploring for gold, we always took 'old fellows' with us. Now that I'm an 'old fellow' myself, I feel a bit awkward using that term, but at the time, that is what we called them, 'old fellows'. In Warlpiri society calling someone old is a mark of respect. Out bush these old fellows blossomed. From being a person asking in poor English for a $20 loan to get a feed or some tobacco, to being a person who could tell you something about every little feature of the country you travelled through, was quite a transformation.

"*Those are warnapari-kartirdi,*" - dingo teeth - as we passed a series of pearly white quartz exposures.

"*That is where Jupurrurla had a fight with Jakamarra,*" (not sure if he was talking about 'ancestral being' or present day people). As we passed a batch of large rounded granite boulders: "*That is a Yankirri-Jukurrpa,*" - an Emu dreaming - the round boulders being emu eggs if you haven't worked it out.

"*That is where I had my first nookie,*" and so on.

Not a dull moment. Magical mystery tours are what they were. Too late, but I wish now I had stopped the vehicle more often and taken notes, but then, that may have spoiled those moments.

On quite a few occasions, the old fellow in the passenger seat would hand me a box of matches and tell me in Aboriginal English to "*Light-im.*" Remember out bush they were in charge. I would duly set the spinifex on fire. This far from happened every trip. Quite uncanny, invariably a fortnight or so after I'd been commanded to "*Light-im,*" it would rain. Formal Central Land Council negotiated agreements that prohibited mining company exploration personnel or contractors from lighting fires were the furthest from my mind when an old fellow told me to *"Light-im."* Old fellows ought to be obeyed. I did what I was told to by those I considered myself to be answerable to. Besides, it was good fun.

Germinating fires were caused by lightning or started by Yapa and were usually followed by a downpour from thunderstorms, which had caused the lightning in the first place. Very clever is nature! Very smart are Yapa.

Sadly as Yapa are restrained or discouraged from, or not interested in roaming their homelands and light fires as they used to, destructive wildfires are increasingly common. The fine ecological balance which has developed over millennia has been seriously disrupted in a matter of decades. Ecological diversity is being much degraded. The number of critters, small mammals and reptiles, has seriously declined. Once plentiful, bettongs, bilbys, possums and bandicoots are extinct or have all but disappeared. The happy days of hunting these tasty animals were still in the living memory of our oldest people until very recently.

Counter-intuitively, guns had nothing to do with this decline as these animals were caught by digging. Yapa also refrained from killing the larger individuals so that they could continue to breed.

No it wasn't guns, but largely degradation of habitat that caused the demise of these creatures. The animals are gone but their Jukurrpa remain, their names, stories and places go on in the Warlpiri collective memory, just like Kardiya's mammoths and do-do birds. Before first contact and even until fairly recent times and within living memory, there were Yapa living off their land. I doubt that the land today could still sustain a significant number of freely roaming Yapa.

When it comes to fire management and reclamation of ecosystems, the recent introduction of Ranger programmes in IPAs (Indigenous Protected Areas) offers some hope for the future but the Rangers have a lot of ecological damage to repair, a lot of catching up to do, not least in the way these programmes are implemented, often with a superimposed Kardiya administrative and operational hierarchy. Caring for country has been tamed, controlled, administrated, usurped and monetised. When the Ranger programme started in Yuendumu there was one

Kardiya and a dozen Yapa Rangers, at present there are a few Kardiya and three Yapa.

Large areas have been denuded of vegetation, and as spinifex has no commercial value, this leaves only old Yapa who can remember, to cry for their homelands. In Xavier Herbert's words, *Poor fellow my country.*

Emus...

It isn't just the vegetation and the small critters which are in serious rapid decline, just as we're seeing more feral camels we are also seeing fewer emus.

My first encounter with emus in the wild, was half a century ago during the Nickel Boom. We were camped at a place called Waitekauri north-east of Leonora. Our caravan was parked under the shadow of a windmill near a wire fence corner. One morning we were woken by a strange sound: Grlmp, grlmp, grlmp!

As we peered out of a caravan window to find out what made the sound, we saw an emu family bobbing up and down. There was father emu, mother emu and their three teenage emu children. Bobbing up and down, grlmp, grlmp, grlmp, contemplating the fence which was hindering their morning walk. Bob, bob, bob, grlmp, grlmp, grlmp, when suddenly father emu took a few steps back and then ran full tilt towards the fence... bang, crash. Father emu picked himself up and rejoined his bobbing family, grlmp, grlmp, grlmp. Then it was mother's turn. A few bobbing steps back, then a run up...bang crash. This went on for an eternity. They didn't realise they were being observed. It was a riveting sight. Bob, bob, bob, grlmp, grlmp, grlmp, a few steps back... bang, crash. The whole family took it in turns. Their perseverance was admirable. We thought it would never end, when unexpectedly, grlmp, grlmp, grlmp, bob, bob, bob, a few steps back, a run up and voila a somersault and there was one of the teenagers picking him (her?) self up on the other side of the fence. Bob, bob, bob, grlmp, grlmp, grlmp, with a smug grin on its beak.

As I said, it took an eternity, but eventually the whole emu family made it across the wire and trotted off together into the distance. Despite the fence, this family was able to pursue an activity their ilk had pursued unhindered for possibly over 40,000 years. La promenade.

Not all emus had been as lucky as the family we observed. From time to time, we would come across a bit of the fence with crossed wires. Tangled in the wire would be the remnants of an emu or a kangaroo. The erection of wire fences had radically curtailed the emu's and other wildlife's right to roam as they always had.

How presumptuous of these recalcitrant emus, to assume they have rights. Why don't they get over it and learn to respect these fences and those who had erected them?

I was taken to a small circular clay-pan not far from the boundary fence with Mt. Allan Station. Clay-pans after a decent rain, fill up with water. These clay-pans often retain water long after the surrounding country has dried out. I was told that certain plants when mashed up and thrown in the water would have a soporific effect on emus that drank the water. The plant is called *warrkalpa*, which Latz's book tells me is *Duboisia hopwoodii*- also known as 'pituri bush' or 'emu poison bush'. It contains the poison nornicotine. Half the world's production of the common medicine, Buscopan, relies on this plant. Unsurprisingly Buscopan packets carry the warning not to drive while taking it.

At the edge of the claypan there was a neat crescent shaped wall made up of stacked rocks. Less than a century had transpired since the last hunter at Yamirringi, with his boomerangs and spears, had hidden behind the rock wall waiting for emus to stagger around like drunks and fall over.

Trick or treat...

Ever since we arrived in Yuendumu, I have been conscious of the fact that all of us Kardiya are, whether we like it or not, agents of assimilation. So how could I reconcile this complicity with taking on managing a mining company, albeit Aboriginal owned? There is nothing much wrong with assimilation, nor its less virulent manifestation, integration, provided it is an option, a matter of free choice, of freely given consent. No one forced me to become an Australian. It is in coercive assimilation wherein lies the problem, especially when it is concurrent with disempowerment in an already very skewed power imbalance and when it is concurrent with prejudice based on stigma, stereotypes and ignorance. Yapa are offered a place at the bottom rung of mainstream society. I recall someone saying, "*I'd rather be a first class Yapa than a second class Kardiya.*" The choice being offered is a moving target of false promises and blatant lies. Again, Kimberley musician Patrick Davies' song 'Rocky Old Road'.

♫ ♫ ♫

It's a rocky old road that we travel
All the tricks that are tried are not new
They're just wrapped up in gift wrapping paper
And handed as favours to you

To Aboriginal Australia, assimilation offered as a free choice couldn't be further from the truth. It is either being delivered in a blatant authoritarian way such as the Stolen Generations or the NT Intervention or it is offered in gift wrapping paper such as Stronger Futures or Closing the Gap or Generation One. Freely given consent is not part of the equation.

The way I rationalised my participation in an assimilationist endeavour is that I saw economic empowerment as a weapon for cultural survival. I have also, with the backing of Yuendumu Mining Directors, tried but not always succeeded in maximising Yapa participation. Without realising it, we were closely following what academic Jon Altman in his research called the 'hybrid economy' whereby economic and cultural imperatives are given equal weight.

I still believe in this, but have been disillusioned by the way that as soon as a pot of gold emerges, control of it, almost invariably is seized by external forces. Ownership of success is almost always usurped. Money trees are not left standing for the common good. Neither are geese that lay golden eggs left to lay in peace. Stealing land, children, languages and wages isn't enough, they've added futures to the list. The latest policy: Stolen Futures.

In the end our naive idealism couldn't save the Yuendumu Mining Company from the reality of the all consuming assimilationist behemoth, but we gave it our best shot.

Wendy also has serious misgivings about the assimilationist aspects of western education. This is why she became so passionate about bilingual education. A passion we share.

The way assimilation in the school system is furthered, apart from overt measures such as the 'four hours English only' policy, is often quite subtle and many of those instrumental in its implementation, both Yapa and Kardiya, are unaware of their complicity. A principal who doesn't understand or believe in bilingual education can by watering it down set the programme back for years.

The most effective way to off-set destructive change is to work at maintaining continuity working within the system, which is why Wendy has continued to work for the bilingual program, supporting Yapa teachers and helping to produce Warlpiri reading resources. For the last more than four decades she has worked long hours which included giving free Warlpiri evening lessons to non-Warlpiri speakers. These lessons are far from producing fluent Warlpiri speakers, but what they teach is respect.

When Wendy offered to help † Jeannie Nungarrayi Egan with lesson planning, Jeannie said, "*We don't need you for that. We need you for Warlpiri singing with the kids with your guitar."* Wendy has kept up singing Warlpiri songs with classes at Yuendumu and Nyirrpi schools ever since. Often middle aged Warlpiri people tell me how they remember with fondness singing in Nangala's class when they went to school as children.

.....Kaarnka ka pinjingka juurl-juurl-pinyi.....

♫ ♫ ♫

(The crow on the wire fence jumps up and down….)

This was part of a well known children's chant, a favourite song for young children, who jump up and down like the crow while singing. Good preparation for traditional dancing.

Another trick used to push the assimilationist agenda is what I dub "The invisible Yapa." It works like this:

At a school council meeting, †Connie Nungarrayi poured her heart out to visiting bureaucrats and officials. *"What matters most to us,"* said Connie, *"is land, family, language and ceremony."* She told the visitors that she wanted her children and grand-children to grow up strong in Warlpiri, to know their country, their Jukurrpa, their family obligations. They need Warlpiri first and then English for work, to look after their families and to grow up as confident smart, well educated, adults with a strong sense of Warlpiri identity and be respected in both worlds. Very eloquent was Connie's speech. When Connie sat down there was a silence and then the visitors thanked her for her contribution, before carrying on with their meeting agenda exactly from whence it had left off before Connie spoke. There was no mention of any of the things Connie had spoken about. It was as if Connie didn't exist. She was invisible.

Despite Connie's invisibility, she succeeded beyond her wildest dreams. Sad she was no longer around when on 4th April 2012, at a Parliamentary Committee inquiry into language learning in indigenous communities hearing in Alice Springs, Connie's son Donovan Jampijinpa Rice spoke as follows (from Hansard):

"*I grew up in Yuendumu, learning both in Warlpiri and English. I work in the language centre in Yuendumu, and my main work is translating and recording stories for new books. I have brought some of them here for you to maybe check out later. They are in Warlpiri. When I was growing up, since I was in preschool, there were two teachers, a kardiya and a yapa, and they both helped in my education in my opinion. I think Warlpiri is a vehicle to move me further towards where I need to go, even in learning different languages such as English. Language keeps me grounded, it gives me identity and a sense of belonging, because I know where I stand, and it gives me a strong sense of pride. I had the opportunity to pick up the English language as I was growing up in the school. I learned both ways, English and Warlpiri. I can read and write in both English and Warlpiri both, so it helps me to learn both ways, to fit into both cultures, English and Warlpiri. I think it helps. I think it is important, especially in younger children because they soak up knowledge very quickly. Especially when they have English coming in and they do not know much about this new language, they have to be slowly fed knowledge. I think the Warlpiri language is the way to help them learn about with English-using both as a way of gaining knowledge, growing up strong and grounded. It helps them get to where they want to go in life. So I think it is important that we keep both languages. That is what we had when I was growing up in Yuendumu.*"

Connie would have been justifiably proud.

Donovan was named after our son Donovan, they are both whizzes on the computer, they both make beautiful music and occasionally they exchange emails, in Warlpiri. Donovan Baarda works as a programmer for Google. He claims that growing up with Warlpiri and English, two very different languages, has enabled him to learn and switch to new computer languages more easily.

In 2008 our son Donovan and I had an email exchange in which we discussed culture and language. This is some of what Don wrote:

Cultural diversity is like bio-diversity... it may seem less efficient and more messy than a "mono-culture", but it is more robust and less vulnerable to events causing "catastrophic crop failures". A diversity of cultures leads to a diversity of ideas that can produce better solutions than a pure mono-culture of like-speaking-minds. It's also much more interesting and fun.

Connie, Jeannie and Awa
(photo - Mary Laughren)

The Aboriginal Problem

The ultimate aim of the authorities' assimilationist agenda amounts to no less than cultural ethnocide. So far they've failed but not through lack of trying. One of their favourite weapons is the concept of 'The Aboriginal Problem' which far too many Kardiya in the coastal voter belt subscribe to. *"Why don't Aborigines grow their own veggies...?"*, *"Why don't they get a job?"*, *"Why don't they get off the grog?"*, *"Why don't they do this.....?"*, *"Why don't they do that...?"*

With the Intervention this campaign intensified. Aboriginal society was portrayed as consisting of victims (women and children) that had to be protected and perpetrators (men) that had to be punished. The reaction from the coastal voter belt? *"Something had to be done"*

Just turn this on its head. A delegation of Warlpiri go to Frankston in Victoria.

"Why don't you Kardiya do this...?", *"Why don't you do that...?"*.

Better still, launch a military backed Intervention... in the Warlpiri language. Why? Because, *"Something had to be done."*

Rosalie Kunoth-Monks put it in a nutshell:

"There is no Aboriginal Problem. There is a white problem."

Or as Sarah Maddison put it in another nutshell in her book 'The Colonial Fantasy; why White Australia Can't Solve Black Problems':

"White Australia can't solve black problems because white Australia is the problem."

Most of the problems seen by both Kardiya and Yapa communities are at the interface of cultural interaction. Within their own society the Warlpiri are unaffected by many of these problems. They are too busy minding their own business.

Another plank of the multi-pronged assimilationist attack on Yapa society are the so-called 'real jobs' which successive Governments have promoted as a panacea for all the problems they perceive or allege are besetting remote communities.

Jimmy Chi's 1990 musical 'Bran Nue Dae' hits one of the nails firmly on the head:

> *Other day I bin longa to social security. I bin ask longa job – They bin say, "Hey, what's your work experience?" I bin tell 'em, "I got nutting". They say, "How come? " I say, "Cause I can't find a job!"*

From the 'role clarity' of the Welfare days when most Yapa were on modest training allowances, to the large number of community and council work jobs to the Community Development Employment Projects (CDEP) scheme, 'Real Jobs for Yapa' has undergone a fairly rapid and confusing evolution. The zenith of local participation was reached during the CDEP scheme. The school for example employed a number of Yapa teachers and literacy workers under CDEP. Administration of CDEP was by local organisations and hence more flexible than would otherwise have been the case. Fifteen hours a week were paid for by the CDEP scheme and employers could and would, if they could afford it, top-up wages for additional hours worked by participants. The scheme thus operated as a form of wage subsidy at a cost considerably less than that under the convoluted and ineffective subsequent systems.

A month after announcing the NT Intervention, the Howard government announced the cessation of CDEP which would be phased out. The likely rationale behind why the government felt the need to phase out the CDEP scheme was that, as these were wages and not welfare, they were unable to tame and control the money as effectively as they could under the Intervention's Income Management. The fact that CDEP had evolved into a fairly effective scheme, which had made a significant contribution to self-determination on remote communities, did not deter the government from killing it, in fact this may well have been their covert reason to do so. Even before the Intervention, ever tightening rules and enforcement and administrative demands had rendered CDEP to be but a shadow of its former self.

The Intervention appointed ITEC as the official 'jobs provider'. ITEC was a Cairns based firm. ITEC quickly sprang into action. ITEC were dairy farmers, milking the system is what they did best. Their first tack seems to have been to spread a rumour, if one didn't register with ITEC, one would lose one's Centrelink benefits. That this was a patent lie, didn't matter. Large numbers of Yapa were spooked into registering.

ITEC would hand-deliver a huge stack of letters addressed to all and sundry to Yuendumu Post Office. So full of their own importance was ITEC, that they were put out when Sascha at the post office insisted they buy and stick postage stamps on the envelopes.

One of the Little Sisters of Jesus came and saw me, obviously distressed. She'd received a letter summoning her to an interview with ITEC to discuss 'Pathways to Employment'. She asked me what she should do. I tore up the letter, put her at ease and told her not to do anything. The fact that the Little Sister was an octogenarian pensioner would not have deterred ITEC when they included Sister Claire on their invoice to the Commonwealth claiming payments for letters and interviews.

Quite a few times I'd receive a phone call, *"We've noticed such and such working for you. Can you tell us when she started work and what her hours are. We've got her on our books."* Call me recalcitrant, I refused to give them the information. *"I know you are only the messenger but tell your bosses that if anyone should get payment from the Commonwealth for having got this person a job, it should be Yuendumu Mining and not ITEC,"* and I'd hang up. ITEC had a vested interest in NOT getting clients employed, all the longer to keep them on their lucrative books. I believe the Australia wide "jobs provider" scam continues unabated, a bit like Water Rights and Offshore Detention, all money-trees ripe for plunder. ITEC Employment has morphed into ITEC-Health, they've found another cash-cow to milk, the NDIS (the National Disability Insurance Scheme). There is already an ITEC-Youth. I suspect ITEC-Bushfires and ITEC-Virus are imminent.

The Intervention didn't do things by half. Concurrent with ITEC they appointed a knight in shining armour. Over the horizon he loomed on a bicycle. Quickly he attended any meeting that took place and presented himself to all of us 'stakeholders'. With extended hand he would introduce himself and declare that his brief was "Jobs, jobs, jobs", a mantra to be adopted by subsequent Australian Prime Ministers. I've forgotten his name but recall that in Canberra from whence he emanated, he'd been a champion cyclist. In between training on his bicycle around the airstrip he'd be tilting at the windmills of Yuendumu unemployment. It didn't take long for him to be dubbed 'Jobs, jobs, jobs'. The Intervention had given 'Jobs, jobs, jobs' a contract as a Community Employment Broker to work in tandem with ITEC to deliver the promised 'real jobs'. Whilst I give 'Jobs, jobs, jobs' full marks for enthusiasm and dedication I'm not aware of him having created a single job during his brief residency. He went on a break overseas and on his return I ran into him in front of our Post Office. It was then that he told me that his contract had not been renewed. It dawned on me that 'Jobs, jobs, jobs' had accomplished a job creation tally of minus one!

The NT Government wasn't going to be left out, in 2009 they hatched an ill conceived scheme to "improve" conditions on remote communities. They declared Yuendumu to be one of twenty 'Regional Economic Hubs' soon to be renamed, 'Growth Towns'. NT politicians waxed lyrical when it came to the potential of this latest fantasy. Nigel Scullion, who eventually would climb the political ladder to become the Federal Minister for Indigenous Affairs, even raised the possibility of Vietnamese market gardeners descending on Aboriginal communities to boost local economies. Our son Joe thought there was greater potential in inviting Afghan refugees held in detention to grow opium poppies thereby solving two major problems at once! In reality nothing much changed except for our postal address which used to be 'Yuendumu, via Alice Springs, NT 0872' and is now plain 'Yuendumu NT 0872' (with an optional street address-which is irrelevant as Yuendumu does not have postal delivery, and Yuendumu has only one house with a letter box). The terms 'Hubs' and 'Growth Towns' were the brunt of much scoffing and sneering, and have fallen into disuse despite the fact that the declaration was never rescinded.

As far as I know we are still a Growth Town, but the only industries, apart from local art, which have significantly grown are Law and Order and the so called 'Aboriginal Industry'.

In July 2013 the already much diminished CDEP scheme was finally 'transitioned' into the 'work for the dole' Remote Jobs and Communities Program (RJCP) and in June 2015 it was 'reformed' and renamed the Community Development Program (CDP). Masters of spin they are, "CDP" if you say it quickly enough, sounds just like the old "CDEP" to which it has no resemblance whatsoever.

CDEP provided real, albeit part time jobs, whereas CDP participants are unemployed, income tested and highly breachable. Centrelink and CDP are so linked that, to be able to apply for welfare, you have to register with CDP and actively search for jobs, which in most cases are non-existent or unavailable to Yapa anyway. A form of bureaucratic torture is applied. Failure to tick all the boxes gets you "breached" and your welfare entitlements may be withheld for as long as eight weeks. If it wasn't for Warlpiri reciprocal responsibility- caring and sharing- you'd starve. CDP is managed by the Central Desert Regional Council which is headquartered in Alice Springs.

The very same Council which administers the CDP programme has a vacancy for a cleaner. To apply for the job, a candidate has to obtain a number of the following: a working with children ochre card, a police check, a driver's licence, a tax file number, a birth certificate, a Centrelink number, a medicare card, a bank account statement, a water and sewerage bill showing an address with a street name and number, all of which are intertwined in a Catch-22 matrix.

The cleaner position remains vacant and a Kardiya office worker cleans the office.

Whenever a mining company or road contractor is on a public relations offensive, seeking permission from Traditional Land Owners or remote communities to get access to land for some project or other, they hold up some blankets, beads and mirrors as an incentive to Yapa to accede. The offer of jobs and training are some of these recurring mirrors. Why, *"We'll let you work for us and help us make an obscene amount of money by removing non-renewable resources from your land,"* should be expected to induce paroxysms of gratitude in Yapa, I fail to understand. As a generalisation, large companies operating on Warlpiri land, are laughing all the way to the Swiss or Cayman Island bank.

The Intervention's propaganda kept bandying the phrase "real jobs". These "real jobs" never materialized. One could say that the many lucrative jobs which were created for Kardiya also do not merit the adjective "real". They are better described as bogus or ersatz or parasitic jobs.

Notable among these bullshit jobs is the job to manage the CDP. A former Yuendumu CDP coordinator told me that one of the questions she had to ask applicants was whether they needed and wanted an alarm clock to help them get up for work and therefore support them in their job search. One of her all too few clients declined the offer of an alarm clock week after week. When she finally persuaded this client to accept the offer, she realized that she hadn't been supplied with alarm clocks, the alarm clocks existed only on paper. She then had to persuade her client that he didn't want an alarm clock after all. Alarming don't you think?

When Yapa are asked what do they want, they often reply *"jobs"*, which is what Kardiya like to hear, yet when jobs occasionally become locally available, the organization offering the job doesn't exactly get run over in the rush. Administrative hurdles have a fair bit to do with this.

One young man after trying for a job and having been confronted by the bureaucratic brick wall was heard to say:

"Why would I want to work for a bunch of fucking white fellas anyway?"

Go West young man…

Northwest from Yuendumu there are vast spinifex covered plains. Feeding on this biomass there is a huge army of white ants (presumably several species) and these plains characteristically are strewn with termite mounds of variable shape and size. Famous are the monumental so-called "magnetic" termite mounds, which I am told are aligned north-south, so as to better capture warmth from the sun. Whilst there are some large termite mounds and hints of north-south alignment in the Tanami Desert, the famous "magnetic" mounds are confined to further north.

Spinifex hummocks and tussocks capture windblown dust and sand. This in combination with the numerous termite mounds result in an uneven, irregular surface. Traversing these plains in a Toyota Landcruiser results in a very slow jarring bumpy ride. Around six km/hour from memory.

Yuendumu Mining Company put forward a proposal to a number of exploration companies for a multi-client network of tracks. Our Caterpillar 910 front end loader, has a two metre wide bucket fitted with a cutting blade at the front. A single shallow scraping pass with the loader blade would smooth the surface and create a track on which speeds in excess of 60 km/h could be comfortably reached. These tracks would save the exploration companies much time and money, so they all accepted.

The area of the track clearing project is west of the Tanami Road, mostly north of Chilla Well (Jila). The tracks run east-west, are 30 kilometres apart, and are connected by a couple of north-south tracks. The tracks totalled around one thousand kilometres in length. At its western extremity, the southernmost track almost reached Lake Mackay and the northernmost track also almost reached the Western Australian border and ran north of hilly country called *Pakuru* (Golden Bandicoot) in the middle of the Highland Rocks map sheet.

In a fit of optimism we gave the tracks gold and copper related names such as the Klondike track and El Escondido which is erroneously named after Chile's biggest copper mine La Escondida (so who decided on the gender of the mine anyway?). Not that there is a shortage of Yapa names we could have used. It is forever driven home to me just how many Yapa names there are, even in rarely visited country, which is the reason we didn't use them, as each track would have ended up with several names which would have been very confusing to our Kardiya customers.

Whenever we felt we were in country where no one had ever been, we kept stumbling on evidence to the contrary. Occasional vehicle tracks, vestiges of campfires, discarded rusted tobacco tins and even an occasional horse shoe, attested to our non-pioneering status.

So there we were at the edge of the project area, ready with our recently acquired and expensive GPS instrument. It was a large black box like those used during the first Gulf War. On the conclusion of that war-crime which became known as the "Turkey Shoot ", namely the shooting of retreating Iraqi occupiers from Kuwait, these fairly recently developed GPS units had been used to record where they buried the bodies. Our use of the instrument I consider to have been much nicer.

There was Bwana or Sahib Baarda ready to sally forth in a westerly direction. I wasn't wearing a pith helmet, nor a khaki safari shirt with epaulettes, nor Bermuda shorts and long white socks and black shiny shoes, but my demeanour was such I might as well have been.

Reading the GPS was rather slow because we could not afford the external antenna and the US military were still distorting the satellite signals (lest the enemy would turn their technology against them).

None the less we steadily moved forward. The convoy consisted of the GPS equipped Toyota, followed by the Caterpillar 910 loader, followed by the support Toyota. Eight punctures on the lead Toyota and a short length of track later, we settled in for the night. Around the campfire, Micah Hudson, our then main plant operator said: *"Jungarrayi, tomorrow you show me how to use that compass."* I've already told you that Micah is an amazing musician; well he could also make earthmoving machinery dance.

The magnetic declination was three degrees (the difference

between true north and magnetic north). Duly the next morning, Micah held up the prismatic line of sight magnetic compass to his eye.

"See that number 267?"

"Yuwayi."

"Well that is where we're going."

Way off in the distance on the spinifex plain there was a small shrub in the middle of our proposed westerly trajectory. Micah got on the loader and took aim at the shrub. When he got tired someone else would take aim with the compass and have a turn. I followed on the newly smoothed track in the Toyota with the GPS instrument. Once in a blue moon I would have to tell the loader operator to veer a little to the south or north. That evening we had covered a considerable distance and we hadn't had a single puncture all day. No more Bwana or Sahib leading the way.

Throughout the project, and despite the US military distortion of GPS signals, no track deviated by more than 100 metres from its course, a pencil thickness of less than half a millimetre on a 1:250,000 scale map.

The project had two Kardiya, †A. Winwood-Smith and me, who took turns to go "out bush". All we did was record people's times (so we could work out what people should get paid), record distance of track cleared (so we could invoice the customers), record machine hours and fuel consumption for costing purposes and make up lists of supplies needed (fuel, food, spare parts etc.).

At sparrow's fart one fellow would get up, throw a few chops on the grill and boil the billy. Another would peer through the compass. Meanwhile a third crew member would apply the grease gun and check the oil and water on the loader and blow the dust and straw out of the air filter. Another would pump diesel from a drum on the back of the service Toyota into the loader. Compass-man would then mount the loader and set off. We Kardiya would have some breakfast and record GPS readings and catch up with the loader. We operated like a well trained football team. We Kardiya didn't kick the ball, we were a hybrid between a coach and an orange boy. The crew would soon also be able to read the GPS, so the Kardiya recorded readings were mainly for accounting purposes. The billy tea and chops person would catch up with the loader and they would swap over. The driver would descend and have his breakfast and the cook would hop on the loader and set off. A new person would hop on the loader and a more experienced operator would sit side-saddle for a while, whilst the novice learned to operate the machine. This went on until sunset, day after day, week after week.

At night we would sit around a campfire telling jokes and stories and listen to music on the radio before turning into our swags. All the time we'd keep a lookout for the tracks of snakes, centipedes, scorpions and other creatures. One time a set of camel pads followed one of our newly bladed straight tracks for a distance of tens of kilometres. I was told camels are naturally curious. I was also curious to know what the camel was thinking, but I never found out. Once I saw a ginger feral cat crossing one of our tracks in daylight. It was more than twice the size of a household cat. No waterholes we knew of existed within at least 50 kilometres from where I saw the cat. Feral cats in the desert don't need to drink water as they derive all necessary moisture from the blood of their prey. They are very efficient killing machines.

When fuel or supplies were needed, a couple of men would set off to Yuendumu to pick these up. Always two. Yapa always need *marlpa* (company) and rarely travel by themselves or are ever alone. Often two different men would return with the supplies. So desired was this "bush" work, that the men would selflessly give others a turn. It wasn't about the money either. More to do with participation and avoiding boredom and the joy and satisfaction of being 'on country' and of a job well done and of the camaraderie and teamwork with your family and friends.

When the back-up Toyota wasn't needed for a supplies run to Yuendumu, the spare crew would set off hunting and often came back with a bush turkey to supplement our tins of sardines, peas and corned beef. This never ceased to amaze me, as the whole time out there, I never saw a turkey except on one occasion when I saw several during a thunderstorm. One time when we all went to Yuendumu, we had a turkey shoot of our own. The crew on the vanguard Toyota shot eight turkeys which were well received by their families back home.

No high-viz vests, no hard hats, no courses and certificates, no consultants, no workshops, no registration, no insurance, no licences. We just did it and had a lot of laughs and made some money while we were at it. Alas such couldn't happen now. The authorities have tightened their grip. Rules and regulations and compliance and above all else ethnocentric control and administrative hurdles preclude such initiative and enthusiasm and independence from ever flourishing again.

On our annual pilgrimage to the Australian coastal voter belt, I often have to keep my cool and bite my tongue when long suffering Australian Taxpayers come out with utterances such as, *"Why don't those Abo's get off their arses and get themselves a job."* I think I know the answer to the question, but I have no illusions that the long suffering Australian Taxpayer busybodies would want to understand.

†Henry Jakamarra Wilson at our camp at Highland Rocks photo - Jim Allender

♫ ♫ ♫

Solid Rock..

The multi-client track project benefited the exploration industry greatly. To date no economic mineral deposits have been found in the area but our tracks had greatly improved access. In hindsight we under-quoted for line clearing, which we had to do out of necessity as we had to forever prove that we could deliver and overcome the industry's reluctance to hire an Aboriginal owned enterprise. Our customers saved much more by using the tracks than we had charged them for. None the less there were spin-offs that benefited us.

Geologist † Tony Hosking and geophysicist Jim Allender ran a company called Desertex which had an Exploration Licence in the Highland Rocks area. They hired us and we joined them in a lag-sampling programme. Lag samples consist of grit and pebbles that lie at the surface and are sieved out of sandy soil, and is a sampling technique used out of desperation in areas blanketed by barren alluvial or windblown cover.

We ranged over sand dunes, laterite ridges and occasional rocky outcrops and dry creek beds and at night settled down at a campfire and yarned. Henry Wilson, who had previously worked on the exploration tracks project, told of his time as a pearl diver in the top end, Jim and Tony of various exploration adventures and I obsessively told of 'matters German' (I'd been writing up my father's anecdotes from his childhood and youth at the time). As is usual in such a setting we enjoyed a lot of jokes. Some optimism was derived from the fact that at night we could see the glow of the lights at the Granites gold mining operations in the distant north.

To my eternal shame I managed to break a spring on one of the vehicles, which in true 'bush mechanic' style we temporarily fixed by inserting a tyre lever. I had yet to learn that the time saved by driving fast does not compensate for the increased risk.

Some weeks later Tony and Jim called in at Yuendumu. They had a special gift for me, a 'Rock' cassette tape, which I wasn't allowed to listen to until after they'd left.

With some anticipation I inserted the tape into a cassette player expecting something by Chuck Berry or Suzy Quatro or such. This is what I got:

....Wenn Sie nach links schauen, sehen Sie den Mount Conner ..... In der Ferne sehen Sie den Ayers Rock, den die Eingeborenen Uluru nennen ....

(....When you look to your left you will see Mt Conner...

In the distance you will see Ayers Rock which the natives call Uluru.)

Joining the dots...

When we first arrived in Central Australia en route to Yuendumu, on every street corner in Alice Springs you'd be accosted by an Aboriginal man trying to sell you a Namatjira style watercolour painting on a cardboard board, (you know the ones- a couple of ghost gum trees, framing a blue or purple range of hills in the background). The quality varied from excellent to pathetic, but the market had clearly been saturated and only a few dollars was the asking price even for good ones.

So called 'dot art' got off the ground in Papunya around 1972. The bush telegraph did its job and within a year men in other communities started painting traditional designs using acrylic paint on boards and pieces of three-ply. Yuendumu was no exception and as mentioned soon thereafter some men had also painted traditional designs onto slabs of flatstone and then of course there was that QSL card that George Robertson did for me. That was around 1974.

There was a gradual shift from traditional colours, white, yellow, red and brown ochre and black to much brighter and varied colours. I wish I'd kept them but even at this embryonic stage as ceremonial art morphed into commercial art there was some amazing psychedelic stuff crossing my path.

Initially 'dot art' was produced exclusively by men. The women had got involved in batik production. As word got around that some of the dyes used in batik are poisonous, and as the market for 'dot art' gradually opened up, women joined the men in producing 'dot art', especially as the latter is often more lucrative and is far less time consuming than batik.

The way this art was perceived and valued by Yapa and by Kardiya differed radically. †Daisy Napanangka Nelson did a painting featuring two snakes (*Pikilyi Jukurrpa*). The Kardiya running the art centre offered her a paltry price. The colours on the painting were rather dull and it didn't have much commercial appeal. Daisy was deeply offended, as the painting represented an important Jukurrpa which she had inherited from her ancestors and she considered invaluable. Rather than accepting the low price offered, she gave the painting to Wendy. It wasn't the money that mattered, it was about respect and acknowledgment.

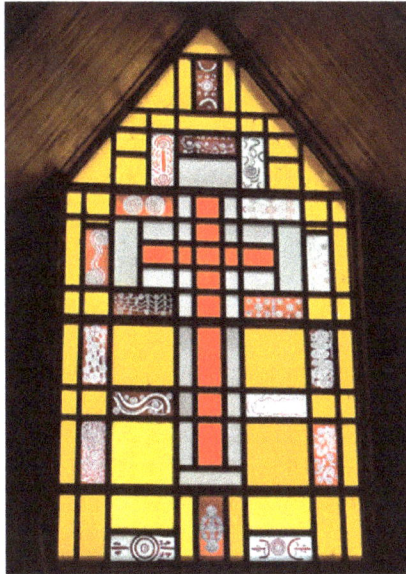

The Yuendumu Baptist Church was dedicated and opened on 10 March 1968. It is a rather beautiful A-frame building that was built by Sitzler Brothers. Incidentally Bruce Farrands of Rabbit Flat fame had been one of Sitzler's labourers who built our church. In 1977 a large stained glass window which has a large central cross surrounded by *jukurrpa* designs, one for each of the skin groups as well as the *yurrampi jukurrpa* - a honey ant dreaming, representing Yuendumu itself, was installed at the apex of a western extension of the building.

The designs were drawn by members of the congregation each for their own particular sub-section. The stained glass window was installed by Lindsay Johannsen, who some years earlier, had installed a stained glass window at the Catholic Church in Alice Springs. Inside the church there are some magnificent dot art paintings depicting biblical themes such as the Stations of the Cross and the Holy Trinity.

You don't have to be a practising Christian to appreciate the evocative beauty and symbolism of these works of art.

More than a decade of cultural adjustment by the artists had transpired when the Warlukurlangu Artists Aboriginal Corporation was registered on 15th April 1986. The Warlukurlangu art centre is named after a Jukurrpa site south-west of Yuendumu, across the fence and just inside the Mt. Doreen Pastoral lease, not far from Ngama (Snake Cave). Warlukurlangu means 'belonging or pertaining to fire'. Before I tell you about our art centre, to put you into the right mood, I suggest you feast your eyes on Warlukurlangu's website. Even better, after hearing this story, instead of a virtual visit in cyberspace, come to Yuendumu and visit our art centre in the real world, and inject some non-externally controlled money into our local economy! You might even find the time to pop in and see us.

Warlukurlangu is Yuendumu's most successful commercial enterprise. It is owned by the artists and is the only Yuendumu organisation which could not function without Yapa. Its Yapa artists are its very raison d'etre. Four days a week, artists wander in and out and paint. They paint and get paid. Art buyers, tourists and visitors are blown away by the explosion of colour as they wander in and out, chat with the artists and volunteers, rummage through a stack of canvases and admire the for sale paintings displayed on shelves, racks and walls and they buy art. Some of the best genuine Central Australian 'dot art' available, in my opinion. The place is a hive of activity. A joyful, enthusiastic and productive atmosphere prevails. All under the supervision of Cecilia Alfonso and Gloria Morales, the Kardiya who manage Warlukurlangu's operations on behalf of the artists and the Yapa Board of Directors. Unlike workers in most other Yuendumu organisations, at the art centre, Yapa are not continuously badgered to conform to Kardiya norms.

During construction of the mill at the Granites Gold mine, one of the settling tanks was installed by a Perth firm. On completion of the tank, three Irishmen working for the Perth firm, were on their way back home when they ran into Peter Toyne in Yuendumu. Peter, the

Yuendumu School principal at the time, had been the driving force behind setting up Warlukurlangu.

Travellers were few and far between back then, so Peter invited the Irish trio in for a cup of tea. One of these Irishmen was Brendan Rooney who showed much interest in the art that was being produced in Yuendumu. He rolled up a batch of canvases and took them to Perth. As I understand it, Janet Holmes a Court had just started her famous collection of Aboriginal art, and Brendan sold her the paintings. He sent a $15,000 cheque to Warlukurlangu, the most money Yuendumu artists had ever seen.

The following year Brendan the hero resurfaced in Yuendumu. He had this idea, to go to Portsmouth in England, where Australia's 'first fleet' had set sail from. Brendan was confident he could sell paintings there at events celebrating Australia's Bicentennial.

A batch of huge magnificent canvases worth an estimated $50,000, which back then was a shitload of money, was produced and Brendan headed off on his selling foray. A $5,000 remittance ensued and Brendan was never heard of again.

Australia Day 26th January 1988, was the bicentennial of Governor Arthur Phillip's raising of the flag of Great Britain at Sydney Cove, on the arrival of the First Fleet of British ships at Port Jackson. On this same day, as Brendan Rooney was flogging stolen Aboriginal paintings at Portsmouth, a mere 170 km further east, † Burnum Burnum was planting the Aboriginal Flag at the white cliffs of Dover claiming Britain for Aboriginal Australia. It is rumoured that Brendan returned to Australia via the art markets of New York.

Like the cargo cultists of New Guinea, Yuendumu artists no longer did any painting nor anything much else but wistfully stared heavenward waiting for Brendan's manna to descend.

A little aside: Years earlier I had the privilege of meeting the magnificently bearded Aboriginal activist, actor and author † Burnum Burnum when he visited Yuendumu. I gave him a boomerang which he was very pleased with.

†Frankie (Bronson) Jakamarra Nelson, Harry Nelson's brother, was

the chairperson of Warlukurlangu. In 1986 Bronson won the NATSIAA (National Aboriginal and Torres Strait Islander Art Award), the longest running and most prestigious award for Indigenous artists in Australia. This was also the year of Halley's Comet's most recent visit and the comet featured in many of Bronson's beautiful paintings. Bronson's wife † Norah Napaljarri Nelson (who everyone called NNN or Ngalyirri) later became a very successful artist in her own right. Norah designed the mosaic for the forecourt of the Supreme Court of the NT complex in Darwin which was opened in 1991.

Warlukurlangu in its post Brendan Rooney catatonic state had ground to a halt and was in dire straits. Felicity 'Flick' Wright was the Kardiya manager. Flick and I sat down at my Osborne prototype computer and did a "what if" spreadsheet using Lotus 1-2-3 software. The conclusion we came to was that for the Art Centre to be sustainable, henceforth artists would receive 50% of the proceeds for their paintings. The other 50% was for running costs and promotion. With the exception of the Holmes a Court bonanza and Papunya Tula artists, the "dot art" market was still in its infancy and Warlukurlangu was struggling to survive.

Bronson had a key to the then art centre (in the Adult Education building, now occupied by PAW media). One weekend he sold one of his own paintings to a passing tourist for $1,500. Promptly on Monday he handed $750 to Flick. That is the sort of person Bronson was. Norah was Yuendumu Mining Company's main 'shop lady'. She was a whizz on the pre-scanning cash register. She was a whizz with acrylic paint.

A delegation consisting of Norah, Bronson and several Directors of YMC, approached me. A discussion ensued in which it was decided that YMC would lend Warlukurlangu $10,000, at the at the time, low interest rate of 10% per annum. Canvas and paints were purchased, artists received modest advances on their paintings, renewed production of paintings was kick started, a few exhibitions were mounted, YMC got reimbursed with interest and Warlukurlangu never looked back. Warlukurlangu was to repay the favour several fold. Such financial flexibility, independence and cooperation no longer exists. Like a wet blanket 'Governance' and the ever watchful eye of ORIC (the Federal Office of Remote Indigenous Corporations) have put out that fire.

Ever since the Rooney fiasco, Warlukurlangu has in co-operation with the South Australian Museum documented its output. Archival duplicate records of all paintings are maintained in Adelaide. Currently the bulk of paintings are done by women. Significant income results from royalties on designs used in all sorts of merchandise sold through a very successful art distribution firm.

There is no doubt that as far as Yuendumu exports are concerned Warlukurlangu gets the gold medal. The silver medal goes to Yuendumu Mining. Gravel products, services to exploration, small scale earthmoving, at one stage cattle, and the already mentioned seeds and bush tucker business, whilst nowhere near reaching Warlukurlangu's dizzying financial heights, none the less add up to a commendable effort.

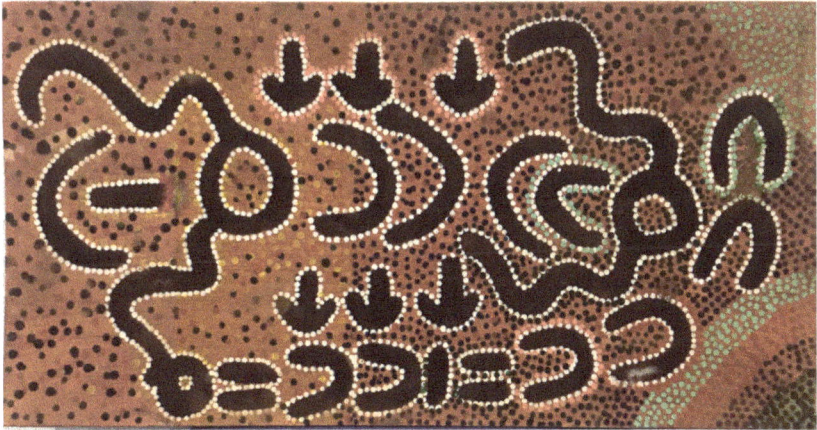

Pre-Warlukurlangu Artists painting on canvas board by †Edith Nangala Daniels – Wayililinpa Warlu-kurlangu jukurrpa

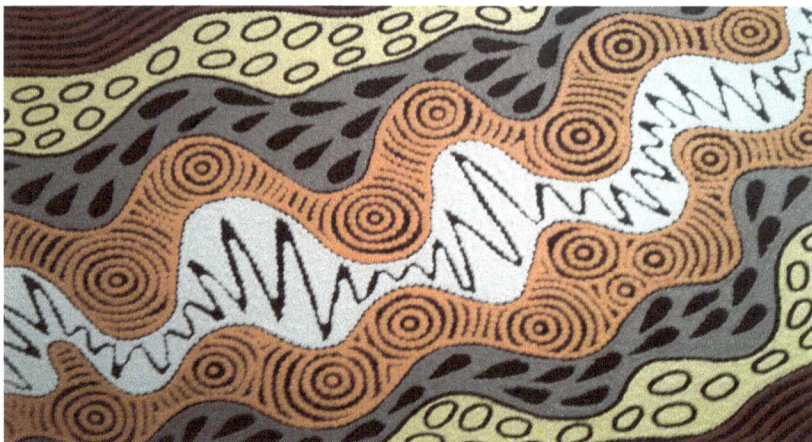

Pikilyi Jukurrpa by Ursula Napangardi Hudson

Can of worms...

Peter Toyne, as well as setting up Warlukurlangu Artists, was a driving force behind setting up the Warlpiri Media Association, Yurrampi Crafts and the Tanami Network. During Peter's stint as Principal, much progress was also made in making Yuendumu School more relevant to Yapa.

Yurrampi Crafts, like so many new initiatives, started with a burst of local enthusiasm. Yapa created Jukurrpa designs were used on screen printed material, bags, printed T-shirts and other garments and products. These were very popular with Yuendumu people and visitors alike. Yapa were particularly keen on having their own Jukurrpa designs on their own things. These products were sold at the local Social Club shop and supply couldn't keep up with demand. Yurrampi crafts had tapped into local demand and was self-sustaining.

Then an adult educator, who came after Peter Toyne, thought more money could be made by selling outside the community. He took on a contract to produce a thousand T-shirts for World Vision, all with an identical honey ant design. Yapa workers soon became bored with this, lost interest, and stopped coming to work. It was left to the one Kardiya worker to slave away by herself to fill the contract on time and avoid penalties. She ended up getting Repetitive Strain Injury (RSI) and had to leave Yuendumu. That was the end of Yurrampi crafts. Yet one more casualty of Industrial Infanticide. Yet one more example of a Kardiya who, like a cuckoo bird chick, pushes Yapa chicks out of the nest, feeds and grows fat and flies off, eventually to find another nest to lay its egg in and leaving an empty nest behind.

Some initiatives are behind the times and fail. Such was the Tanami Network. By the time it was set up, the satellite link, which was supposed to revolutionise communication between communities was obsolete, inadequate and way too expensive.

Jail link-ups were the most appreciated activity by the Tanami Network. Mothers, wives, brothers and others were happy to see their sons and husbands waving and smiling at them and importantly to reas-suringly see them physically unharmed. For the guys in jail it was probably a break from boring routine and a reminder they had families who loved and worried for them. None cared nor had any inkling of what all this cost.

I cannot match Lee Cataldi's poem, 'Beam me to Kintore Japanangka', to capture Tanami Network's essence:

the jet-lagged
coal-eyed prophet
who can sell himself anything
even a can of worms
goes around waving
his arms like aerials
his right-hand man
a telephone plugged into each ear
barely stops to dial
a new level of bliss
and the dollars pour out
like tap water into sand
the sky dreaming
its icons the round white bowls
dotted across the Tanami
signifying heaven
hums to the satisfying buzz
of human conversation
Japanangka's mothers
gather to visit their sisters
with a murmur like doves
they go into the building
on the other television someone
wakes up in Kintore
they are not disappointed
they smile at their sisters
who seeing them
disembodied diminished but moving

smile in return
a far cry
from the men with the cheque books
who expect something like answers

Lee has kindly given me permission to use her poem.

Once I sat on the sidelines and watched the Tanami Network in action. On a television screen, flickering squares would gradually reveal a recognisable group of women in Lajamanu smiling and waving at us:,

"Ngurrju mayinkili?" (*"Are you good?"*) The Yuendumu women smiled and waved back:

"Yuwayi!" ("Yes!")

Scintillating conversation it was. It all reminded me of that Black Books episode in which Bernard and Manny drink that very expensive bottle of wine. On the upper left of the screen a counter tallies the amount poured so far. With the last drop of wine and with a cash register 'kah-ching' the counter ticks over to £7,000! Only the Tanami Network tallied up a much larger amount.

Lee Cataldi absolutely nailed it.

Double Dutch…

Les Hiddens was granted an Army Defence Fellowship in 1987 to research bush survival, as part of the Australian Army's strategic planning. Les was to prepare maps showing where native foods could be found. I believe I may have been the first Kardiya he bumped into in Yuendumu when he fuelled up his trusty Land Rover at Yuendumu Mining's diesel pump. He sought local assistance and I recommended some Yapa and suggested he'd get the Army to fund him so he could pay his informants. I'd met too many well paid Kardiya who thought unemployed Yapa should jump at the privilege of assisting them for free. Darby Jampijinpa was one of the people Les enlisted. To his credit Les paid Darby and the others.

Les later became famous as "the bush tucker man" of the TV series. The series was very popular in Yuendumu. The kids called Les the *'bush jaka man'*. The Warlpiri word for 'bum' (buttocks) is j*aka.* Similar sniggering amusement had been derived from a preceding TV series *'Jaka* Zulu', which had resulted in gangs of boys keenly swarming the streets of Yuendumu and holding mock battles with bamboo spears and cardboard shields.

The Bush Tucker Man TV series coincided with and complemented some serious promotion of the then emerging bush tucker industry. Demand for bush tomatoes has greatly exceeded supply ever since. We used to call *yakajirri - Solanum centrale* 'bush raisins' but just like jew fish became gem fish and crayfish became Australian rock lobsters, so too bush raisins became bush tomatoes, a bit confusing as *wanakiji,* another solanum, are called bush tomatoes. But such is the power of marketing and advertising.

Yuendumu Mining became involved with *yakajirri* in 1990 and since then it has traded almost ten tonne of bush tomatoes. The term 'bush tomatoes' is rather apt in that both potatoes and tomatoes are also *Solanacea,* as is deadly nightshade. *Yakajirri,* potatoes and tomatoes have very similar flowers, five petals enclosing prominent yellow pollen laden stamens. These flowers differ mainly in colour and size. *Yakajirri* flowers are purple.

Some of the *yakajirri* was sold in the Lajamanu store. The residents of Lajamanu are mostly Warlpiri. Lajamanu is not on Warlpiri land and Central Australian *yakajirri* actually doesn't grow there. It is like Australian Kardiya buying Vegemite when they're overseas.

The last significant crop of *yakajirri* was in 2015. YMC could have sold many tonnes of it, if it had been available. At the beginning of 2020 there was a bit of rain and we were hoping for a crop. There was virtually no follow up rain until late October and so far there are only flowers on a few scattered low bushes and a significant crop seems most unlikely. Yakajirri seeds only germinate after fires.

At some stage Les Hiddens had become obsessed with an 1834 article in the Leeds Mercury in Yorkshire. Over the next months and years the story was repeated in other newspapers including a Perth newspaper. A nineteenth century version of 'going viral'. To cut the story short, the article tells of a Lieutenant Nixon who in a secret expedition to Central Australia, chances upon a mile wide stretch of water complete with numerous canoes manned by fishing natives, a grove of palm trees and - wait for it - a Dutch colony, the descendants of survivors of a shipwreck 170 years earlier. A veritable Xanadu. Coleridge wrote Kubla Khan, which features Xanadu, after an opium induced dream and I do wonder what substance induced Lieutenant Nixon's tale. In true evangelical style, Les delves deeply into historical records and through a series of non-sequitur quantum leaps, reaches the conclusion that the story is true and that it explains such as the blonde hair of some central Australian Yapa children.

A credible rumour did the rounds that army enthusiast Bruce Farrands had requested the Army to train him in how to operate a tank and to position such at Rabbit Flat. At the time of Bruce's alleged request, there reigned a fair bit of paranoia about the possibility of invasion from the north, and Bruce is alleged to have suggested the tank as a very economical way to put up a line of defence. Whether it is true or not, it makes a good story. Good ideas never get much traction. Bruce's request was apparently declined, so it was not without a tinge of envy that Bruce hosted Les Hiddens and his party who in his quest to find proof of his pet Dutch colony turned up with a helicopter that the army had kindly provided.

Returning from one sortie, an over the moon Les announced he'd found a stone building which he declared had quite clearly been built by the descendants of the Dutch castaways, only to be disillusioned by Bruce who informed him the structure had been erected by a couple of poddy dodgers in the present century. Remember the Elliott brothers, the cattle rustlers of the Black Hills?

"The only Dutchman you're likely to find in the Tanami is Frank Baarda at Yuendumu." Bruce told Les.

Yakajirri (bush tomatoes)

Trousers...

From an inauspicious start when I was on Bruce Farrands' hit list and despite being on opposite sides of the political spectrum, Bruce and I developed a friendship which found expression in the form of very enjoyable and interesting telephone conversations. We taught each other a lot and gave each other many laughs. I miss our phone calls now we are both retired.

The record rains of the deluge I told you about were followed by much drier years and included a ten year drought from around 1989 to 1999.

Bruce had been assigned the Jangala skin-name. The Jangala/ Jampijinpa father/son pair are the rain-makers. During this prolonged drought, Bruce told me he'd complained to an old Warlpiri man that whereas he'd been dancing and dancing, he'd only managed to raise clouds of dust. *"Were you wearing trousers when you were dancing?"* asked the old man. *"Yes of course."* With his tongue in his cheek and a twinkle in his eye, the old man told Bruce:

"Well, that explains everything. To make it rain you have to dance naked!"

The continuing drought confirmed my suspicion that Bruce never followed this advice.

Safe as houses...

At no time during the events I've been telling you about, was there any let up in the assimilationist push. Yet another assimilationist obsession is 'Community Safety'. As with so much else imposed on communities, when it came to 'Community Safety' the dominant society applies the deficit model to the Yapa/Kardiya dichotomy. It is taken as a given that these communities are not safe, especially not for women, children and Kardiya. Yet another deliberate lie, that is very difficult to debunk.

Many who are convinced that Yuendumu is an unsafe, violent community, do so believing that their stance is in sympathy with what they assume are the numerous victims. They don't realise that they are being rather condescending and insulting to the proud strong women and happy healthy children of Yuendumu, not to mention to the much maligned men.

Yuendumu has a Counter Disaster Plan. Over the years several meetings were held to which representatives from the Granites Gold Mine, surrounding pastoral properties, Alice Springs bureaucracies and Yuendumu organisations were invited as well as the local police, clinic and school.

A thick folder had been produced and distributed which contained such vital information as fuel tank capacities, stocks of aircraft fuel, availability or lack of safety equipment such as jaws of life, life support equipment at the clinic, water carts and earthmoving equipment (for fighting bushfires) and contact telephone numbers and email addresses. Sections in the folder dealt with such as what to do and who to contact in case of fire, floods, road accidents, aircraft mishaps, etc. It did concern me at the time that in the handbook there were no contingency plans to deal with a plague of locusts. Neither had a pandemic been anticipated. Periodically, meetings were held to discuss and update the Plan.

After a seven year hiatus during which Yuendumu's $7.6 million Police Complex had been built, it was decided it was high time that the Counter Disaster Plan be revisited, particularly in view of the Intervention's "Safe Communities" obsession. For some reason, on this latter occasion, the pastoralists and Yuendumu Mining Company had not been invited.

I received a phone call from Paul Davis, the community liaison officer, at the Granites Gold Mine. Paul asked me if I had been invited to the proposed meeting. He expressed a desire not to attend. Solution: Yuendumu Mining Co. was appointed by Paul as Newmont Mining's proxy.

The meeting, held in the school library, was attended by the school principal, the Government Engagement Coordinator (as Government Business Managers had been re-badged), the police lady in charge of Yuendumu police station, a high ranking policeman in charge of Counter Disasters in the Southern Region of the NT, and proxy me. No Yapa. It is not without intended irony that I consider the meeting to have been rather a disaster.

At this meeting, the big knob from Alice Springs told us of counter disaster plans at other communities. What local participation was there? I asked. He told us that at Haasts Bluff there was an Aboriginal man involved and at Ampilatwatja, recently an old lady suffering from dementia had wandered off into the bush and the local 'boys' had promptly tracked her down. Again that thought bubble of mine: 'boys'? In Yapa society to call an initiated man a 'boy' is rather insulting, but the high ranking policeman wouldn't have known that. The high ranking policeman took pride in the fact that his own daughter had obtained a certificate in search and rescue. A bit like Vladimir Putin bragging that his own daughter had been inoculated by the Russian miracle vaccine. What relevance either of these have to Yuendumu I can't begin to fathom.

The need for a local volunteer fire brigade was discussed, as it had been discussed a decade earlier. All counter disaster activities were to be coordinated and directed from the Yuendumu police station, (the term 'Yuendumu Police Complex' having been discarded once the $7.6 million construction money had been expended). In which case, all volunteers would have to apply for a 'criminal history check' piped up the police lady in charge of Yuendumu police station.

Most Warlpiri men have at sometime in their lives been ensnared by the criminal justice system. It could almost be regarded as a rite of passage. Their chance to get accredition is thus severely hampered. When I discussed the counter disaster meeting with some Yapa, Purnpajardu ruefully declared in exaggerated seriousness, that the next time he came across a road accident he'd have to decline being of assistance.

"I'm terribly sorry, but I am not accredited to help," he would tell the victims.

In hindsight I am now almost sure the big knob is the same previously mentioned but unnamed Sergeant Plod who castigated A. Miravitchi's rescuers.

The NT Police's motto is:

Working in partnership with the community to ensure a safe and resilient Northern Territory.

All this emphasis on 'safety' reminds me of an experience we had in the deep South of the United States when returning to Australia in 1971. Late one night in Alabama we asked an old toothless 'gas jockey' in a trench coat if we could camp overnight in his service station parking lot. We were sleeping in our panel van. No problem, and as we were settling in, the old guy schlepped his way across and reassured us that we were perfectly safe. He reiterated his assurance that we were perfectly safe whilst opening his trench coat to reveal a large revolver in a holster hanging from his belt. He then told us of what must have been the highlight of his life:

"One time this feller tried to hold me up (pause) a niggra he was, he'd gotten hold of the gun I kept under the counter. Imagine!! He was holdin' me up WITH MAH OWN GUN! MAH OWN GUN!!!! He didn't know I had another gun. 'Boy, youse in big enuff trouble already,' I hollered at him. He wavered and then I shot him. The bullet went in he'ahr (indicating the middle of his forehead) and came out he'ahr (indicating the back of his head). Hee hee hee hee (he chuckled)."

The old feller then proceeded to tell us his wife had 'done run away', and that he regularly went to church and that he was a real sucker for 'them travelin' preachers' to whom he made generous donations. As you can imagine we felt perfectly safe! This feeling of safety turned out to be a precursor for our life in Yuendumu.

Yes sir, that is what we have in Yuendumu, armed police and a squad of gun toting safety enforcers, ready to fly here at short notice when outsiders decide we need them. The NT Police's Territory Response Group, armed with Remington R5 RGP and SIG Sauer SIG716 rifles, and wearing A-TACS AU (Arid/Urban) camouflage, are only an alleged bout of civil unrest or a demonstration away.

For all it's worth, our $7 million plus police complex includes accomodation for 14 extra law enforcers, which although rarely used, I'm told is slated for an upgrade.

The alibi...

The evolution, from Community Policing to Policing the Community, and from the way the Kardiya Justice system used to work on communities, to the way it is presently implemented, is an interesting but somewhat disturbing story.

Scrubby' Hall was a "bush" magistrate who used to travel around remote Central Australia holding court. He'd turn up in Yuendumu once in a while. A small room, in what was then the "new" Police Station, was our 'courthouse'. A number of elders wearing long sleeved white shirts, and the inevitable bush hats would file into the back row. When Scrubby appeared in front of them, they would 'be upstanding' and with some pomp take off their hats. When Scrubby sat down, they would follow suit, sit down, put their hats back on and stare into the distance past the defendant. The prosecution and defence would have their say and Scrubby would look at them over his glasses.

Just before passing sentence, Scrubby would mumble something about needing to have a piss or a cigarette and he'd leave the room. A coincidence, but the elders would simultaneously also have an urgent need to leave the room. The defendant would be left upstanding as the elders filed out. After a while, the elders and Scrubby would return. Scrubby would then pass sentence: *"I reckon you're a mongrel bastard, I'm going heavy on you to set an example,"* or *"I reckon you're basically a good lad. I'll give you a second chance."*

Elders were then much more respected than they are now. Not hard to work out why.

I had the dubious honour of being the first Kardiya to be locked up at this "new" police station. It had been one of those rare occasions on which I'd had a family problem. Tim Langdon came to the door and I invited him in and we got drunk together. I invited myself to sleep in Tim's camp that night.

"No, Jungarrayi, she's a good woman. You make up with her," Tim said.

"No Japangardi, tomorrow I'll make up with her, but tonight I

won't be sleeping with that woman, I'll be sleeping in your camp." I replied.

After much of this, I prevailed and we staggered to Tim's camp. There we were met by an apprehensive †Perry Japanangka Langdon, Tim's oldest son. I dived under the nearest blanket. I now suspect Perry had alerted the Police, because it wasn't long before I heard the rattling of the cage on the back of the police Toyota and I had the blanket torn off me with a *"Hello, hello, hello, what have we here?"* Tim told me afterwards, he'd been staggering along, only to find he was suddenly treading air. We were both thrown into adjacent cells. Tim with some old fellows, and me with some young fellows.

I remember asking for toilet paper, and being refused. I must have started to sober up, because I muttered, *"Do you think I'll twist it into a rope to try and escape?"* Tim and his cellmates sang traditional songs until daybreak, and us young blokes spent all night hunting large hungry mosquitoes. Much to the amusement of others and my embarrassment, it transpired that I'd dived under the blanket in the middle of a *jilimi* (single women's quarters). Warlpiri are very polite I have no doubt everyone knew what happened, but no one ever mentioned the incident to me, all sniggering had been out of my earshot.

Next morning the local police 'processed' me. My fingerprints were taken and a policeman filled in a lengthy form using two fingers on a typewriter- remember those? When he got to what vessel I had arrived in Australia on, I got some warped pleasure in spelling out *'Johan van Oldenbarnevelt'*: Tick-tick, tick-tick, tick-tick…. It was then that Herman N. the school's principal, marched into the station, *"They have broken into the preschool again!"* *"It wasn't me, I've got an alibi,"* I mumbled.

Tim Langdon was released with a slap on the wrist and told not to do it again. I on the other hand, a Kardiya having been sprung pissed, under a blanket in the single women's camp, wasn't to be the recipient of such forbearance. I was charged with consuming alcohol on a Native Reserve. So it came to pass that on Scrubby Hall's next visit I was to front him. At my hearing, Harry Nelson who was a Justice of the Peace at the time, eloquently told Scrubby that I was a terrific fellow and that the very future of Yuendumu hinged on people like me. As I blushed, Scrubby disconcertingly peered over his glasses as he found me guilty, but did not record the charges. He then gave me a slap on the wrist and told me not to do it again, which I didn't.

MS Johan van Oldenbarnevelt

The Torch of Justice…

Forty-three years ago some young lawyers who had joined the recently formed Central Australian Aboriginal Legal Aid Service (CAALAS) came to Yuendumu.

An election was being held at the time. The policeman's wife sat on the saddle of her motorbike handing out how to vote cards. The rear part of her anatomy protruded invitingly. This proved too much for a very drunk Japanangka, an affable gentle giant of a man, who couldn't resist the temptation of clutching her in an inappropriate manner. I'm not saying this was connected in any way, but Japanangka found himself sobering up in a Yuendumu police cell with two broken ribs to keep him company. The young lawyers were jubilant. Here was an opportunity to score a significant win over the constabulary, a veritable "gotcha" moment in more ways than one.

This is also when the lawyers struck one of many differences between Kardiya and Yapa world views, attitudes, values, priorities etc. They were on a steep learning curve. Japanangka wasn't having any of it. *"I did the wrong thing and I deserved what I got."* End of story. Their "gotcha" moment proved to be ephemeral. Some of these young lawyers went on to forge brilliant legal careers, their baptism of fire at the cross-cultural legal frontier stood them in good stead.

On the 10th Anniversary of the Intervention, 'Concerned Australians', invited Harry Nelson and myself to speak at a forum in Melbourne held at RMIT (Royal Melbourne Institute of Technology) University. Concerned Australians is a group who have been opposed to the Intervention from the outset and which famously included former prime minister the late Malcolm Fraser. I wasn't going to attend. Too many times had I seen Yapa elbowed off the podium by egocentric Kardiya. At Harry's insistence I changed my mind when Harry appointed me as his 'Cultural Adviser'.

Mutual cultural advisers H. Nelson and F. Baarda

In Melbourne, during preparations for the forum, Harry invited Frank Vincent, who had been one of the young CAALAS lawyers, to catch up with us. In a blend of pride and nostalgia Frank, now a High Court Judge, retold that when CAALAS was first set up, they had some very satisfying wins over the NT Police. The police had got so used to having everything in court their way that they'd become slack and complacent. When effective legal representation became available to Yapa, defendants started to plead not guilty, questions were being asked, interpreters were used when necessary, evidence and procedures were being tested and suddenly cases were being thrown out or defendants found not guilty. Magistrates admonished and criticised members of the constabulary, who as a result became very antagonistic towards CAALAS lawyers.

When I told Frank Vincent that these days CAALAS lawyers were so overworked, underfunded and over-run that in desperation their best advice to their clients was to plead guilty, and that these days magistrates tended to err on the side of police prosecutors, he was horrified. All that good hard work back then, down the tube!

These days typically, a defendant is summoned to appear in court on a certain day, and ends up sitting on the ground outside the Yuendumu Police Complex, or under the small, shady *wajarnpi* tree across the road, together with the other 50 or so defendants and their families and supporters. Much in Yuendumu comes to a stand still as essential personnel are busy waiting outside the court. Some defendants sit there for three days and their case still doesn't come up. Some sit there for two days, get sick of it and wander off to buy something to eat, and their case does come up, their name is called out and then they are guilty of "failing to appear" and a warrant is issued for their arrest.

During the three day court session, a couple of defence lawyers have twenty minutes at most per defendant, to receive instructions and advise their client before presenting their case in court, that is if they skip lunch. Invariably if a defendant chooses to plead not guilty (possibly because he/she didn't do it!) the case is adjourned. A month later the defendant again spends from an hour to three days sitting outside the police complex waiting to be called, only to have the case once again adjourned, unless in the meantime the defendant has changed the plea to guilty. When the defendant is due to appear for a third time, he (these are mostly young men) may have been delayed by a flat tyre, or the car he is travelling in is pulled off the road for being unroadworthy and/or unregistered, which then results in additional charges being laid against the defendant or his friend who offered to drive him to Yuendumu to attend court. An alternative scenario is that the defendant considers that taking part in ceremonies or attending a funeral has a higher priority than turning up in court. People who have warrants out for them, are arrested and placed in remand in Alice Springs till their case is finally heard.

They get to rue not having taken their lawyer's advice to plead guilty in the first place.

On 30th October 2017, that shining beacon of Justice, Senator Brandis, our then Attorney General, wrote to CAALAS,

" ... *The Australian Government is committed to ensuring access to justice for Indigenous Australians and improving the lives of Aborig-*

inal and Torres Strait Islander people ... I acknowledge CAALAS' long history in providing legal assistance services to the Aboriginal and Torres Strait Islander people of Central Australia ... I have decided to offer the North Australian Aboriginal Justice Agency Ltd. (NAAJA) grant funding under the Indigenous Legal Assistance Program .... NAAJA will be the funded provider in the southern region of the Northern Territory ...."

The Torres Strait Islander people of Central Australia indeed!

In 2014 George Brandis had famously declared in Parliament, *"People have the right to be bigots."*

No sooner had I penned this, when that same evening, (9th April 2019,) on ABC TV NT News, there was an item featuring Yuendumu. NAAJA advised that due to insufficient funds it was unable to meet its obligations in the bush and that some of its clients would have to go to court unrepresented. Our current Attorney General, Christian Porter, when asked about this, responded by stating that national funding for legal services had increased (by 43% as compared to ten years earlier), which was a bit of a furphy. That the Law Council of Australia considers funding to be inadequate and that Indigenous incarceration continues to be at scandalous high levels wasn't mentioned.

Coincidentally 43 also happens to be the Answer to Life, the Universe and Everything in Douglas Adams' Hitchhiker's Guide to the Galaxy. Oops it is 42 i.e. not quite the answer!

BS-detector…

Just as Murray Wood had opened my eyes when I first landed in Yuendumu, so too had my eyes been gradually opened during my varied and enchanted infancy, childhood and youth.

As mentioned, two years after the war, my father got a job with a Dutch bank in Buenos Aires. We stayed in Argentina for nine years and by the time I was twelve years old we'd crossed the Atlantic Ocean by ship four times.

Argentina had stayed neutral and profited greatly from WWII. There was an economic boom in Argentina at the time we settled. Many people from all over the world had emigrated to Argentina. The population of our newly created well-off middle class suburb was very eclectic.

In the two streets our corner house abutted there were people from Holland, Belgium, South-West Africa (now Namibia), England, Trieste (now part of Italy), France, Austria, USA, Guatemala, Japan, Chile, Switzerland, Germany and naturally Argentina. Germans were in the majority amongst the foreigners. All types of Germans: those who had fled prewar Germany for political or economic reasons or because they were Jews, as well as those who had euphemistically 'arrived on U-boats' in 1945 or subsequently via the Vatican on the so-called Rat Lines.

At the time, our parents did not burden us with prejudices or hatreds. I wasn't told until after we'd left Argentina that the little boy next door I played with, was probably the son of a Nazi war criminal. We were never told, "You can't play with that kid". No visiting of the sins of the father, about it. Our parents let us be children. Soon enough we would grow out of this and join the messy real world.

Argentina was run by General Juan Domingo Perón until 1955 when he was ousted in a military coup. Perón's government can best be described as a populist dictatorship. With his wife Evita, Perón ran the country like Robin Hood and his band of Merry Men and Maid Marian only in this case Robin and his associates all had Swiss bank accounts. There are many similarities to Ferdinand and Imelda Marcos of the

Philippines and I do wonder how many pairs of shoes Eva Perón had. Argentina was, and probably still is a kleptocracy, as most of the world is rapidly becoming.

It wasn't till later in life that I tweaked to the fact that dad's Dutch Bank was one of many that had been complicit in Argentina's postwar flight of capital which has to this day kept many Argentinians in poverty.

.....*Don't cry for me Argentina*...

♫ ♫ ♫

In 1952, after five years with the bank, dad had earned three months of long service leave. Our whole family travelled by ship to Holland. At the end of dad's break on the way back to Buenos Aires, the ship we were on, anchored in the harbour of the island of Sao Vicente. Sao Vicente is part of the Cape Verde Archipelago in the middle of the Atlantic Ocean and which has since gained independence from Portugal and is now called Cabo Verde. As for most, if not all Portuguese colonies, the population of Sao Vicente was extremely poor. I've never forgotten the boys who sidled up to our ship in little row boats and who would dive for coins thrown into the sea by the ship's crew. Neither have I forgotten the crew members who thought it very amusing to make the boys dive for cakes of slippery soap. The boys were my age but I'm not sure if I'd yet learned to swim. The rows of large rich shiny white ocean going yachts lining the Sao Vicente harbour is another memory I've not erased. Such ostentatious opulence facing utter poverty. Such bullshit. Not unlike contrasting the luxurious International Yulara tourist resort with the poorly resourced Aboriginal community of Mutitjulu at Uluru (Ayers Rock), the rock they own. Such bullshit.

Yachts in Sao Vicente harbour

The fine tuning of my bullshit detector didn't stop there. My child-hood experiences, observations and impressions were much magnified by being the avid reader my mother had encouraged me to be. One of many books I'd read was a book on the Amazonian Indians. A party of Jesuit missionaries had been killed by poisoned darts when they marched into the jungle holding crosses aloft. The Indians thought the crosses were weapons!

On the Castel Bianco the ship that took us back to Europe at the height of the cold war, there was a large contingent of Russian/Argentinians. Many of these had been in Argentina for several generations. All of them spoke perfect 'native' Spanish as spoken in Argentina. They also spoke fluent Russian and delighted us on board with spectacular Cossack dances. At this time, around the world, the Soviet Union was coercing people of Russian descent to return to the USSR. In Australia two years earlier there had been the Petrov affair when Australian officials physically dragged Mrs. Petrov, a Russian spy, away from Soviet agents on a departing plane in Darwin. The Spanish/Russian bilingual speakers on our ship would make ideal Soviet spies, and undoubtedly did. The cold war with its doctrine of Mutually

Assured Destruction (and its apt acronym 'MAD') ultimately was an extreme manifestation of Bullshit.

My BS-detector was to receive a significant boost when I did Matriculation (year 12) at Moe High School. Mr. Lesley, who was our English teacher, used to bring newspapers purchased out of his own pocket to class, a copy for each student. We'd discuss the front page, question it, analyse the stories for verifiable truths or the lack thereof and check them out for bias and question the sources and so on. We'd look at syntax and semantics and expression while we were at it and were introduced to précis as an art form. Mr. Lesley got into trouble once when the class discussed a newspaper article dealing with abortion and some parents had him called on the carpet. Mr. Lesley made a significant contribution to the reduction of ovine and asinine tendencies in society. It is obvious from the current sociopolitical landscape that there are not enough Mr. Lesley's.

I have a head full of memories, but I must refrain from further digressing as I'm trying to tell you my Yuendumu story. Suffice it to say that having been blessed with a well honed BS-detector (or was it a curse?) made Yuendumu an ideal place for me to end up in.

Yuendumu after all, is wallowing in a quagmire of Kardiya bullshit.

The olympics

Despite, and one could almost say in defiance of, the relentless assimilationist assault and the many tragedies and setbacks, joyful and exciting life continued in Yuendumu.

Started in 1959 the annual Yuendumu Sports Weekend was one such joyful occasion.

By the time we arrived, Yuendumu Sports Weekend was a truly big event and already famous. It was known as the Aboriginal Olympics and attracted thousands of visitors and competitors from places as far away as the Tiwi Islands and South Australia.

The Yuendumu Sports weekend was opened with a march past led by twenty or so men proudly holding their long spears upright and followed by many uniformed teams. There were bucket races in which women ran, balancing sand filled buckets on their heads (no hands). There was a long distance run up to the water tank on the hills south of the Tanami road. There was fire making, *purlapa* and *yawulyu* dances, a full range of athletics. There was a tug of war and children's events, basketball, softball, and it almost goes without saying, the main event, football.

Not only did athletics and football, basketball and softball teams descend on Yuendumu, but so did bands and musicians. The Saturday night Battle of the Bands became a highlight, soon to be complemented by a jam session at my Sunday night birthday party.

As mentioned, it was at the 29th Yuendumu SportsWeekend that Martin Flanagan's glass tower of preconceptions about Aboriginal Australia had been shattered into countless brilliant fragments. Over time, as other communities started holding copy-cat Sports Weekends, the prominence of Yuendumu Sports Weekend diminished. The first Barunga Festival was held in 1985 and by 1999 when the first Garma Festival was held, Yuendumu Sports Weekend had been totally eclipsed. The once proud and unique Yuendumu Sports Weekend, the Aboriginal Olympics, is increasingly referred to as a Football Carnival. One of many.

Yuendumu Sports Weekend is held during the first weekend in

August when Central Australia has the Picnic Day public holiday on the Monday. I've heard it said that the Reverend Tom Fleming instigated the Sports Weekend as a way of dissuading his flock from attending and gambling at the Harts Range Races. In jest I have often claimed the Yuendumu Sports Weekend was held to celebrate my birthday.

In 2020 there was no Sports Weekend because of the virus, and my birthday party was more subdued than ever. But then there is always next year.

For many years I had the honour and fun of being the spear throwing convener and judge at the annual Yuendumu Sports Weekend. I would borrow Mary Laughren's carved wooden snake and then R.J. Robertson and I would ceremoniously use the snake to measure out the course. It was usually a 20 *lingka* event.

A hessian covered foam rubber kangaroo tied to a star picket was the target. The realism of the target often required a fair bit of imagination. Fortunately the participants had that in spades. The spear throwing competition was often preceded by an entertaining and stylised act put on for the benefit of video cameras and the audience. For the act, three or four men armed with spears crouched in line and sneaked with exaggerated caution towards the foam rubber kangaroo. They would be checking the ground for tracks and at intervals a hand would shade the eyes of one of the hunters, and so shaded he would scan the horizon. The leader picked up a carefully placed kangaroo poo pellet and he would squash it with his fingers so as to determine how fresh it was. A hand full of sand was then poured onto the ground from a height to determine which way the wind was blowing. Then in silence and using hand-talk, a hunter suddenly indicated that a kangaroo had been spotted. The hunters would abruptly and simultaneously crouch down and arm their spears onto their woomeras and creeping a bit closer would stand and let fly their spears in unison. The acting was superb and the audience was left in no doubt that the kangaroo had been successfully hunted down and killed.

The spear throwing event started when people were ready, not at the scheduled time. Punctuality is not Yapa's forte. I got a bit tired of answering visitors as to when the spear throwing would start, especially as I usually had no idea myself. My standard answer became 1:43 pm.

When a journalist asked me about the use of the wooden snake to measure out the event, with a straight face, I told him it was a traditional way Yapa had for thousands of years made measurements. I added that recently a standard lingka had been housed in Canberra at the Australian National University. This standard lingka was 93.6 cm long at room temperature. To this day I'm not sure if the journalist was fully aware of my tongue being in my cheek, or thought I was weird, or perhaps even believed it was true. So there you have it, 1:43 pm, and 93.6cm, you couldn't possibly let these communities get away with not having any standards!

From being a highlight at the Sports Weekend, spear throwing has fizzled to a non-event as fewer and fewer spear carrying visitors and locals took part over the years. At its height we even had a participant representing Scotland, Alastair Burns, the then principal of Willowra School, but alas since then the event has got sucked into the vortex of nonexistence. It was fun while it lasted.

Spear throwing 1979 (photo D.Nash)

Incidentally, 'You can't see the wood for the trees ' is a proverbial saying, first found in John Heywood's 1546 glossary:

'*A dialogue conteinyng the nomber in effect of all the prouerbes in the englishe tongue.*'

Mary Laughren's *lingka* is carved out of mulga wood and the grain of the wood faithfully follows its regular sinuous curves. A Yapa person looked into the mulga scrub and exclaimed: "Look there is a snake!"

He was able to discern both the wood and the trees.

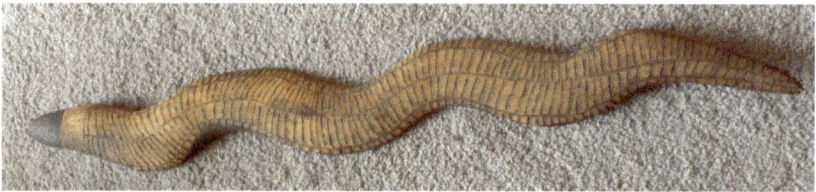

Dog judging

In 1984 Yuendumu School held the first of several annual dog shows. It almost goes without saying that due to my experience as a judge at the Sports Weekend Spear Throwing competition I was expected to be an accomplished judge at dog shows. Spear throwing and dogs, much of a muchness! I rose to the occasion. Clipboard in hand, I would with a serious countenance, judge the dogs as the school pupils dragged their pets by a leash or rope and paraded them in front of me.

Categories were such as 'hairiest dog' and 'fattest dog'. There were as many categories as there were dogs, so they were all winners. Quentin Granites' dog won 'mangiest' dog. Shirley Napanangka Martin's dog Dougie, won 'cheekiest dog' at the inaugural dog show. Dougie had been tied to a star picket which it pulled out of the ground. Dougie took off, clang, clang, clang, towing the star picket at great speed due north towards the horizon, not to be seen again that day. Shirley who teaches at Yuendumu School tells me she has proudly kept her dog show certificate.

A visiting Beijing University Professor was being shown around Central Australia by Mich Bazin, a Frenchman, and Alice Springs based Department of Aboriginal Affairs officer, who had previously worked in Yuendumu. No sooner had Mich introduced the Professor to me, than it was time to go to the school for the dog show. I wondered and still do - what was the Chinese professor thinking when the dog charade unfolded? Did he perhaps think it was a Korean food fair? What did he tell the folks back home? Very eclectic Yuendumu can be.

After a long hiatus the school recently held a dog competition. The new, magnificent blue fence mentioned earlier surrounds the school yard which has as a result been converted into a dog free zone. This year competing pupils could have themselves photographed with their dog at home.

Not quite the same.

Magic Moments

At one Yuendumu Sports Weekend we were graced by the presence of the Milingimbi Gospel Singers. At the concert they sang beautifully. So far so good. However, they could not afford the bus fare back to Darwin. The promise marriage system was still much in effect and the choir boys started forming romantic liaisons with local sheilas and married women. This was cause for much consternation among older Yapa men. The choir boys were running riot. This was to be the first time that Yuendumu Mining Co. (YMC) would fund a non-commercial endeavour. At the insistence of YMC directors we lent each Gospel Singer sufficient money to ensure their exit. Subsequently, two of the Gospel Singers repaid us by mailed cheques. The rest we wrote off as our contribution to social harmony.

†Rex, Robin and †Kurt Granites' father †Tommy Japangardi Granites was one of nature's true gentlemen. He spoke such a beautiful clearly enunciated Warlpiri that he was one of the first Warlpiri speakers that I could begin to understand. At one of my birthday parties, Tommy got up in our lounge room with a long spear and did a very graceful traditional dance. By some miracle he managed to avoid spearing the ceiling. As Tommy danced, Banjo Jungarrayi and his gang were clicking their boomerangs with great gusto in a steady rhythm to the sound of the music that was blaring out of our gramophone player which was 'Brown Sugar' by the Rolling Stones.

A musical highlight happened in 1986 when the Blackfella/ Whitefella tour came to Yuendumu. The tour combined the musical talents of Papunya's Warumpi band and the world famous Midnight Oil. The tour got its name from the Warumpi band's Blackfella/ Whitefella song.

♬ ♬ ♬

Black fella, white fella
Yellow fella, any fella
It doesn't matter, what your colour
As long as you, a true fella

Midnight Oil's most famous song 'Beds are Burning' includes the following lines,

Four wheels scare the cockatoos
From Kintore, east to Yuendumu
The Western Desert lives and breathes
In forty-five degrees

Followed by the chorus,

How can we dance when our earth is turning?
How do we sleep while our beds are burning?

Lead singer Peter Garrett's unique dancing style both intrigued and amused us. When Peter became a politician, he no longer danced. He couldn't. His bed was burning.

At another Sports Weekend the sound equipment at the Battle of the Bands was inadequate to cope with a larger than usual crowd. You couldn't hear a thing at the edges. So a group of us, including the visiting Warumpi Band decided to come to the rescue. Opposite to where I lived there was a seldom used stage which had been the base of a large water tank, next to it was a power outlet on a pole. We set up an alternate venue on this stage and began to play loudly enough so that the people at the periphery of the main concert could hear us. Slowly some of their audience drifted to our stage. As Micah Hudson recalls, most of this crowd were Alyawarra men wearing black cowboy hats with a metal star at the front, which they wore pulled low over their foreheads.

The visitors from the other side of the Stuart Highway were far less extroverted than the locals. As we played, local kids jumped up onto the stage and did incredibly athletic and boisterous sexy dancing. The visitors stood still and stared. Those of us up on the stage, as we peered into the darkness, could only see a silent sea of black hats and glinting eyes and metal stars. It was disconcertingly eerie.

The ABC TV film 'Big Name, No Blankets', is a documentary on the all too brief life of †George Rrurrampu. George was from Elcho Island and married and settled in Papunya. His mother tongue was Gumatj. It is not well known that before joining the newly formed Warumpi Band as lead singer, George lived in Yuendumu. He was a member of Yuendumu's 'Poor Boys' band, who were not destined to become famous. That said, the Poor Boys played some truly brilliant music on their way to anonymous oblivion.

George learnt Warlpiri and rendered a number of Top End stories into readers written in the Warlpiri language for the bilingual programme. These booklets are much liked by Warlpiri children even today.

In the Big Name No Blankets film, Rachel Perkins said:

"I saw George and the Warumpi band play to thousands and thousands and thousands of people all around Australia, and I saw how George could reach out and touch people, open their hearts to make them celebrate and embrace Aboriginality, and just dance with us and sing our song... "

We in Yuendumu got to see that too, we got to sing and dance with George. As in the Warumpi Band's 'Blackfella/Whitefella' song, George was a true fella...and probably best remembered for the now famous song, "My Island Home" first autobiographically performed by him

In 1989, Neil Murray, a founding member of the Warumpi band, who had not long before released his 'Calm and Crystal Clear' album came to my birthday party and played 'Ocean of Regret'. Our local musicians, who had never played the song, instantly backed him to brilliant effect. Whenever I saw an opening I put in the odd trumpet lick, it really was memorable and most enjoyable. Years later Neil, remembering that occasion, said it had been a 'magic moment'. Over the years many visiting musicians have joined with Yuendumu musicians to create such magic moments. Such countless brilliant fragments.

Neil Murray and Frank Baarda

The last nail…

Anyway, I must get back to the serious business of exposing the hypocrites who control Yapa lives.

In front of the now closed Mining Shop, there was a sign:

"*Yuendumu Mining Co. Est. 1969, Locally Owned, Against the Intervention.*"

Often when people saw the sign, they would ask "*What is the Intervention?*" If it had been published, I would have told them to buy this book!

I just went to reminisce by gazing at the sign, but it has been removed. Reminds me of a George Orwell quote from '1984',

"*The past was erased, the erasure was forgotten, the lie became the truth.*"

Wendy's song *'Why are they doing this to us?'* says all you need to know about the Intervention. Here is the chorus.

♫ ♫ ♫

I can still hear the gentle voice of my friend Nungarrayi,
Saying, Why, why, why?
Why are they doing this to us?,
What have we ever done to them?
Why can't they just leave us alone?
We don't need no intervention.

For those of you who are less poetically inclined, see the Intervention's organisation chart on the next page which also says it all, albeit in a different format, in a different font if you like. If you can be bothered I suggest you scan to the bottom of the chart. You will note that on the chart, local input is confined to the bottom two 'boxes'.

Kevin Rudd's famous apology included the lines:

"....not to insist on a one-size-fits-all approach for each of the hundreds of remote and regional Indigenous communities..."

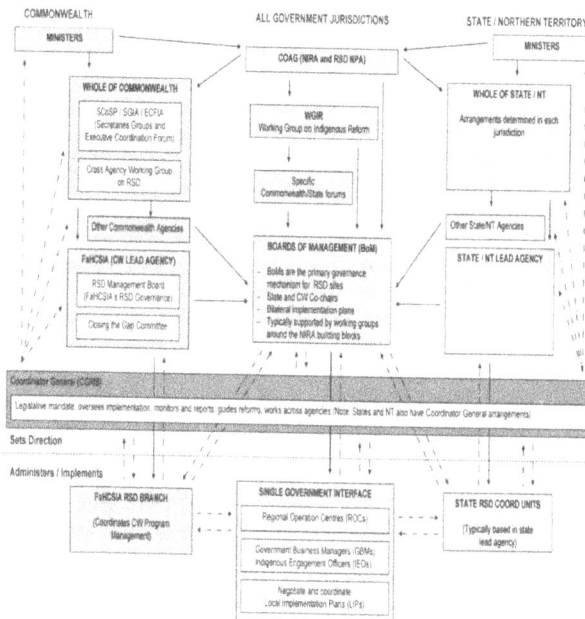

Intervention Organisation Chart

From time to time I carefully peruse the organisation chart and no matter how hard I try, I'm unable to find any evidence of Kevin Rudd's noble intention having been a factor taken into consideration when the chart was being designed.

The organisation chart, that bureaucratic labyrinth, also explains why the Intervention proved to be such a calamity. It explains why the authorities failed to find their road to Damascus or any other road for that matter, when it comes to Aboriginal affairs, only cul de sacs.

The NT's conservative Country Liberal Party (CLP) had stayed in power for 27 years before being ousted by the ALP. Playing the race-card at elections had a fair bit to do with this longevity. The so-called cowboys of the CLP showed their true colours when they spent millions of dollars on fighting Aboriginal land claims in the courts. Shane Stone had been one of the CLP's Chief Ministers. In 1999, he resigned as the Chief Minister and the same year he was appointed the Federal President of the Liberal Party of Australia. It probably is no coincidence, that soon after Shane Stone took up his new role, then Prime Minister John Howard, became a virtuoso of the dog whistle, an accomplished race-card player and a master of fear and loathing elec-toral campaigns. John Howard's methods have been fairly successfully emulated ever since, by politicians from all ends of the political spectrum.

Shane Stone last year was rewarded by being appointed to head The National Drought and North Queensland Flood Response and Recovery Agency, at a reputed annual salary exceeding half a million dollars. Shane Stone famously pleaded that the Drought and Flood Response not be politicized.

I've read a definition of the Yiddish word *chutzpah*: A boy who'd murdered his parents asked the court for mercy because he was an orphan.

That *goy* Shane Stone, he has *chutzpah*.

In 2001 the Howard Government was re-elected, after the so-called Tampa and Children Overboard incidents. Government ministers including Prime Minister, John Howard, had demonised refugees by alleging that the asylum seekers had thrown children overboard from an intercepted boat. After the election the Children Overboard allega-tion was proved by a Senate Committee to have been a deliberate lie. In 2004 the Howard Government won the election with an increased majority, again to a significant extent, due to its mean spirited 'tough on border protection' stance.

Before the subsequent 2007 election however, the Howard Govern-ment was seriously on the nose and the ALP had got their act together with the 'Kevin 007' campaign. In desperation, on the 21st June 2007,

Prime Minister John Howard and his accomplice Mal Brough, the then Minister for Families, Community Services and Indigenous Affairs, announced the Northern Territory Emergency Response (NTER) which soon became known as the Intervention. Someone aptly named the Intervention 'Aboriginal Children Overboard'.

Pat Turner called the Intervention 'the last nail in the coffin of Self-Determination'. Sadly her words were to prove prophetic. Pat Turner is the current CEO of the National Aboriginal Community Controlled Health Organisations and in February last year spoke optimistically about the Government's undertaking to work with Aboriginal Australia on refreshing its Closing the Gap initiative.

This optimism is not shared by those of us whose memory goes back further than just the latest smoke and mirrors olive branch offered by the Federal Government; those of us who remember Neville Chamberlain.

The Intervention

"An unjust law is a code that a numerical or power majority group compels a minority group to obey but does not make binding on itself."

Letter from a Birmingham jail - Martin Luther King Jr.

It isn't well known that in an ironic twist of fate, it was the 1967 Referendum which gave the Commonwealth Government the imprimatur to enact the Northern Territory Emergency Response (NTER) legislation, commonly referred to as the Intervention. The amended constitution empowered the Commonwealth to pass laws meant to favour Aborigines, but which in a hypocritical sleight of hand actually did the opposite. They even cynically suspended the Racial Discrimination Act (passed by the Whitlam Government in 1975) to enable the Intervention to tighten its grip even further.

The triumvirate heading the Intervention consisted of Sue Gordon, Dave Chalmers and Brian Stacey.

Sue Gordon was born the same year I was. As my family sailed to its Argentine adventure, Sue, a member of the Stolen Generations, was being separated from her mother at the age of four. She became the first Aborigine to be appointed a magistrate in Western Australian history. She was the initial chair of the NTER Taskforce.

In 2001/02 Dave Chalmers had been National Commander of Operations in East Timor. In bureaucratic circles, Dave's East Timor experience was seen as a compelling reason as to why the Major-General was eminently suited and should be appointed the Operational Commander of the NTER. Who am I to disagree? I suspect similar criteria were applied to appoint 'Smiling Dave' as had been used to appoint me as the judge at the Yuendumu School dog shows.

Brian Stacey, the Deputy Commander of the NTER, was a career bureaucrat. In 2010 Brian was awarded a Public Service Medal for his 'work supporting Aboriginal people in the Northern Territory'. Reminds me of Henry Kissinger receiving the Nobel Peace Prize.

Not entirely dissimilar to the role of the military in the Australian bushfires and the current pandemic, when the Intervention was launched, much was made of military participation

The highly publicised initial display of military strength and determination was at Mutitjulu, the Aboriginal community that lies in the shadows of Uluru (Ayers Rock). At Mutitjulu there had been countless soldiers wearing camouflage fatigues (who were they hiding from?) The soldiers were seen on national television, kicking footballs with grinning native children. Ironically these children looked healthy and happy and probably were. These were not the abused and neglected children 'crouching in fear', as portrayed in the Intervention's propaganda barrage.

Kintore was the next destination for the by now seriously depleted media caravan. Then it was Yuendumu's turn. The military ranks had shrunk even further to the Major-General and two Norforce soldiers in uniform, one white and one brown- the soldiers that is. Our eleven year old grandson, in his imagination, had anticipated army tanks, rocket launchers and helicopters. After the meeting, at which the Major General lectured and admonished the docile gathering and outlined the new regime the Intervention was imposing, a disappointed Jordon went up to one of the soldiers and asked,

"*Where are the others?*"

Claudia Rowe who had been one of the contestants in the popular 1997 ABC television series 'Race around the world' had worked for Warlpiri Media- now PAW- some years before the Intervention. In 2007 she returned to film the arrival of the military vanguard of the Intervention in Yuendumu. After setting up her camera on a tripod just inside the arch where one enters Yuendumu, Claudia was to be as disappointed as our grandson. No tanks, no helicopters, not even an army squad.

Not wanting to have wasted a trip, Claudia took the opportunity to make a short documentary film critical of the Intervention. So tamed, timid and domesticated had the Australian media become that in contrast to Intervention propaganda, Claudia's incisive little master-piece received virtually no airplay. In the film clip Claudia interviewed †Neville Japangardi Poulson, nicknamed Cobra, a Warlpiri intellectual and philosopher. In the clip Cobra appears standing in front of the dilapidated corrugated iron building which had once been used to hand out rations in the early 'Welfare' days. Cobra was wearing his favourite outfit, military camouflage very similar to that worn by Dave Chalmers! In the clip he speaks of the Interventionists as being *muluru-piya*, like white-ants, a most apt metaphor, as white-anting is what the Interventionists excel at.

> *"I value the time I spent in Yuendumu over those few years (from 1998) immensely. It was the most edifying, mind and heart-expanding experience of my life. It is staggering to me, that for the most part, Australians still do not value the depth and richness and wisdom of Aboriginal people and culture."*
> Claudia Rowe (pers. comm. 2019)

When the ALP's Kevin 007 won the election, we were jubilant. When John Howard and Mal Brough lost their seats to boot, ecstatic and euphoric barely describe our mood. During the election campaign, Jenny Macklin and Warren Snowdon (an NT federal senator) had as much as implied that the ALP would roll back the Intervention if they won, and we were eagerly waiting for this to happen.

Kevin Rudd became Prime Minister of Australia on 3rd December 2007. On the same day the Department of Families, Housing, Community Services and Indigenous Affairs and Tiddlywinks (FaHCSIA - pronounced 'fuckseeyah') was formed. Aboriginal Affairs continued to be relegated to a potpourri ministry.

Jenny Macklin became FaHCSIA's Minister, a position she held until 2013. Opinions on her policies are divided. Jenny Macklin has been much praised and lauded for her achievements in Indigenous Affairs, which is very frustrating for some of us at the coal face, who are of the opinion that she was the politician who in recent times has inflicted the greatest damage to the social fabric of remote Aboriginal Australia.

The 1983 Prices and Incomes Accord was an agreement between the Australian Council of Trade Unions and the Australian Labor Party. Successfully selling the 'Accord' to the media and captains of industry had been a big public relations coup for the Hawke Government. Kevin Rudd's Government tried to emulate that success by holding the Australia 2020 Summit with the aim to, *'Help shape a long-term strategy for the nation's future'.*

One of the topics at the summit was *'Options for the Future of Indigenous Australia'.* † Jeannie Nungarrayi Egan was one of the invited delegates to the conference. She was asked to bring someone along with her, and chose her husband Thomas Jangala Rice. Jeannie had a vision of a self-determining community with strong maintenance of Warlpiri law, language and lifestyle.

Before attending, Jeannie went around all the Yuendumu organisations asking for input. We all availed ourselves of the opportunity. After all, this was the government which was going to roll back the Intervention, which was going to ring in a Bran Nue Dae!

♬ ♬ ♬

On the way to a bran nue day, everybody, everybody say...

'Bran Nue Dae' - †Jimmy Chi

Off to Canberra went Jeannie and Thomas bearing a manila folder of one-pagers containing the communal hopes and wisdom of Yuendumu society. Ideas, comments, suggestions, appeals. A folder full of one of the summit's objectives, 'Options for the Future of Indigenous Australia'.

At the time I said to Wendy that it was a pity that someone younger, with a better command of English didn't go instead.

"You're mistaken there," said Wendy, *"I've seen Nungarrayi in action. She has an uncanny ability of catching the attention of those who matter."*

Jeannie was one of the all too few fully qualified experienced Warlpiri teachers, and Wendy had spent many years working with and for Jeannie at Yuendumu School, and also at Wayililimpa outstation School, which Jeannie had set up.

After their return from the conference Jeannie and Thomas burst into my office. Jeannie proved Wendy right as she reported with infectious exuberance,

"There we were, in a row, Jenny Macklin sitting next to Jangala, and Kevin Rudd sitting next to me. We talked and then I handed Kevin the folder, and yes, he promised me he'd look into it. They listened to us!"

Jeannie was very optimistic that the Intervention would be stopped. This after all was the Prime Minister whose famous sorry speech included,

"The time has now come for the nation to turn a new page in Australia's history by righting the wrongs of the past and so moving forward with confidence to the future."

Jeannie and the rest of us were to be bitterly disappointed. Kevin Rudd and Jenny Macklin got what they wanted - a photo opportunity with the blackest people at the conference.

I do wonder however, what did they do with the folder?

Closing the Gap...

On the heels of the Intervention (NTER) came the Federal 'Closing the Gap' strategy.

Initially 'Closing the Gap' was a source of mirth and amusement. Some wags suggested that the authorities were intent on closing Heavitree Gap at the southern end of Alice Springs, which would have been a massive civil engineering feat. Others thought it would be more likely that The Gap Hotel, a popular and notorious watering hole, would be closed. It soon became apparent however that the Government had successfully sold 'Closing the Gap' to the rest of Australia, including many Indigenous Australians, and that it was no joke. Many Yuendumu residents haven't bought 'Closing the Gap' and are less than enthusiastic about it. Most are indifferent. In Yuendumu 'Closing the Gap' manifested itself as a never ending parade of mentors, consultants, advisors, experts in almost everything and others, intent on boarding the 'Closing the Gap' gravy train.

The government had identified a number of 'gaps' which highlighted 'Indigenous disadvantage' and set targets for these gaps to be closed. The prime minister was to report to the parliament on an annual basis, on what had been 'achieved' in Closing the Gap.

A lot of ethnocentric nonsense is written about Reconciliation and 'Closing the Gap'. Racism and culturism are confused. Racism is plain ignorant and nasty. Culturism is a Trojan Horse, *"Everyone has the right to live and be like me"*, the implication being that this is somehow better than how "they" are living and what "they" are like. At the coal face, it wasn't easy to distinguish what was NTER (Northern Territory Emergency Response) and what was 'Closing the Gap', as they seemed intrinsically interwoven and simultaneously deployed by the same protagonists. The distinction hasn't become any clearer since the NTER segued into 'Stronger Futures'.

Closing the Gap is a construct of non-Indigenous Australia. The defined gaps are derived from Kardiya values and priorities and perspectives. No attention is paid to the Communication Gap, the

Understanding Gap and the Mutual Respect Gap. The Gap is rooted in an unshakeable belief in Kardiya superiority.

One needs only consider the most discussed gap, namely the life expectancy gap, to perceive the flawed assumptions on which the objectives of this initiative are based. The life expectancy gap between the richest and poorest suburbs of Glasgow is of the same magnitude as that between Indigenous and non-Indigenous Australians.

From the 2020 Closing the Gap Report:

Target: Halve the gap in employment outcomes between Indigenous and non-Indigenous Australians within a decade (by 2018).

In the 2008-2018 decade the Indigenous employment rate increased by 0.9% and the non-Indigenous rate decreased by 0.4% - thus the Gap decreased by 1.3%. Employment rates were 75% for nonIndigenous and 49% for Indigenous, i.e. half a gap of 13%. At the present rate halving this gap will take ten decades i.e. a century. The report dryly states, *The target to halve the gap in employment outcomes within a decade was not met.*

Closing the Gap uses a sledge hammer approach to nuanced problems. Forgive them Father for they know not what they do.

The Closing the Gap initiative hasn't travelled so well. Thus the authorities came up with an ingenious solution. They renamed it. They now referred to 'Closing the Gap Refresh'.

"That'll fix it!" they thought. Well it didn't seem to, so in mid-pandemic Prime Minister Scott Morrison announced an 'historic' Closing the Gap Partnership Agreement. A formal agreement between the Commonwealth, State and Territory governments, the National Coalition of Aboriginal and Torres Strait Islander Peak Organisations, and the Australian Local Government Association.

We now have the New Closing the Gap initiative. To avoid Albert Einstein's definition of insanity (doing the same thing over and over and expecting different results) the New Closing the Gap initiative. has increased the number of targets from seven to sixteen. For brevity's sake I'll only mention one of these new targets:

Target 10: *By 2031, reduce the rate of Aboriginal and Torres Strait Islander adults held in incarceration by at least 15%.*

I calculate this to be an annual decrease of at least around one and a half percent. Unlike previous targets, this one is achievable! It only needs for unpaid fines to be taken off the list of jailable offences or any other of the minor jailable offences committed by people who are no danger to the public.

An unmentioned gap is the closing the 'Becoming a Kardiya Gap'. It is a gap Yapa society fails to close, nay, refuses to close. Recalcitrant or resilient- take your pick. Possibly unclosable, even if anyone did want to. How possible for instance would it be for us to close a 'Becoming a blackfella' gap?

♫ ♫ ♫

Let me tell you Mr Teacher,
When you say you'll make me right,
In five hundred years of fighting,
Not one Indian turned white......

(Indian) Drums- Peter la Farge, sung by Johnny Cash

Closing Heavitree Gap

Sisyphus - A painting by Alice Springs artist, Rod Moss,
(Collection of Yael and Raimond Gaita)

Someone once said, *"What these government mob seem to think is, that if you squeeze a blackfella hard enough, a whitefella will pop out."* When I told Harry Nelson this he said it wouldn't work. All you get is a squashed blackfella.

Piggybacking...

It fairly soon became evident to us that the Rudd Government had no intention to roll back the Intervention. They took over ownership of the Intervention instead. They told us all that their predecessors had failed to properly consult and engage with Indigenous Australia, and that they were going to do a much better job. They didn't.

Soon after Kevin Rudd came to power Francis Kelly cried out at a public meeting at the basketball court in Yuendumu: *"Why is Kevin Rudd using John Howard's shoes and piggybacking his policies?"* Francis' anguished rhetorical question has never been satisfactorily answered. Neither have the subsequent five (if you count Kevin Rudd's second tenure) Prime Ministers adequately provided an answer. To paraphrase the Bob Dylan song:

...How many Prime Ministers will it take, before...

♫ ♫ ♫

...The answer my friend is blowing in the wind...

Once again we were to be distracted and seduced by false hope. The Government announced that they would be guided by an independent review, to be conducted a year after the Intervention had been launched. The Peter Yu Review, as it became known, submitted their report in October 2008. Peter Yu and his team had spent a full day in Yuendumu, escorted by Harry Nelson, and we were given ample opportunity to express our concerns to the board of enquiry. We were optimistically looking forward to the report, as we felt we'd been listened to.

When the report came out, Darwin based journalist Paul Toohey, alleged in a newspaper article, that he'd seen the draft review and that it had been substantially doctored to better align it with the Government agenda. I have little doubt Paul Toohey's allegation was true, as I've been told by a reliable source that contrary to convention, the draft had been submitted to FaHCSIA for vetting, prior to the release of the report. It was even rumoured that fees were withheld so as to force redaction of the report, which Jenny Macklin was then able to cherry pick, so as to portray it as a glowing endorsement of the Intervention. If you read between the lines it was anything but.

The second NTER visit to Yuendumu included Sue Gordon. Valerie Napaljarri Martin was showing Sue Gordon and Dave Chalmers around. When they entered the Mining shop, Dave showed he wasn't just a pretty face. In amongst the many notices he quickly spotted Wendy's Warlpiri lessons notice, and expressed his approval.

Valerie must have referred to me as Jungarrayi, because when Sue Gordon shook my hand she said, *"You must be very respected. You've got a skin-name."* As explained before, I was labelled 'Jungarrayi', because I'm married to Wendy Nangala. Respect didn't have anything to do with it.

On the same day, Wendy attended a meeting at the Yuendumu Women's Centre. A small group of Yapa women had invited Sue Gordon to come and listen to their suggestions about how the Intervention might be able to help improve the things that mattered to them, such as more housing and better housing maintenance. They had installed Sue on a chair whilst they sat cross-legged on the ground in a semi-circle around Sue. So there was Sue pontificating about this wonderful Intervention that would set the women free from all those violent men who abused their children. The most vocal person in this group of women was Barbara Martin. Barbara and the women interjected and disagreed with much of what Sue Gordon said. The proud women of Yuendumu refused to accept the role the Intervention had assigned to them. They did not see themselves as helpless victims who had to be saved. So here we had someone being appointed the chair of a multi billion dollar Federal Government initiative, yet who didn't listen.

Sue Gordon wasn't alone in being confronted by the women of

Yuendumu refusing to embrace victim mentality. A lady was invited by the Women's Centre to talk to the women about how to rise above their poverty and oppression. The women asked the lady, *"What is poverty and oppression?"* and after her explanation they exclaimed *"Oh, we don't have that!"*

Early during the Intervention, Harry Nelson said that the Government was using the Stolen Generation mob to help the authorities destroy Yapa culture. Divide and rule in action. Harry despised those urban Aborigines, who knowingly and willingly allow themselves to be so used. The quislings and sell-outs. The 'white sheep of the family' as Gary Foley was heard to label one such. The assimilationists and the assimilated.

As for Sue Gordon, I'm prepared to give her the benefit of the doubt. After all Napoleon is reputed to have said, *"Never ascribe to malice that which is adequately explained by incompetence."* He would have said it in French: *"Ne jamais attribuer à la malice de ce qui est bien expliqué par l'incompétence"* ...with a Corsican accent.

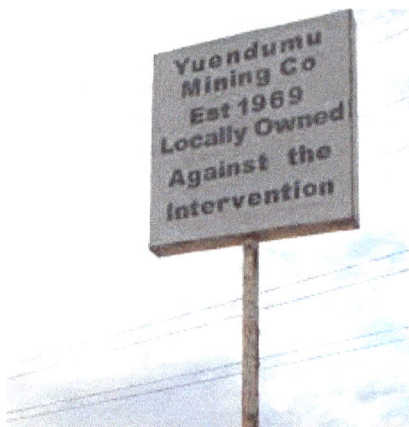

The Ginger-Bread Man (GBM)...

Noel Mason was Yuendumu's first Government Business Manager (GBM) appointed by the Intervention. At a rumoured annual salary of $180,000 plus perks, he was Yuendumu's highest paid individual. He kept a low profile, and we dubbed him 'The Invisible Man'. Yapa called him *ngipiri* (egg). Why *ngipiri*? Well, what does an egg do? It sits in its nest all day knowing nothing and doing nothing. I told you didn't I? Yapa are masters of metaphor.

As a manifestation of the fact that he really existed, Noel sent an email 'To all stakeholders and agencies'. In a two-pager, he suggested among other things, that to improve school attendance, truants should be made to pick up rubbish under the supervision of elders. Cecilia Alfonso, the co-manager of the arts centre, immediately shot back with a 'reply to all': "*I was under the impression that the Emergency Response aimed at protecting children rather than turn them into slave labour.*"

Cecilia's email got traction. Prime Minister, John Howard, was in Darwin at the time, and on the TV news we saw him being asked questions about his Government's Aboriginal policies in the light of the Yuendumu GBM's directive. "*I will look into it,*" John Howard replied; one of his countless non-core promises. As a geologist I like to use the word 'metamorphism'. You may have noticed how Noel's 'suggestion' had metamorphosed into a 'directive'.

Noel became even more invisible than he'd been. In fact he left the community. Later we were to find out he hadn't been sacked. He'd been transferred to neighbouring Yuelamu instead, there to become Yuelamu's highest paid individual and to continue his hermit existence.

At a meeting at the Yuendumu basketball court Ned Jampijinpa grabbed the microphone and loudly spoke up:

"*In Africa children are made to work in the mines. In India they're made to weave carpets. Here, what do they want our children to do? Pick up rubbish!*"

The affront of it all!

Later I will tell you about the community "consultations" the government held when the Northern Territory Emergency Response's five-year term was about to expire. These consultations revealed two main objections to the Intervention on which there was wide consensus, namely that the no alcohol, no pornography signs were offensive and should be removed and that the GBMs were a waste of money and a return to pre-self-determination days and should likewise be removed.

The signs were to stay, on the grounds that they "informed" community residents. My thinking is that these signs were like a dog pissing on trees to mark its territory. All they informed us of, was who was in charge.

In a rare case of listening to us, the government did indeed get rid of the GBMs. But, just as throughout Australia 'rubbish tips' became 'refuse disposal sites' and later 'landfill', so too in the NT, our Government Business Managers became Government Engagement Co-ordinators (GECs).

The main role of the GECs that we perceive, is for them to spy on us and keep the government informed, so as to assist them in imposing total control. No different to the GBMs.

The middle of nowhere

Every now and then a gem of a book lands in your lap which is mind altering. One such for me was Wade Davis' 'The Wayfinders - Why Ancient Wisdom Matters in the Modern World'. If you're getting bored with this story, I strongly suggest you put it down and get hold of that book instead. My favourite bit in the book is where the Navigator tells the author:

"We don't travel to the islands, we make the islands come to us."

In a Radio National, Big Ideas program (The Massey Lectures, 'Century of the Wind', 25-2-2010) Wade Davis stated:

"Cultural survival is not about preservation, sequestering indigenous peoples in enclaves like some sort of zoological specimens. Change itself does not destroy a culture. All societies are constantly evolving. Indeed a culture survives when it has enough confidence in its past and enough say in its future to maintain its spirit and essence through all the changes it will inevitably undergo.....It is not change that will destroy a culture but power...."

Without a doubt Wade Davis was referring to the power of an external dominant culture. This so encapsulates what I've come to realise living in Yuendumu that I simply had to include it in my story.

My first geologist boss, †Jim Cundill, introduced me to the concept of 'home is where your suitcase is'. He explained that whereas the well-site we were at right now was our centre of the universe, once we flew home on completion of the well it would shrink to a dot on the map, and our home would expand to again be our centre of the universe. Not unlike the 'blue dot' of NASA astronauts or looking down a microscope. It's all a matter of perspective and scale.

Whenever visitors or tourists allude to Yuendumu as being 'in the middle of nowhere' I respond with, *"This is not the middle of nowhere, this is the centre of everywhere."* Yuendumu is labelled as a 'remote Aboriginal community'. We are considered to be part of remote Aboriginal Australia, yet we don't consider ourselves to be remote at all, we are right here. To us, those seats of power, Darwin and Canberra are remote, even Alice Springs is a little remote. In this story I have nonetheless referred to Yuendumu as a remote Aboriginal community because that is what we are called in the Australian coastal voter belt. We are part of remote Aboriginal Australia, in the eyes of those politicians and bureaucrats who push our buttons, those who govern us by remote control.

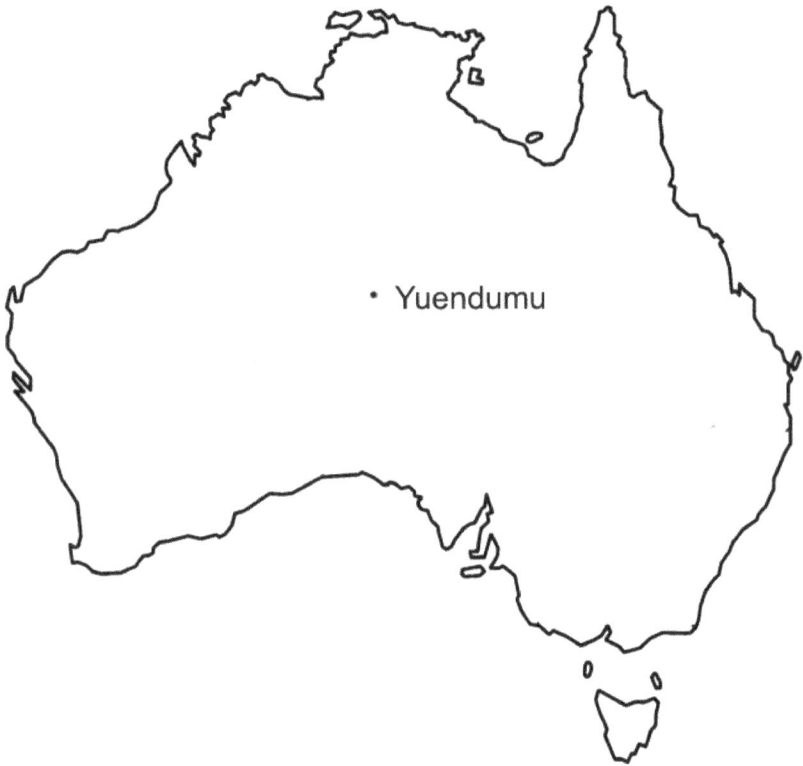

Lip service...

The Intervention created Local Reference Groups (LRGs). The LRGs were under the direction of Regional Operations Centres (ROCs). Bureaucrats love acronyms. I recall a feeling of *schadenfreude* when at the meeting called to set up the Yuendumu LRG we kept nominating more and more members, most of them in absentia. I think we ended up with around 40 members, much to the discomfiture of the organising Kardiya who unsuccessfully tried to limit the numbers. None of us had any illusions that the numerous members would regularly attend LRG meetings. Yuendumu was suffering, and still is, from 'meetings fatigue'. We just enjoy our occasional small victories against overwhelming control pressures. It's known as taking the piss.

The LRG met to take part in one of those recurring reinventions of the wheel sessions. The LRG met to decide on a Local Implementation Plan (LIP), as if planning sessions had never been held in Yuendumu. A brick wall was drawn on a white board with bricks labelled 'Education', 'Employment', 'Health', 'Law and Order', 'Housing', 'Garbage Collection', 'Safety' etc. No bricks were labelled '*Ngurrara*' (homeland), '*Kuruwarri*' (Yapa law), '*Purlapa*' (ceremony), '*Jaru*' (Language) or '*Warlalja*' (family-kin).

An answer to Ned Hargraves's repeated question, *"What I want to know is, what is behind this wall?"* wasn't forthcoming. I am sure that what was concealed behind the white board was a hidden agenda.

Yuendumu's LIP was launched in 2010. At the inaugural LIP meeting, Kenny Japangardi Lechleitner, an urban Aborigine who spent some of his childhood in Yuendumu, had been hired as a 'facilitator' by FaHCSIA. Kenny gave us all a pep talk. He brandished a plastic trident and a bicycle bell as props, and told us that he'd ring the bell or threaten us with the trident, whenever we got out of hand.

It was around the time that the NT Department of Education's infamous 'Four Hours English Only' policy had come into force. We kept harping on about our strong desire for bilingual education to be restored at Yuendumu school. Kenny, in frustrated desperation, asserted that the Warlpiri language had held us back, *"You could never have sent a man to the moon with Warlpiri language,"* he blurted out.

My immediate thought was that this is absolute claptrap. We Kardiya sprung to the defence of the Warlpiri language. A visiting linguist thought she had seen a paper, possibly written by the late Ken Hale, in which the splitting of the atom or some such is explained using the Warlpiri language, and we raised other reasons as to why we thought Kenny was wrong. After the meeting Neville Poulson joined us in discussion. His reaction to the moon assertion was much more to the point. *"We don't want to send a man to the moon."*

A week later Neville in conversation with me ridiculed the use of the bell and the plastic trident and pointed out that the first man into space had been a Russian. We decided that the '4 hours English only' policy should be replaced by the '4 hours Russian only' policy.

Варлпири так и не смогли отправить человека на Луну. Может быть, это их язык удерживал их от этого?

I'll be back...

The Intervention was extended beyond its initial five year term by the Stronger Futures legislation, which has a ten year term. The seamless transition was preceded by a propaganda blitz.

As part of this propaganda, FaHCSIA commissioned the 'Community Safety and Wellbeing research project'. I won't bore you with the twenty pages of questions. A sample will do:

Under the heading 'Social Problems':

*"This next part of the survey is asking you what things you think might be keeping **Yuendumu** back - making it a worse place to live."* (The bold insertion of Yuendumu being indicative that other "lucky" communities were subjected to the same survey).

Question 13: Tell me which of these are still a problem in Yuendumu.

Men hurting women

Other types of family fighting

Adults hurting kids or younger people

Young people hurting older people

Young people not listening to their parents and older people

Drinking too much grog and 11 more items....Anyway you get the drift.

The answers were multiple choice:

4. Very big problem (happens all the time)

3. Big problem (happens a lot of the time)

2. Small problem (happens a bit of the time)

1. Not a problem (doesn't happen here)

0. Don't know

Other questions they might have asked are,

"Do you think the Warlpiri language is keeping Yuendumu back, making it a worse place to live?" and *"Do you think Aboriginal languages are preventing Aborigines from landing a man on the moon?"*

I couldn't find the question *"When did you stop beating your wife?"* I wouldn't have been surprised if it had been there.

Cunning bastards. If the survey showed an improvement in safety and wellbeing, this would "prove" that the Intervention was working and therefore should be extended. Should the situation have got worse according to the survey, this would show that the 'emergency' wasn't over and that the Intervention was still needed. Heads you lose, tails I win.

A visiting Melbourne University lecturer took a photocopy of the survey. She was going to use it to teach her students about leading questions and other tricks of the trade.

At the farcical roadshow to "consult" with communities regarding the Stronger Futures Legislation, we were handed a 28 page 'Discussion Paper', which until then we hadn't seen. We were being asked to have an instant opinion and comment on the proposed legislation which would regulate remote community life for the next ten years.

I was sitting next to Ned Hargraves who took the ball and ran with it. In his inimitable loud style, he let fly: *"How do you expect us to have a sensible discussion when we've only just now been given this book....."* and on and on he went. It was an Oscar winning performance which had the public servants squirming. Highly paid squirming that is. Ned concluded with,

"You know what I think of this paper? This is what I think of it!" as he ceremoniously tore it up into little pieces.

I leant over to Ned and handed him a note.

During the lunch break one of the public servants came over to me, she didn't think it appropriate that I'd tried to influence Ned. She clearly didn't know Ned! Not in my wildest imagination would I think I'd be able to influence Ned, of all people! My note said:

"Ngurrjunpa wangkaja." (You spoke well) - seditious old me!

The final conclusion at this meeting was that we'd not been given enough time to think about the proposed legislation (genius!).

The public servants (who'd flown in from Western Australia) promised they'd be back for further discussions. It was a non-core promise. Unlike the Terminator and the cat, they never came back.

The Stronger Futures legislation expires in 2022. Governments usually apply the ratchet method of negotiation and legislation. I wouldn't be surprised therefore if the road show will at last keep their promise and return in 2022, shortly before Stronger Futures reaches its use by date.

Guantanamo Bay...

Stronger Futures was soon often accurately referred to as 'Intervention Mark II'. The Stronger Futures legislation, if anything, tightened the grip authorities had on Yapa society even further. A graffiti appeared on a water tank next to the Tanami Road: 'Strangler Futures' it proclaimed.

If the aim of the Intervention was to gain greater control of remote communities, it succeeded way beyond Minister Macklin's wildest wet dreams. If the aim was to make these better places, the Intervention was a miserable failure.

The day after the Australian Parliament passed the Stronger Futures legislation, I was at Yuendumu airstrip when a charter plane landed and disgorged three passengers. I offered them a lift into town that they gratefully accepted, as they'd made no arrangements, and there was no one there to meet them. They had come to Yuendumu to inspect the Men's Safe House.

At the beginning of the Intervention a contractor had installed a converted shipping container as a 'Men's cooling-off place'. At the time I came to the conclusion that the 'cooling-off place' had been designed by the same architect who had designed Camp Delta at Guantanamo Bay. The several strands of barbed wire at the top of the chain-wire mesh fence, the padlocked chain on the gate and the spotlights surrounding the Spartan building are reminiscent of TV images I had seen during the time, that Australian David Hicks was a guest at Guantanamo Bay.

I'd found it hard to envisage Warlpiri men embracing the facility as a cooling-off place. It was nothing like the Men's Centre the community had asked for, a place for men to hang out, similar to the Women's Centre, a comfortable place for women to meet.

The perceived and implied need for these 'cooling-off' places is yet another example of how remote Aboriginal communities have been stigmatised. No discussion or consultation with Yapa preceded the decision to install these facilities, they simply assumed and asserted they were a good idea. The intervention had tens of these converted containers installed throughout the NT. The contractor made a killing.

I drove the two men and the lady to the padlocked 'cooling-off' place which I found out had been renamed the 'Men's Safe House'. The lady exclaimed, "*It looks like it has never been used!*" Well spotted! It never had.

An hour later the charter plane took off on its way to another community made safer by the erection of an Intervention Men's Safe House. To pay a local organisation to inspect the safe house, take a few photos and knock on a few walls to check for termites would require a paradigm shift the interventionists are incapable of making.

A much more likely scenario is that a plane load of experts, consultants, mentors and trainers lands at Yuendumu airstrip to run a course leading to 'Safe House Termite Inspector' certificates.

The green green grass of home...

♫ ♫ ♫

Early last year when driving to our annual holiday destination, while I was concentrating on the road, Wendy was looking at the landscape and providing a running commentary. Never, in the almost half a century we've been in this part of the world, did the country look so poorly. After she paid attention for a while she concluded that around one quarter of the mulga trees were dead or dying. I think the mulga scrub was trying to tell us something.

It never ceases to amaze me though how quickly after a decent shower of rain the country springs to life. Frogs in the dam and a carpet of green materialise seemingly out of nowhere. *Wajirrki* is what the Warlpiri call that bright green new growth that can so uplift the spirit.

In football obsessed Yuendumu a bright green footie oval is the stuff of dreams. Grassing the oval has been a political football in more ways than one.

Last century Yuendumu Mining got a contract to install drip irrigation on a Yuendumu football oval. Recycled water from the sewage ponds was to be pumped a short distance to the northern oval. A trenching machine was hired and with great enthusiasm and quickly learned skills, the contract was completed.

The northern oval however was never grassed. The people responsible for the planning designing and budgeting of the project had underestimated the size and cost of the required pumping equipment. Their funds had dried up.

Remote Aboriginal Australia is littered with expensive unfinished abandoned projects-did I mention the brick making machine? After the next ice age, archaeologists will puzzle over an oval shaped network of polythene pipes with no apparent purpose.

When the NT cabinet meets other than in Darwin this is referred to as a "bush cabinet meeting". During one such bush cabinet meeting held in Yuendumu, the Chief Minister and the Minister for Sport of the NT promised that the Government would fund the grassing of the Yuendumu football oval.

At a Local Implementation Plan (LIP) meeting it was suggested that grassing of the oval should be made conditional on improved school attendance (similar to the "Yes School-Yes Pool" policy being implemented at the swimming pool). The idea was dropped when it was pointed out that none of our footballers go to school, but it is yet another example of subtle yet relentless moves at control. Social engineering without conscience or consent

After a hiatus, the grassing of the oval idea resurfaced. The grassing would be in three phases. Each phase to be triggered by School attendance reaching a certain level. The LIP discussion rejecting the idea that grassing of the oval should be contingent on improved school attendance had been conveniently forgotten. Local implementation had once again fallen by the wayside.

The NT Government engaged a consultant to look into the logistics of grassing the oval. Yuendumu Mining (YMC) was invited to a meeting with a view of becoming involved in the proposed project. Purnpajardu who was a YMC director and who has been involved in Yuendumu football all his life, and myself went to the Yuendumu office of the Central Desert Shire, at which a three hour meeting ensued during which suitable grass types, source of water, fertilisers, fencing and other grave matters were discussed at length. Towards the end of the meeting, spectator seating was discussed. Purnpajardu, who had been silent throughout, suddenly sprang to attention. *"The seats that are there now, we made them ourselves!."*

The Government Business Manager (GBM) seized on this, and thought that ITEC or some such organisation could run a welding course leading to certificates and 'real jobs'. Call me cynical, I think the GBM missed Purnpajardu's point.

I've seen it time and time again, whenever Kardiya, as they're inclined to do (and I admit there have been occasions I've been derelict myself in this regard) take over, Yapa will fade into the background and lose interest. They become silent and invisible; they exit the Kardiya world and retire through their Stargate to their own world.

Wendy tells me that at a school staff discussion regarding the role of Kardiya in communities, Purnpajardu had advised Kardiya to '*talk slowly and encourage*'.

At the grassing of the oval meeting, the consultant and GBM had not talked slowly and neither had they encouraged. Purnpajardu spoke no more.

Yuendumu oval remains red and barren, but I must admit some progress has been made. An Alice Springs contractor installed some tall steel poles. The oval now has night lighting. Football till midnight and beyond!

We are all happy.

The deep end…

Yuendumu has a long history of plans and consultations and meetings and arguments and discussions about a swimming pool. Would a swimming pool cause the spread of infections? Would a swimming pool be a silver bullet for improving children's health? Could a swimming pool be used as a weapon against school truancy?

I've already told you of the tiny swimming pool at Yuendumu school. In November 1982, at the rear of what had been the hospital, the YMCA, as the school holiday youth programmes had become known, opened a small but functional swimming pool. It ran for a number of years, but in due course the pool became a dark green slimy algal mess and was duly filled in. The old hospital building itself, after sustained termite attack, collapsed. The site is now occupied by YKNAC, Yuendumu's outstation resource organisation. All that remained of the old hospital were a few concrete foundations now being covered over as YKNAC builds a large shed. Memories obliterated by a large shed. Progress.

Alice Springs based Tangentyere Design had been commissioned to come up with a culturally appropriate design for a Yuendumu swimming pool. The lady leading community consultations suggested a boomerang shaped pool! Can you just picture it? There is Yuendumu's best swimmer at the Australian Olympic trials. He or she is leading, when suddenly spectators are flummoxed as he or she takes off at a tangent.

At one stage planning had progressed so far that the discussion centred on how much various alternative swimming pool designs would cost to build. Our recently arrived town clerk, threw a spanner in the works. A swimming pool would have to be under cover, he insisted, thereby increasing the potential cost several fold.

In the last several decades, Yuendumu has experienced fewer dust storms than I have fingers on my hands. The biggest dust storm occurred one week after the town clerk arrived, hence his insistence on a pool roof.

A government initiative to improve Indigenous health, was the dollar for dollar subsidising of the building of community swimming pools. The Yuendumu Council having not long before been under Administration and soon to be swallowed up by the Central Desert Shire in any case, was in no position to lodge an application. Alice Springs based pro-bono business consultant, Christine Godden took the initiative to meet the application deadline by having WYDAC support the application as a proxy for the council. WYDAC the Warlpiri Youth Development Aboriginal Corporation was formerly the Mt.Theo Substance Misuse initiative which had successfully eradicated petrol sniffing in Yuendumu.

I learned something new. I thought a swimming pool consisted of a hole in the ground suitably clad to prevent water loss, and filled with water with a few chemicals thrown in for good measure. Something which Yuendumu Mining with local labour and some outside help could easily handle. Total cost- perhaps $50,000. Very naive of me. No Sir, after dealing with an entanglement of rules and regulations the swimming pool evolved into a multi-million dollar project, complete with a business plan and landscaping and flood mitigation.

Christine Godden, Susie Low (Nangala) the CEO of WYDAC and a lady from the relevant government department in Darwin, successfully dealt with the application and the necessary fundraising. A substantial donation was received from the late Tom Kantor's family. Tom (Jampijinpa) had worked at Warlpiri Media. A large stone from Juka-juka (a spectacular water dreaming site west of and not far from Yuendumu) was erected in front of the pool with a plaque in memory of that young Jampijinpa. Warlukurlangu Artists paid for the landscaping. Even after the money had been raised, the swimming pool was subjected to a lot of bureaucratic sabotage. The fierceness of external opposition to the pool was beyond our comprehension.

I may be wrong, but as I recall, a misogynist government official took umbrage because the swimming pool show was run by women, and he floated a rumour that the proposed pool site may have been contaminated with cyanide from the old Yuendumu Mining Company (YMC) copper leaching operations. That this was plainly not true didn't make much difference. The closest source of cyanide would have been minute quantities in almonds in kitchen pantries and discarded orange peels and from certain species of native cockroach which spray cyanide as a defence mechanism.

Sodium cyanide (NaCN) is used in the gold mining industry. Strict protocols are in place to ensure the safe handling and use of cyanide. An irresponsible truck driver on the way back from having delivered a load of cyanide to the Granites gold mine discharged the flushing fluid on the side of the Tanami road. A large number of birds and a few dingoes died from drinking this poisoned water. It could have been worse, it could have been people. A panic driven public relations offensive was launched by Newmont Mining. Suddenly cyanide was believed to be everywhere. YMC's defunct copper leaching plant is not far from Yuendumu's present day swimming pool. Sulphuric acid was sprayed over crushed ore containing carbonates of copper. The chemical reaction produces copper sulphate solution. Copper was then precipitated by adding scrap iron tins to the solution. In hindsight, we now know that much sulphuric acid was consumed by reacting with iron oxides (rust) contained in the ore, producing ferrous sulphate, a fertiliser which was worth less than it would have cost to transport it to market, and certainly less than the cost of the acid. I won't bore you with the chemical formulae, but assure you that cyanide was never used at the copper leaching plant.

Yuendumu Mining Co., which had been involved in many geochemical sampling surveys in its own right, or under contract to mineral exploration companies, could have, for a modest fee, confirmed that no cyanide was present at the proposed pool site.

But no, a Darwin based firm of geotechnical engineers was engaged. A small excavator was ferried to Yuendumu and a friendly, lucky, young man got to travel to Yuendumu to dig a few sampling pits and take a batch of samples. I went to check out the sampling operation and spoke (nicely) to the friendly, lucky, young man. He knew bugger-all about chemistry or geology. I think this sampling exercise cost $20,000.

Minister Macklin, by now firmly in control of the Intervention, opened the Yuendumu Swimming pool. The Intervention had had nothing to do with the pool, but this wasn't mentioned by 'photo-opportunity Jenny' when on 27th October 2008 she cut the ribbon.

When WYDAC had run the swimming pool for one year, as agreed, the pool would revert back to the Council. In the meantime the Central Desert Shire had appropriated the Yuendumu Council and despite having undertaken to take on the responsibility for running the swimming pool, had failed to budget for this and was thus unable and unwilling to meet this commitment.

Susie Low called an emergency meeting to discuss fund raising to keep the pool open. My tongue in cheek suggestion that Yuendumu could make the sacrifice of managing without the Intervention installed Government Business Manager, and that the money thus saved could run the pool for the next few years, got a big laugh, but no follow up action. As I previously mentioned, in Yuendumu, good ideas usually fall flat especially if they are locally generated. In the end, the meeting could not come up with a solution, and the possibility that the pool would have to close, was very real.

It was then that I suggested that seeing as Jenny Macklin had with great fanfare opened the pool, she should be invited to close it, if it came to that.

The cartoon is by MacAdams and accompanied an article by Jack Waterford which appeared in the Canberra Times, soon after the WYDAC meeting. The article and cartoon were prompted by emails from a whistle-blower. Wonder who that might have been?

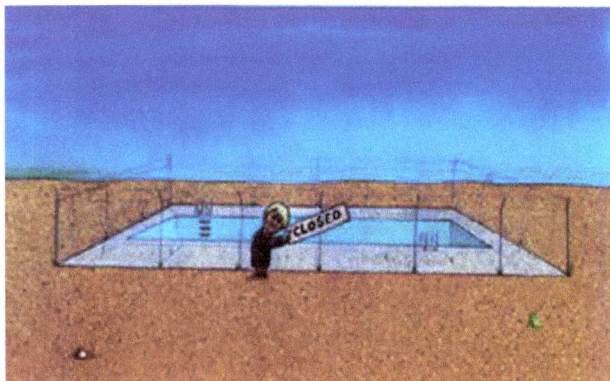

I have just checked out the pool - there is a 'Closed due to COVID-19' sign. The magnificent water dreaming rock, from Juka-Juka, (one of the clouds thrown down by the Water ancestor, which Traditional Owner, †Jack Jangala Cook had so graciously allowed to be moved), and its brass plaque in memory of Jampijinpa Kantor, are nowhere to be seen.

A shame job…

In Moe there was a large billboard featuring a thermometer. This was the Moe swimming pool appeal. Not long before, Australia had dominated the swimming events at the 1956 Melbourne Olympics, and every country town in Australia yearned to have its own Olympic swimming pool. Moe was no exception and in red paint on the thermometer was marked the level of donations reached so far and the top of the thermometer signified the target when construction could begin. When donations had reached the halfway mark on the thermometer, the treasurer of the appeal absconded with the funds to Queensland. These days ill gotten gains end up in exotic places such as the Cayman Islands or Luxembourg, back then Queensland was the destination of choice. As you can imagine donations dried up and it was to be long after I'd left, that Moe finally got its pool.

The closest swimming pool to Moe was at Yallourn. Keen and well off parents would regularly drive through the Haunted Hills and take their children to swimming training at the Yallourn Swimming Club, leaving the rest of us to flounder on dry land.

When the first inter-school swimming sports were held, four High schools took part. These were Yallourn and Morwell both with swimming pools and Moe and Drouin without. The Moe team consisted of a small core of excellently trained swimmers and the rest of us mediocre at best. The winner of each event would score three points for their team, the runner up two points and the third placegetter, one point. When I swam a backstroke event I got absolutely nowhere. Then the 800 metre freestyle event was announced with only two entrants. All Moe's good swimmers had declined to swim the 800 metres as they preferred to save their energy for the many shorter events they had entered. Here was a point up for grabs and I quickly volunteered to be the third entrant.

By the time I'd swum the first length, the other two contestants had shot past me on their second lap and by the time they finished placing first and second I was only halfway and had 400 metres to go. I can still picture the anxious look on the face of Mr. Curtain, who was to become my chemistry teacher, as he shouted from the end of the pool *"Frank if you want to give up that's OK!"* What, give up? I could have swum the English Channel at the leisurely pace I'd set myself, no, it was just a matter of time and I'd get that point. I think it was a good twenty minutes later when I finished. Moe High School came third in the swimming sports. We beat Drouin by one point.

The next day at school assembly the headmaster, as principals were then known, waxed lyrical about the example of sportsmanship he had witnessed. It wasn't about winning he told the assembled students who turned to me with looks of envy or admiration. It was most embarrassing. In the Annual School Magazine in the school sports section there was an entry that read: *"The most notable swim was by Frank Baarda."*

A bit like when Yuendumu won the "most improved community" award in the Annual Territory Tidy Towns competition.

So what is the point of this story? When Warlpiri people play sport there is a reticence to personal stardom, it is more about the team, no tall poppies in traditional Warlpiri society, no chiefs only indians. I know how Yapa feel when they're put on a pedestal. They are *kurnta*.

In Aboriginal English this is known as a 'shame job'.

Tall poppies

Kardiya are often blown away when they watch Yapa play sports. Such agility, such flair, such anticipation! As with many amazing things there is often a simple rational explanation.

Wendy recalls when a Yapa literacy worker was walking along carrying her baby who was about 18 months old, and a Yapa bystander called out to the child to get its attention. The child heard the voice but could not locate the person, so the speaker called out again. This time the bystander mentioned the direction in which the child should look. The bystander said, '*Kakarrara*', meaning towards the east. Immediately the baby turned its head and looked in the right direction towards the speaker.

You ask any five year old Yapa child in Yuendumu, where is Alice Springs, Papunya or Nyirrpi, and without hesitation they will accurately point in the right direction. Any five year old Kardiya child who grew up in Yuendumu will as likely as not, also point in the right direction.

Our son Donovan, who learned Warlpiri by immersion, used to play basketball with Yuendumu teams whenever he was around and the opportunity arose. As Donovan explained to me: when a Kardiya player yells out at a teammate 'Here!', that is one dimension. When a Yapa player yells at a teammate '*Yatijarra*!' (North!) that isn't where he is, that is the direction he wants him to throw the ball in – two dimensions.

Thus it is no mystery that Yapa excel at sports. Their culturally and linguistically inculcated spatial perception has much to do with this.

Yuendumu's most famous native son footballer is Liam Jungarrayi Jurrah. Liam is the first indigenous person from a remote community in Central Australia to have played senior football in the Australian Football League, the AFL. In 2010 at the zenith of his brief meteoric football career he was awarded Mark of the Year. For non-Australians a 'mark' is catching a ball which hasn't touched the ground after being kicked.

A mark entitles the catcher to a free kick. Marks can be very spectacular when they involve soaring onto and above other players who are clamouring for the ball. During an almost three year period after he left the AFL, Liam fell foul of the law, was in and out of court and even spent time in jail.

Liam returned to playing football in August 2014. TV crews and journalists descended on Yuendumu in anticipation of filming the former star in action. They were to be disappointed. Liam was playing with his friends and family. He duly passed the ball and helped his team to win. He was playing for Yuendumu, not for the cameras. He had no tickets on himself.

On 29th September 2020, Yuendumu defeated Mt Allan in the Grand Final of the Centralian Football League held at Traegar Park in Alice Springs. Yuendumu's highest scorer was Liam Jurrah. In one instance during the game, Liam gained possession of the ball a few metres in front of the goal posts. So did he kick the goal to add to his score? No, he didn't. He hand-balled the ball to another nearby team member, who then kicked the goal.

Kirsty-Anne Napanangka burst into the shop bearing a big grin and the big brass Best Actor award trophy her great uncle Hamilton Japaljarri Morris had won at the Australian Academy of Cinema and Television Arts Awards in Sydney. Hamilton had won the award for his role in the film 'Sweet Country'. Hamilton modestly followed out of the car Kirsty-Anne had taken the trophy from. The award, he declared, was something we could all be proud of, all of us Yuendumu and Nyirrpi-*wardingki*. He saw it as a Warlpiri achievement, not his own. When he told us that, there was not a hint that Kardiya residents like myself were to be excluded from his magnanimity.

It is this collectivism which is one of the things that makes being Warlpiri or amongst the Warlpiri special. It also makes the Warlpiri vulnerable. To be modest and generous in a competitive world of greed and individualism and political and commercial opportunism, can be perilous.

To turn Warlpiri society from collectivism to individualism, supposedly 'for their own good', is one of the assimilationist aims of Kardiya society. I hope the bastards never do, but if colonialism reaches its ultimate goal of total control and ethnocide, we will all be the poorer for it. If the assimilationists succeed we would no longer be able to feel proud of such as Hamilton's award.We would no longer have a sense of communal ownership of 'Sweet Country'.

Liam and Hammo are no tall poppies, they're mere ordinary members of an extraordinary society.

Little Children are Sacred...

Clare Martin's Government commissioned an inquiry into the sexual abuse of Aboriginal children on 8th August 2006. Wild and Anderson's *Ampe Akelyernemane Meke Mekarle* (Little Children are Sacred) report was dated 30th April 2007 but wasn't released to the NT Government until 16th June. One justification offered for the sudden launch of the draconian Intervention, which I have already described as a nasty political ambush, was that the NT Government had sat on the report and hadn't acted on it. Indeed they'd sat on it a lengthy five days!

At the time, linguist David Moore alerted me to the fact that the report title was based on a mistranslation from the Alyawarr language and could equally well have been mistranslated as 'Little Children are Dangerous'.

A decade of conservative government had already disempowered remote communities by social, bureaucratic and fiscal sabotage when, thirteen years ago, John Howard and Mal Brough sprung their desperate political opportunistic stunt on the most marginalised section of Australian society.

Remote communities were portrayed as dysfunctional, depraved places. As well as Mal Brough's alleged paedophile rings, Senator Heffernan, under the cowardly legal refuge of Parliamentary privilege, claimed that he'd been in Yuendumu only twenty minutes to find out who the drug runners at Yuendumu School were, as well as alleging sexual misconduct at the acclaimed Mt. Theo programme. Bill Heffernan's political career as a conservative Federal Senator was punctuated by alleged unethical controversial and dishonest statements and ended in May 2016. He never proved nor retracted his Yuendumu allegations.

As UN Special Rapporteur on the Rights of Indigenous Peoples, James Anaya, who visited Yuendumu, was to say later about the Intervention, that it *"further stigmatised already stigmatised societies"*. The stigma of alleged depravity and dysfunction in remote Aboriginal Australia has never been erased, and continues to be used by political opportunists, and probably will be so used forever.

The second verse of Wendy's Intervention song:

It's all for the children, that's what they said,
Our kids are in danger that's what they read,
When those ladies first came to talk and find out,
We told them all, we all knew about.
There had been cases but only a few.
White people have some child abuse too,
But when it is found in a white people's town,
They don't blame all the men, put them all down,
They don't bring in the army and check all the kids,
They don't put up big signs where everyone lives,
Maybe their thinking goes back to the past,
One black did a crime so they shot lots of us.

The last two lines refer to the earlier mentioned Coniston massacre and what Wendy calls the 'massacre mentality' which is very much a feature of the Intervention. Erect straw men and then tar everyone with the same brush.

Dingo trapper, Fred Brookes, who had taken liberties with the wife of Kamalyarrpa (Bullfrog), was murdered in 1928 at Yurrkuru on Coniston Station, 55 Km north east of Yuendumu and not far from present day Yuelamu (Mt. Allan Station). This triggered the so called Coniston Massacre in which, during a series of punitive raids led by Gallipoli veteran, police constable William Murray, probably more than a hundred Yapa, men, women and children, were indiscriminately killed. This is not unlike WWII reprisals when random civilians were put up against the wall. A subsequent official inquiry into the Coniston Massacre acknowledged only 31 victims and found the killing of 'blacks' to be 'justified'.

The children who were killed in 1928 were back then certainly not regarded as sacred! Bullfrog died of old age in Yuendumu in the 1970s.

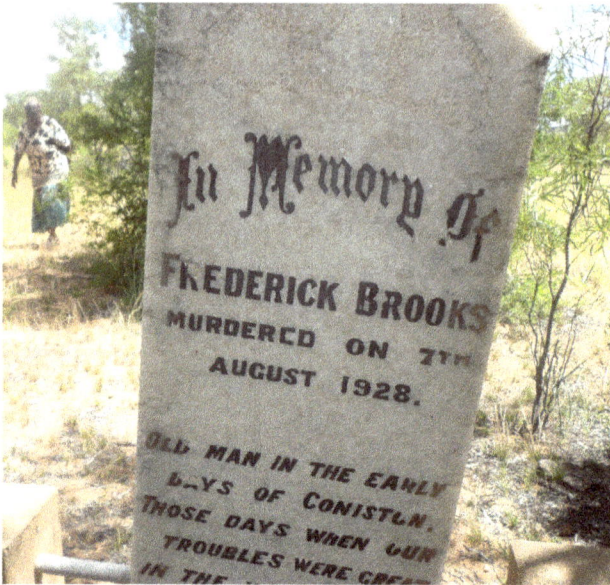

Over the years much has been written and filmed on the Coniston Massacre and in 2013, yet another Coniston film, co-directed by David Batty (Rebel Films) and Francis Kelly (PAW-Warlpiri Media), was produced. But what made this movie refreshingly different is that the story is told from a Yapa perspective.

One evening many of us drove to Yuelamu 35 Km east of Yuendumu on the 'back-road'. The language spoken at Yuelamu is Anmatyerre, though most Yuelamu residents also speak Warlpiri, which is as different to their language as Polish is to French. A screening of PAW's Coniston film was held at the Yuelamu Basketball Court which had been opened the previous day.

In this film, which has some very funny scenes, there is an absence of rancour and animosity which could be a lesson to peace makers everywhere.

There is an old 'joke', I think originally from the Pacific:

"*We had the land and the missionaries had the Bible, then they came and now they have the land and we have the Bible.*"

In this film it was gently stated,

"Our land is no longer ours, it now belongs to the pastoralists and the miners. We never got justice,"

all said without anger or blame.

Just as I was starting to despair for the fate of Warlpiridom under the sustained multipronged assimilationist attack, along came this film showcasing Yapa strength and humor. Any society that can experience deep sorrow yet so heartily laugh at the oppressors and themselves, surely has a future.

On the 90th anniversary of the massacre, we attended the memorial gathering at Yurrkuru. Yapa are very pleased that descendants of constable Murray come on these occasions in a true spirit of reconciliation. Politicians and government officials also attend. I suggested to Japangardi, it might be an an idea to bring up some ongoing injustices. He said this was not the time. This was for families to remember and feel sorry for the ones they lost. Political opportunism is not part of the Warlpiri psyche.

There is a 'Conistonn' street in Yuendumu. Never mind the misspelling, but I have on occasion pondered how many Srebrenica Streets there might be in the former Yugoslavia.

When the Intervention's allegations of child sexual abuse were "launched", Wendy spoke to someone who'd been in charge of WYN Health from the year 2000. Since disbanded, WYN (Willowra, Yuendumu, Nyirrpi) Health, was an organisation which had been set up in the hope that it would take over local control of health clinics. Wendy was told that in the preceding seven years, not a single case of a sexually transmitted infection had been detected in Yuendumu for children under the age of thirteen. This important fact is nowhere to be found in official reports.

From memory it was $45 million, which was allocated to the Australian Federal Police (AFP) to investigate Mal Brough's alleged 'paedophile rings'. Despite the AFP pursuing the alleged perpetrators, armed with Star Chamber Powers bequeathed under the Crimes Act

1914, not a single case of paedophilia was prosecuted. No more were there paedophile rings in Remote Aboriginal Australia than there were weapons of mass destruction in Iraq. Or reds under the beds in 1950s Australia.

Kamalyarrpa
(Bullfrog)

Give me the child…

"Give me the child for the first seven years and I will give you the man." An axiom attributed to Saint Ignatius of Loyola, the founder of the Jesuits.

With the Intervention came an intensified focus on early childhood education and child care. This concerted attempt at assimilation starts at a very early age. From memory there were seven initiatives imposed on Yuendumu relating to early child care and education, including a lady who'd been sent to Yuendumu to deal specifically with '0 to 3' year old children.

Another lady came out to coordinate the efforts of this plethora of participants. This lady joined a small group of Yapa women who were gathered outside of where a meeting was to be held. She told this group that despite a large amount of money having been spent, there had been no improvement. The group told the lady coordinator that Yuendumu children were happy, healthy and learning well. How were their children failing and what could they do to "improve" them, they asked. The lady told them that all remote Aboriginal children were down when measured on several criteria. When asked what these criteria might be, she was not able to enlighten the group. She didn't know.

Afterwards the group discussed among themselves how their children might be lacking. They couldn't think of anything. Finally a Yapa school teacher came up with, *"white children in preschool are better at colouring-in."*

The third verse of Wendy's Intervention Song.

♫ ♫ ♫

They say our little children are not good enough,
In what ways they are not telling us,
Our kids are happy they don't suck their thumb,

They're loved and cared for by every-one,
They're bright and alert, and nimble and quick,
They catch little lizards they dig with a stick,
They can bounce, they can catch and they surely can throw,
They know a few things white children don't know.
Well maybe it's just about colouring in,
Surely there's time for that kind of thing.
For them we would like education that works,
We want them to learn in our own language first.

We have known F. Nangala all her life. When she became a mother, Wendy was invited to baby Japalyi's 'smoking' - a ceremony attended by a few close women friends and relatives, such as grandmothers, aunts and sisters. Baby Japalyi displayed symptoms of what in western society, we call autism; for instance he would ignore and look away from anyone talking to him. Nangala wasn't having it. She would hold her baby's face towards the person, until he looked at the person's face and then would repeatedly say the person's name and relationship, for example *"jaja nyuntuku"* (Grandmother for you), while alternately touching the child and the person.

Japalyi is now a healthy, happy, very sociable thirteen year old who plays football and actively plays with his equally sociable siblings. Last week Nangala gave birth to her 5th boy. Wendy asked her if she was going to keep trying for a girl. No, enough was enough, said Nangala with a smile.

Warlpiri babies lead a blessed life. They receive constant attention from their extended family and are expected to reciprocate. Warlpiri mothers, friends and relatives constantly talk to babies and remind them who they and how they relate to them, *"I'm your pimi,"* (aunty, father's sister), *"That is your yapirli,"* (father's mother). Warlpiri passersby will usually address a baby or child before talking to the adults.

In Warlpiri society, most childhood disorders such as thumb suck-ing, stuttering, eating disorders, and toilet problems are virtually non-existent. Warlpiri parents and extended families could teach main-stream society a thing or two about child rearing.

Kardiya teachers often comment on Warlpiri children, they're magic, so lively, responsive, and affectionate. A teacher who left and went to another school said, "*I wish I could have Warlpiri children in this school.*"

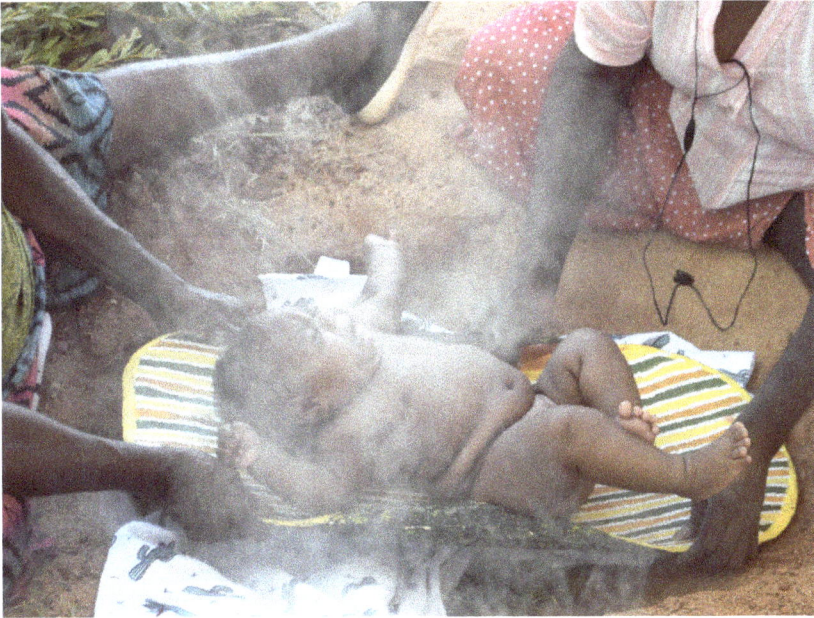

Operationalising dingoes...

We had a dog once who, despite having produced a litter of puppies, insisted on adding another dog's puppies to her own litter. There she was, with a smug grin on her snout, surrounded by numerous puppies, while nearby the other dog could be heard whimpering in heartrending distress. Chocolate was our dog's name, because of her colour. Wendy eventually managed to return the stolen puppies to their rightful mother and then had to keep both litters segregated.

A veterinarian who regularly came to Yuendumu was doing research to find out if dog ticks could transmit diseases to humans. Always willing to help, I recall once sending him a matchbox full of live ticks by Australia Post. Anyway, this veterinarian had told me that DNA tests had shown that most dogs in Yuendumu had at least some dingo blood. I also found out that it was typical dingo behaviour for dominant bitches to take over the rearing of other bitches' pups. Like cuckoo birds in reverse.

During the previous Stolen Generations, lighter skinned children were at greater risk of being taken away than the darker skinned children. Francis Kelly, was one of those lighter skinned kids, but he had narrowly escaped being abducted by "the Welfare". I discussed all of this with him, including what was happening at present. Our discussion concluded with Francis declaring that the Welfare mob are *wanaparipiya* - they are like dingoes.

A lady was sent to Yuendumu whose job was to prevent 'children at risk', being removed by welfare agencies. She introduced herself at an 'agencies' meeting, and told us that the previous week only one child had been removed, as if this was some sort of an achievement. You could hear the air being sucked in by those Yapa present as they gazed at the floor and said nothing.

In hindsight the newly appointed 'dingo lady' failed utterly in her brief. Despite this being something which isn't freely spoken about because of a misplaced notion of guilt and shame, I personally know of several children that were removed during her reign.

The Stolen Generations fiasco, whereby thousands of Indigenous children were removed from their families, is now recognised as a grave past injustice. A fuck-up of gargantuan proportions.

The Stolen Generations is second only to the introduction of smallpox in 1788 in its calamitous effect on Australia's First People's societies.

When on the 13th February 2008, Kevin Rudd opened the Australian Parliament with his now famous and inspirational National Apology to the Stolen Generations, we sat riveted to our television screens. We were emotionally touched and believed the Promised Land had truly arrived:

"...that the injustices of the past must never, never happen again..."

The long overdue Apology meant a lot to the traumatized members of the Stolen Generations, robbed of their families and culture, but for the rest of Aboriginal Australia, subsequent events proved that nothing had changed and the past injustices, the removal of children, would happen again and again.

Kevin Rudd, has dined out and basked in glory about his Sorry speech ever since, yet his and subsequent governments did little to implement those noble sentiments and words.

Removal of children continues unabated. A disingenuous distinction is made however. The old Stolen Generations were stolen without due process. Due process is meticulously applied with this new wave of child stealing. Only one problem, the current due process is seriously flawed as it takes little consideration of Yapa social structure and operates on the basis of Kardiya style nuclear families, the 'regular' family as portrayed on high fibre cereal packets.

Nguyu is a generic term for organic material which can be used for blackening body parts. Cork-wood charcoal is one such material, another is a pointy shaped fungus (*ngupu-ngupu*), the stalked puffball-which grows in Central Australia. Yapa used these puffballs as an insect repellent and to blacken the skin of half-caste children to prevent them from being taken by patrol officers.

Just as the modern fishing industry has become more "efficient", so has the child 'protection' industry. And just as over-fishing has serious long term deleterious consequences, so have the "improved" nets and increased catches of the child 'protection' industry. No mere pointy shaped mushrooms will stand in their way.

† Jupurrurla and Napanangka were looking after Napanangka's sister's two children. The children's mother had gone off the rails and was drinking in Alice Springs. Jupurrurla had spent many years as Yuendumu's Police Tracker. He was a Director of Yuendumu Mining Co. He was pensioned off from the NT Police when his diabetes prevented him from staying at work. Jupurrurla had had a foot amputated. Jupurrurla and Napanangka were model citizens, the ideal couple to look after the children, yet despite this, the 'Welfare' had taken the children off Napanangka.

Jupurrurla and Napanangka engaged a lawyer at CAALAS and embarked on jumping the many hurdles placed in the path of Yapa when they try to retrieve removed children. Eventually they got the children back, but that had taken much longer than it had taken for them to be taken away in the first place. Thus functions the New Stolen Generation. Indigenous children in Australia continue to be removed from their families at a greater rate than ever.

A Warlpiri mother got into strife in Alice Springs. Her baby was taken and 'placed'. A few years later, the rehabilitated mother who had in the meantime returned to Yuendumu, had, after a lengthy court battle, regained custody of her child. The child returned, only to bawl his eyes out. He did not recognise his mother, he was not used to seeing so many black faces, he did not understand the language. The mother was also greatly distressed. And that is saying nothing about the Kardiya family who had in the meantime cared for and loved the baby boy. There are no winners. The child should not have been removed from his extended Warlpiri family in the first place. So much for the multi million dollar 'Child Protection' industry.

L. Nangala's little boy developed a nasty rash on his leg, caused by scabies. She often bathed her little boy and cleaned his leg, but despite all her efforts, her little boy's rash got worse, and eventually got infected. It looked terrible, so in the end she took her boy to the clinic. In the same year, the Intervention was foisted on remote Aboriginal Australia, mandatory reporting was legislated for by the NT Government. The Care and Protection of Children Act 2007 was enacted. Even if you only suspect children are being harmed, it is your legal obligation to report it.

Thus it came to pass that Nangala was reported and charged with "child neglect". Nangala's parents, Jampijinpa and Napangardi (the grandparents of the little boy) were questioned and naively, as proof that they were caring grandparents said, *"We told her she should go to the clinic."* This was seized on as evidence of Nangala's neglect.

That Jampijinpa and Napangardi were both working at the Yuendumu Clinic for the Department of Health's 'Stronger Families' initiative did not dissuade the dingoes from trying to bag a catch to add to their tally. Jampijinpa and Napangardi were promptly subpoenaed to appear in court as witnesses against their daughter. At stake was that the little boy would be declared to be at risk and removed. On court day, Jampijinpa and Napangardi "went bush" and could not be found. On the strength of a few character references, the non-appearance of witnesses, and a lack of proof of deliberate neglect, the charges were dropped. Not everyone caught up in the net has such backup. The now, not so little, boy has grown up to be a healthy teenager and is happily cared for by his mother who is a successful artist. On the way to school he greets me with a wave and a big grin and has no idea he'd nearly been taken by the dingoes.

A 2020 productivity commission study report, 'Expenditure on Children in the Northern Territory', has 'Annexure B – Case Study Yuendumu'. The case study includes a section sub-titled 'Operationalising the Child and Family Centre' from which I quote:

> ...the previous Child and Family Centre manager had approved for 'Territory Families, family support services', to operate out of the Child and Family Centre. When Territory Families recently merged their operations, the child protection staff commenced operating out

of the facility. There is a perception from some people in the commu-nity that the presence of these workers has made some families unwilling to visit the facility due to the perceived threat of child protection intervening...

Which I'll translate for you:

...Since the dingoes moved into the Child and Family Centre, some people avoid the place like the plague because they're shit scared of the 'welfare mob' stealing their children...

"But Grandmother! What big eyes you have," said † Little Red Riding Hood. *"All the better to see you with my dear,"* replied the wolf ...."*What big teeth you have,"* said Little Red Riding Hood, her voice quivering slightly.

Incidentally, don't you love that verb 'operationalising'?

The big house...

Back in the days of unregulated freedom, shop break-ins were mostly for food. On one occasion a couple of lads broke in, heated themselves some pies in the pie warmer and dined on pie and coke, before absconding sated and empty handed. Then there was the occasion that Bill McKell and myself caught a young lad in flagrante delicto, breaking into the 'Mining Shop'. Rather than call the police we thought we'd give the lad a fright and locked him in the then non-functioning cool room. The claustrophobic lad sang out from his dark prison, *"Let me out. I want to go to the big house!"* (jail).

The Intervention increased police powers and also the number of police. NT police numbers were significantly boosted by officers transferred from the AFP (Australian Federal Police) on six month contracts. These AFP officers were like fish out of water and mostly brought with them, a "them and us" mentality. They had been used to regard Aborigines as a criminal cohort from which mainstream society and property had to be protected. They could not adjust to the reality that on communities, the racial profiling they brought with them didn't fit, as the community they were there to protect now consisted mostly of aborigines. A comprehensive survey in 2010, into policing conducted on communities, where police stations had been installed by the Intervention, found that, generally speaking, a majority of residents welcomed the police presence. But this varied very much depending on the attitudes and actions (or in-actions!) of individual police officers. It comes as no surprise to me that the most vehement complaints against police revealed by the survey relate to house searches.

In 2015, a group of women who were in 'sorry camp', mourning the death of a Yuendumu man, witnessed some serious activity emanating from the new police complex across the road. They witnessed a 'shock and awe' operation by the police. From around midnight to the next day, police were looking for people with outstanding warrants. They made several arrests. In one instance eight members of the NT police's ninja squad surrounded a residence (two officers for each cardinal point) and caught an alleged criminal, waking several children in the process. It was 5:30 am. The alleged criminal was quite angry and told me afterwards, that 'someone' had informed the police of his whereabouts. The possibility of a generation of children growing up fearing and hating the police, and of conflict resulting from the paranoid suspicion that "someone" dobbed 'someone' in is, I suppose, a small price to pay for us being made safer by these night time raids.

Most of these warrants are for such nefarious activities as 'failing to appear in court' or breaching bail conditions such as travel restrictions or reporting requirements, or for unpaid fines. Calendars are not ubiquitous in Yuendumu and not many Yapa keep diaries. All the same, the Law is the Law and has to be enforced and obeyed (or so I'm often reminded). We all feel much safer in the knowledge that those court skipping, bail breaking criminals are being actively pursued even in the middle of the night. If you didn't perceive the irony in the aforementioned, you shouldn't be reading this.

NT police are legally able to enter a residence without a warrant. All that is required of them is that they allege that they suspect there is grog in the house or that a person for whom a warrant is outstanding, is holed up there.

A few houses down the road from where we live, such a legally sanctioned middle of the night raid took place. As described to Wendy by an elderly lady who resides in that dwelling, the residents were made to stand against a wall. A mother was prevented from picking up her crying baby lying on a blanket on the other side of the room. She had to remain standing against the wall whilst the baby continued crying and the police searched the premises for grog or drugs.

Such raids are not uncommon. Japangardi, our local Aboriginal Community Police Officer (ACPO), told me of one occasion when he dissuaded a member of the riot squad flown into Yuendumu from using a battering ram to smash in a door. *"We don't use those in Yuendumu, we knock on the door."* Our ACPO has been issued with a gun which is locked in the police station safe. He doesn't wear it. Occasionally some other Yuendumu police, as a matter of personal choice, also do not carry arms, which begs the question, do they need to be armed in the first place.

Long after I'd written the preceding part of my story, on the 9th of November 2019, the NT police entered a residence in Yuendumu and a 19 year old Yapa man was shot and died. A policeman has been charged with murder and the whole situation is sub-judice and I have nothing further to say about it.

Nyirrpi Community had lobbied for a police presence and finally got one. It's not for me to say if this is a good thing or not, but that old adage *"Be careful what you wish for"* does spring to mind.

Wendy regularly works at Nyirrpi school on Wednesdays. At a Nyirrpi school staff meeting, Kardiya teachers were commenting on a Yapa man who only two days earlier had been charged with driving an unregistered vehicle without a driver's license, and yet had managed to be charged again with the same offences. The consensus was that the man wasn't too bright.

This man used to regularly take his unregistered (unregistrable) ute on short trips along traffic-less bush tracks and return with a load of firewood for his family and in-laws. That is what he did. That was his purpose. He had role clarity.

Should he go to jail for repeat offences, so be it. No stigma, no regrets. He'd come out of prison and be welcomed back with open arms by his family. He would reoffend and resume gathering firewood. Kardiya would continue to regard him as 'not too bright'.

If he had refused to get firewood for fear of police, he would have lost family respect. By Warlpiri law a man is supposed to obey his family, particularly his wife's family.

It's no contest, Warlpiri law or Kardiya law?

The Intervention installed Nyirrpi police station (a converted shipping container) is now vacant. Firewood gathering has reverted to being un-noticed and unpunished by the police.

Every now and then some serious open minded research backs our emotive assertions with facts:

In 2012, Thalia Anthony, and Harry Blagg authored the 'Report to the Criminology Research Council Grant: CRC 38/09-10- Addressing

The "Crime Problem" Of The Northern Territory Intervention- Alternate Paths To Regulating Minor Driving Offences In Remote Indigenous Communities'.

The authors have kindly given me permission to cite and quote from their report, and as they said it so much better in their 90 page report than I can, I'm taking the liberty to do so. The emphases are mine. Bear with me, it's written in academeze but is really very good:

> *"...This study of the incidence of Indigenous driving offending was conducted by the authors in the Northern Territory from 2006 to 2010 on two central Australian communities. It demonstrates how new patterns of law enforcement, set in train by the 2007 'intervention', inevitably led to a dramatic increase in the criminalization of Indigenous people for driving related offending....Our research suggests that* **the criminalization of driving related offending represented an attempt to construct a new form of coercive, neo-assimilationist governmentality in the NT through which the state seeks to discipline, normalise and incorporate elements of the Indigenous domain into the mainstream.** *In Simon's (2001, 2002) phase the state is effectively 'governing through crime': amplifying and dramatizing a particular crime problem (child sexual abuse)* **to legitimate an aggressive annexation of Aboriginal space....the processes and outcomes have been solidly fixated on eradicating key cultural differences between mainstream Australia and its Indigenous Other.** *Over the lifetime of the study we witnessed few indications that the state was effectively uncovering, let alone prosecuting, cases of child sexual abuse and/or family violence, but we did see* **significant changes taking place in the physical layout of the community and a significant increase in the numbers of Indigenous people being prosecuted for failing to adhere to new rules.** *The issue of driving and roads became a site of contestation and conflict between mainstream government and Indigenous communities..."*

You'll recall how Yuendumu's unique patchwork of integrated houses was eroded by external decisions on house building and allocation and such as the erection of high fences. These were some of the significant changes in the physical layout of the community that Thalia Anthony and Harry Blagg so shrewdly observed.

An entry on Bruno Jupurrurla Wilson's Facebook page reads:

"Was pulled up again for DWB - Driving whilst Black".

Thalia and Harry's report was based on the Warlpiri communities of Yuendumu and Lajamanu. From mid-2006 to 2010 the incidence of driving criminalisation increased 250% in the NT. The prison population includes 25% driving offenders. More than 80% of the prisoners are Indigenous.

An Alice Springs friend of ours, Kay Smith, who spent many years in Yuendumu and maintains close relations with many Warlpiri people, was going to visit someone at Alice Springs jail. A Warlpiri friend asked her to take some money for another prisoner.

"Where do I take it to?"
  "Take it to rejection. You just take it to the rejection desk."

I suppose the person at the desk is the 'rejectionist'. Hotels and motels have 'rejectionists': *"Sorry! We have no vacancies!"* is a common experience for Yapa, even if they have previously booked accommodation on the internet, or have been seduced by the lit up 'Vacancies' sign at the front of the establishment.

Meanwhile at the jail, a notice appeared. Several typed paragraphs are taped to the door of the signing-in room where visitors first assemble. The notice reads in part:

'' ....all visitors must give their full address that includes the house number and street name as well as the name of the community (just Yuendumu is no longer acceptable)...."

If visitors clear this first hurdle they proceed to the rejection room where they're subjected to a second signing-in and wait before entering the double layer of doors into the jail.

The choice of Yuendumu on the notice as the example is no coincidence. I estimate close to half of Yuendumu's young men are in jail, the majority for such heinous crimes as repeat traffic offences like driving with a suspended or expired licence, or for not paying their fines, or for missing their court appearances. A significant number because of the overloaded justice system are held in remand and haven't even been found guilty. Just like those people held in Australia's offshore detention centres they have no idea when they will be 'processed'. They're in trouble for being in trouble. Except for those kept in the remand holding pens, who have no diversionary activities whatsoever, it isn't all doom and gloom at the Alice Springs Prison. There is a silver lining to this dark cloud. The prison has a Warlpiri football team! They compete against other inmate teams. They probably win. They are winners.

Street names are a fairly recent addition to Yuendumu. Many street signs have fallen down or are pointing the wrong way. I live in Quandong Street, so named despite the fact that quandongs grow much further south and the nearest quandong tree grows at the Olive Pink Botanic Gardens in Alice Springs. Neither have I been able to solve the mystery of where Ral Ral Avenue got its name. Street names are hardly used in Yuendumu, none the less street names and numbers are demanded from jail visitors. How can Yapa ever hope to Close the Gap and aspire to Stronger Futures if they persist in using *kakarrara* (east) and *yatijara* (north) rather than learn what the street their house is in, has been named, and what its house number is?

A young man, having just returned from Yuendumu police station, told dejectedly of failing to get his car registered. The reason his application had been rejected was that he had unpaid fines. He'd been fined for driving an unregistered vehicle. He didn't have enough money to pay for both his unpaid fines and the car registration.

"*I hate the police,*" said the young man. Then in quick succession, "*I hate Centrelink, I hate the Government, I hate the Land Council.*"

I expect the young man would soon thereafter be again fined… for driving an unregistered vehicle. He may even go to jail for unpaid fines.

I have already mentioned that what we are witnessing is community policing morphing into policing the community. What I didn't mention is, that just like the melting of the polar ice caps, this is happening at an ever accelerating pace.

Role models...

One side-effect of the mentioned mass incarceration, is that many Warlpiri children grow up without a father. The closest I myself came to growing up without a father was when Dad was interrogated by the Gestapo. As he told it to me in Dutch:

> *"A group of German officers were having a party in a hotel in Bloe-mendaal. They'd taken off their weapons and Jan Lucas and I grabbed some of them and took them to the resistance. For some reason, the Germans rightly suspected me of having been involved in the weapons theft. I was arrested by the Gestapo and taken to Ferdinand aus der Fünten, at their headquarters in the Euterpe Street in Amsterdam. He told the others to leave me alone with him. He knew everything about my youth in Germany, the names of my school teachers, what street I'd lived in, everything. I told him that I'd been playing cards all night in Heemstede. It was important I'd used 'I' and not 'we', otherwise he'd have asked me who 'we' were, and I'd have been caught out. At one point he slammed the table and shouted: 'Was sind Sie eigentlich Holländer oder Deutscher?' (What exactly are you, Dutch or German?) I answered: 'Papiermäßig bin ich Holländer, aber im Herzen, wie könnte ich etwas anderes sein, als ein Deutscher?' (On paper I'm Dutch, but in my heart, how could I be anything but German?)*
>
> *Because I so thoroughly knew the Germans and the German language, I was able to convince him of my innocence. The Gestapo never even checked my alibi!*
>
> *Suddenly aus der Fünten tells me I can go. Often, in such circumstances, people got shot in the back. This was known as 'Auf der Flucht Erschossen' (shot whilst fleeing). I dared him: 'Herr Obergruppenführer, wenn Sie auch nur den geringsten Zweifel haben, möchte ich, dass Sie ihre Pflicht tun' (Sir Obergruppenführer, should you have the slightest doubt, I want you to do your duty!) and then I turned and walked out.*
>
> *When I got down to the street I had to suppress a strong urge to*

run, as this would have looked very suspicious. At home, Guurt asked me, 'How come you look five years older than you did this morning?'

This was one of the few occasions during the war in which your mother asked me anything about my activities.

'I had a bad day at the office' I told her.

It was well known, that no one got out of aus der Fünten's clutches alive. I may well have been the only one."

SS-Hauptsturmführer
Ferdinand Hugo aus der Fünten

You may have noticed Dad had used the Jewish semantic trick of answering a question with a question, (how could I be anything but?) Even in mortal danger, he'd avoided surrendering his Dutch identity.

I have since googled *aus der Fünten and Euterpestraat*. Such are memories, aus der Fünten wasn't an *Obergruppenführer* as Dad remembered, but a *Hauptsturmführer* and coincidentally came from Mülheim an der Ruhr where Dad grew up. At the notorious Euterpes-traat HQ, aus der Fünten was in charge of the 'processing' (interroga-tion and torture) of countless Jews and others. Anne Frank and her family were 'processed' there before transportation to their deaths. Euterpe street has since been renamed.

Ferdinand Hugo aus der Fünten was one of only four Nazi war criminals to be sentenced to life in prison in the Netherlands. He was controversially released from the special prison at Breda in 1989. Three months later he died in Duisburg on 19th April, one day before Hitler's birthday.

Dad survived the war by the skin of his teeth. Growing up without my father would have had a devastating effect on my future life, yet the many children in Yuendumu whose fathers are either locked up in jail, or drinking in Alice Springs, or buried in the ground, don't lack care and attention nor male role models. This is because the resilient Warlpiri social fabric, the extended family structure, the *warlalja,* enables them to cope, as I most likely wouldn't have.

Sealing our fate...

When I was still working for Central Pacific Minerals in Darwin, my then boss, †John Ivanac, got me to check out a sand deposit. When I expressed surprise, he pointed out a little appreciated fact, the value of the world wide production of building materials, far exceeds that of base and precious metals combined.

The built in resilience resulting from the Warlpiri social fabric, the mutual obligations, extended to local organizations. I have already told you how Yuendumu Mining Company (YMC) had helped Warlukurlangu Artists to, phoenix-like, rise from the Brendan Rooney rip-off ashes. So let me tell you of when the Yuendumu Social Club (YSC) gave YMC a much needed shot in the arm.

When North Flinders Mines committed to mine gold at the Granites, YMC geared up to supply gravel and sand during the construction of the mineral processing plant. I'd inherited a Scoopmobile LD5 front end loader, when I first started to manage YMC. It was a piece of shit, and clearly wouldn't do.

YSC lent YMC $15,000 with which we bought a second hand Caterpillar 910 front end loader for $30,000. The same front end loader we were to use on our epic exploration tracks contract.

Our suppliers never knew, but by us delaying payments due to them, they effectively financed the other half of the loader. I'm sure they were a bit concerned when the usually prompt payer that YMC was, made them wait for their money but as it turned out they didn't have to wait for too long.

Over a three month period we supplied the mine with $60,000 worth of gravel and sand. It cost us $30,000 to pay Putland for his trucks to transport our products to the mine site. It cost us another $15,000 to produce the gravel and screen the sand. Thus in three months, we had earned enough cash surplus to pay for half of the cost of the front end loader. It took much longer to earn the other half.

In September 1973 the Federal Department of North Australia proposed the construction of five Northern Territory Development Roads. One of these roads was the Tanami Road from the Stuart

Highway to Yuendumu, a distance of 271 km. In 1976 YMC made a submission to a Parliamentary Standing Committee on Public Works, which in hindsight was premature. YMC's submission urged that the Tanami Road be prioritized so that it could get involved and grow local participation. The proposed sealing of the Tanami Road, back then often referred to as the Tanami Track, was to suffer many delays. As I'm putting the finishing touches to this story, so too are contractors preparing to complete the seal. Recent rain has turned this final 10 km strech of road construction into a sea of mud, but despite this latest delay we still expect the seal to be completed within a mere 48 years after the original proposal

The 1973 proposal included these optimistic words:

"Sealing the four road sections proposed for the Centre will also facilitate greater involvement and participation of local communities in their own economic and social development...."

We were to hear similar sentiments many times over. Reminds me of a graffiti mentioned in a book by Eduardo Galeano

"Basta de hechos. ¡Queremos promesas!" (Enough of deeds. We want promises!).

Concrete aggregate is a graded product, thus smaller sized particles fill the spaces between larger particles. Sealing aggregate on the other hand consists of single sized gravel. The natural gravel scree slope at the Yuendumu quarry contains 12% of the size adequate as sealing aggregate, thus a very large quantity of raw material has to be handled to produce a relatively small quantity of product. To make it viable for Yuendumu Mining Co. to produce sealing aggregate, it would have had to invest in crushing equipment rather than use screening on its own. We produced a sample of sealing aggregate material by screening out the 12% falling within the appropriate size parameters, and had it tested. It met all criteria except for the Los Angeles Abrasion Test. In an LA Abrasion test, a weighed sample of aggregate retained on a 1.7 mm sieve, is placed in a rotating drum charged with steel balls. The drum is rotated a standard number of rotations over a standard period of time and the weight of abraded material now passing through the 1.7 mm sieve, is expressed as a percentage of the original weight. The maximum was supposed to be 30% LA abrasion, Yuendumu sealing aggregate, produced by screening alone, was 33% LA abrasion. In road making, it is common practice to use material of greater than 30% LA abrasion when alternative complying sourced product cost a lot more to transport. But we didn't know this and the authorities had an excuse to ignore our approaches.

For decades we were stonewalled when it came to supplying sealing aggregate for the Tanami Road. In 2005 we finally managed to convince someone in the NT Government to give us a fair go. We back-loaded two trailer loads of over-sized material on a semi trailer returning empty from the Granites gold mines. In Alice Springs the Department of Transport and Works crushed and screened that material and produced a batch of sealing aggregate. We were never told what the LA abrasion of this batch was but it was irrelevant as the batch was laid down on a trial basis on a 100 meter section of the Tanami Road, 180 kilometers from Alice Springs. This was the ultimate test and for years we were able to admire the fact that the Yuendumu aggregate stood up much better than Alice Springs sealing aggregate. We were also unaware that research had found that there is a poor correlation between the empirical laboratory LA abrasion test results and field performance of sealing aggregates. If the authorities knew this, they never let on.

The 2005 trial seal has since been covered over by a fresh layer of asphalt. Our sign advertising the trial and provenance of the gravel is still clearly visible to be pondered and puzzled over by tourists and historians alike as there is nothing to see.

Our friend Jeremy Drew at the gravel sign
(Photo-Andy Sutherland)

Chief Minister Clare Martin and the Minister of Employment, Education and Training, Paul Henderson came to Yuendumu, chaperoned by our then local member Karl Hampton. I dubbed Karl the Minister for Football (including to his face). He was a driving force behind the proposed grassing of Yuendumu football oval, which just wasn't happening. On many occasions, I'd earbashed Karl, who has family in Yuendumu, on bilingual education, self-determination, local participation, respect for cultural differences and more, ad nauseam. I admire Karl and consider him a friend, but I'd had a gutful of wasting my time on him and of being ignored by him. I insisted that as well as showing Paul and Clare the barren football oval, they should spend some time at our gravel quarry.

The quarry is on a scree slope, consisting predominantly of Vaughan Springs Quartzite. It is two kilometres south of Yuendumu just across the Tanami Road. At the quarry, looking down on the splendid vista which includes Yuendumu, and pointing and waving my arms, I told Clare and Paul of our long held dream to develop the gravel deposit and supply sealing aggregate for the asphalt paving of the Tanami Road from Napperby Creek to Yuendumu and beyond. My exuberance was matched by the response. Paul Henderson in particular could see that our dream neatly dovetailed with the purported aims of his portfolio. Paul was to become the Chief Minister on Clare Martin's Intervention prompted resignation. A pity that their sincere enthusiasm vanished the moment they crossed the boundary grid on their way back to Alice Springs. Our worn out Powerscreen was eventually sold for scrap. The one hundred metre trial was to be the only bit of the Tanami Road sealed by Yuendumu gravel.

The only landmark…

Kim Mahood the author of *Position Doubtful* grew up on Mongrel Downs Station, since renamed Tanami Downs, not far from Newmont's present day gold mining operations in the Granites Gold Field.

In *Position Doubtful* Kim quotes from her father's diary, who, when referring to a 1962 expedition in search of a stock route had written:

> *"… didn't auger too well for the rest of the trip, particularly as the only landmark marked anywhere near our route (another fifty miles on) was marked Position Doubtful…"*

As Kim explains in her book, her father was referring to a landmark labelled McFarlane's Peak, on an aeronautical one is to a million scale map. Printed on the map, under McFarlane's Peak was 'PD'.

On page six of this masterpiece Kim wrote:

> *"The term (Position Doubtful) lodged in my mind as a metaphor for the way in which white Australians move through and occupy the country…it seems to me that our position in relation to the remote parts of the country is more doubtful than it has ever been."*

This so resonated with me that I felt compelled to recommend the book to all visitors to Yuendumu who crossed my path. At the Yuendumu Mining Co. store we sold over one hundred copies of *Position Doubtful* and received not a single complaint.

There is nothing doubtful about my assertion that, whereas the Kardiya map had only one landmark on Joe Mahood's proposed route, a Yapa map of the same itinerary would have been festooned with countless named landmarks, with little doubt as to their position.

Country

"Aborigine (sic) and Torres Strait islanders used the word 'country' to describe their profound connection to place.

Country embodies the spirit ancestors who made the land, sea and all living creatures as well as the knowledge, stories and responsibilities tied to those places."

The British Museum 2015 exhibition - Indigenous Australia: Enduring Civilisation.

Nguru, Walya (country), is a central tenet of Warlpiri existence. It is far too often assumed that Australian Aboriginal connection to land is a thing of the past. You may even have noticed that the well-meaning British Museum proclaimed that Indigenous Australians 'used' the word 'country', as if they no longer do.

A highlight of the Yuendumu school year are the so called "country visits". Several homelands are decided on, where school children with their teachers and families, camp out for up to a week at a place they belong to. They are told about the Jukurrpa of the country and how they are related to it. They are shown and told about animals and plants and how they connect to country in a way they can't be shown in the community, or at school, or in a book.

Earlier on I told you how Jimija had solved the Native Title conundrum (*"my country, your land"* in case you've forgotten). Jimija knew exactly what he meant by 'country'.

If you've read this far you will have noticed that I, even with my tenuous grip on Warlpiri geography, have named numerous Yapa place names. Every outcrop, every rock hole, soakage, creek and large claypan, every area of Warlpiri land is named and owned or cared for by an extended family group. Jukurrpa dreaming paths, the so called 'songlines' and stories pass through from one set of owners to the next and onto another tribe's country. All of these places are part of and have Jukurrpa. All of these places have *kirda* (owners) and *kurdungurlu* (care takers), and they have stories, many have songs and designs and they are on many maps of the mind.

Just check out this map and you'll see what I mean. And it actually shows only a fraction of the jukurrpa places in Warlpiri country.

Map from Warlpiri Picture Dictionary - pp 20-21 (IAD Press 2012)

Dancing ladies...

Whilst I was traversing the land, chasing pots of gold at the end of rainbows, Wendy, as well as teaching and working in the bilingual program, was digging up witchetty grubs and honey ants and being told about the country.

Frank: That is a sinkhole typical of karst topography in limestone formations. There is an occurrence of barytes with minor galena south of the sinkhole. The area of dolomitic limestone stretching from 4-mile to past White Point has some potential for Mississippi Valley type lead-zinc deposits. It is overlain by terra rosa soil which is ideal for growing grapes.

Wendy: The area is called Kanaji, the Kinki (cannibal monster) lives in the Giant's hole. At the school printery we have a Warlpiri language book that tells the story of the giant lady.

Faultlines and songlines. Dollars and cents versus connection to country.

Whenever we head to Alice Springs along the Tanami Road, Wendy comments on the scenery:

> "*Its amazing how the juntala trees come up green when there has been no rain for so long... Unusual for those mantarla trees to be flowering this time of year.... Even the mistletoe on the mulga looks like it is dying.... Look up high over there, there is a karlantirri soaring (*a buzzard which Wendy told me smash emu eggs using a stone clutched in their claw*).... Those hills going towards the salt lake are a giant python (ngawininyi).... Those ghost gums (*as we go through the gap approaching Tilmouth roadhouse*) are dancing ladies... The coolibahs are suffering.... The plains are completely bare.... Those two pointy hills are a woman's dreaming, they are nipples.*"

Real estate...

Terms such as 'Stock Exchange' and 'Real Estate' slightly amuse me.
These are English Kardiya terms for which I'm not aware that there are
Warlpiri equivalents. I envisage someone at the Stock Exchange swap-
ping seven rabbits for two goats or exchanging five cows for two
camels and a sheep.

As for 'Real Estate', all I need to consider is its antonym, 'Unreal
Estate', which illustrates the subjective nature of reality.

Thus when a geologist working for an exploration company, enters
Aboriginal land chasing that elusive mineral deposit, he/she is treading
on real estate.

Exploration Licenses are 'granted' by the Department of Mines and
Energy, conditional on an Exploration Agreement negotiated on behalf
of the Traditional Land Owners by the Central Land Council. A mountain of paperwork is involved in this almost entirely Kardiya driven
endeavour. The barely visible and often uncomprehending Yapa, the
Traditional Land Owners, denizens of a different reality, are sidelined
and provided with rubber stamps. Not unlike defendants in court.

On several occasions I have mentioned 4-Mile, a piece of real
estate seven kilometres south of Yuendumu. It is the land where Ted
Egan and his gang built the cattle yards. It is from where the Ngalikirlangu Pastoral Company trucked the cattle which topped the southern
markets after having been fattened at a sacred site. It is where Penhall's
bore was drilled and where as a precursor to self-determination, a pig
farm and vegetable garden had been set up. It is where the road to
Nyirrpi and Papunya goes through a gap in the hills and another road
branches off to the bore field. It is where the Central Desert Regional
Council spent a large amount of money constructing a concrete
causeway in case it rains again. It is where the Intervention drew a
square on the map to include it in the Yuendumu Prescribed Area.

It is also where for years we saw a native fig tree growing on a
rocky slope at the gap. It is the country where two giant men were
hunting *janganpa (*possums). One of the men, thinking he was seeing a

possum through the tree leaves, accidentally hit his mate, and instead of helping him, he went on hitting him, killed him and finally cooked and ate him. Once common, possums are now extinct in the area, but they live on in Warlpiri communal consciousness. The Yuendumu hills are a Possum dreaming with a well known story, a song, a comical dance and many Jukurrpa paintings.

Ramarra is Warlpiri for 'ribs'. *Kujurnu* is the Warlpiri verb 'threw'. The Warlpiri name for 4-mile is *Ramarra-kujurnu,* it is where the giant man discarded the ribs after he ate his companion. It doesn't take a lot of imagination to see that the outcrop of thinly bedded quartzite at the gap south of the stock yards does indeed look like ribs.

Then there was the time I cracked a rock at Ramara-kujurnu which revealed a beautiful black moss like pattern. This was dendritically crystallised pyrolusite - manganese dioxide. When I showed it to Japanangka, he immediately declared this to be a Jukurrpa. He mentioned several other places where he had seen this. All of the sites he mentioned had been mapped by geologists as the Cambrian Djaga-mara (sic) Formation. I doubt that many of that veritable venue of vultures, the army of well paid bureaucrats who have embarked on 'Closing the Gap', would appreciate the beauty of dendritic pyrolusite crystals. Where we see countless brilliant fragments they see only rocks, if anything at all.

As the manager of Yuendumu Mining Company I was privileged to get to tread on both Real Estate and Unreal Estate. Both on land and on country.

I asked Courtney Nampijinpa why she thought some Kardiya stay in Yuendumu. Her succinct answer was, *"You know that song 'The Desert calling you back Home'?"*

♫ ♫ ♫

It is a song written by her late father, Patrick Jangala Singleton, a

member of 'Blackstorm', one of the many bands we used to jam with.
I'm sure Courtney wasn't talking about real estate.

Ramarra-kujurnu (photo - BRDU)

*The groove where the giant man dragged the body of his mate. The
discarded ribs are to the right (north) of this photograph.*

El Dorado…

From a high price, when I worked for Central Pacific Minerals, the price of uranium rapidly declined to an all time low in 2001. The price of gold on the other hand, from a low in 1970, peaked in 1979 and despite some significant fluctuations has remained high ever since, in fact is at an all time high, as I write these notes. Yuendumu Mining Company, as a result of these price variations switched its main exploration focus from uranium to gold.

Old †Alex Wilson had heard about the soaring gold price and asked me about it. I told Alex that gold was $900 an ounce (it's about three times that now). *"How much for a full tobacco tin?"* he wanted to know. I made a calculation and told him that he could buy a brand new Toyota Landcruiser (a Warlpiri measure of wealth!) with the money he'd get if he sold a tobacco tin full of gold. Alex's eyes lit up at the thought of the opportunity this presented. He looked forward to replacing his decrepit old vehicle. The next day Alex took his three wives up to the known gold occurrences at the Granites. This was long before the mine's revival. Oozing disappointment, Alex with his wives returned a week later with just a tiny bit of fine gold which he brought to me at my office.

I told him he'd been wasting his time, then opened my desk drawer, and pulled out a small gold nugget. Alex's eyes lit up again and, heavy with anticipation asked where I had found the nugget. I told him I'd found it at our gravel quarry. He gave me a funny look and I could read his thought bubble *"Bullshit, you're a bloody liar."* I cracked a smile and then told him the truth that a few days earlier a prospector, on his way back from Halls Creek, had pulled up at the fuel bowser. The prospector needed petrol but he had no money. Instead, because he'd been prospecting with a metal detector, he had some gold with which to pay.

In 1983 North Flinders Mines Ltd., through the Central Land Council, had reached a pioneering agreement with the Traditional Land Owners (TLOs) and were planning to commence exploration drilling at the Granites. Shortly after, Geoff Stewart, North Flinders' managing director and major shareholder, called in to the Yuendumu Mining office on his way to the North Flinders Mines leases. Several days later on his way back to their Adelaide head office Geoff told me: *"Frank, we've got ourselves a mine!"*

My geological training and experience made me sceptical of this claim. I judged North Flinders to have only a 10% chance. My assessment proved to be very wrong, big time, and Geoff 's assessment on the other hand to be prophetic. Current production from the Granites Gold Field easily exceeds a billion dollars worth per year. Later I found out that Geoff was dyslexic, so that when he sat on Chapman's Hill at the Granites looking along the long line of low hills extending westward, his atypical brain enabled him to conceptualise a three dimensional picture which convinced him they were onto a winner. I've also been reminded that Geoff Stewart when negotiating the agreement, and note this was prior to North Flinders' successful drilling programme, had offered equity in the proposed mine to the TLOs in the form of a sizeable parcel of North Flinders shares. The Central Land Council advised the Traditional Land Owners against taking up the share offer. Regarding the rejection of the share offer I have no further comment. Royalty equivalents paid on production to the Traditional Land Owners are I believe around 2%. The way these moneys are disbursed, all under Central Land Council supervision and control is another matter I shall refrain from commenting on. The image of a pack of dogs fighting over bones, which springs to my mind, is purely fictional and bears no resemblance to Royalty Distributions and is entirely coincidental, (this is what a lawyer friend told me to say).

A week of Royalty meetings, 4.3.2021

In 1987 Yuendumu Mining Co. was approached by David Barra-clough, a geologist who had worked in the region. David alerted me to a major tectonic feature, the Willowra Gravity High, which extends from the Tanami gold deposits straddling the Western Australia/Northern Territory border, all the way to the Stuart Highway, via a gold occurrence at Waldron's Hill (Munyupanji) north of Willowra. At this stage Yuendumu Mining was ahead of the game and applied for a number of Exploration Licences, but through lack of finance had no hope of exploring these in its own right. The licences were duly farmed out to Posgold which was controlled by Normandy, who would eventually control the Granites gold mines before selling out to Newmont. Newmont Corporation, the current owners of the Callie gold mine at the Granites, are the world's biggest gold miner and are based in Colorado U.S.A. Callie's annual production exceeds half a million ounces of gold.

The Barrow Creek Joint Venture agreement with Posgold included clauses, which gave Yuendumu Mining priority to be awarded any contracts it was able to fulfil. As a result we took part in what at the time was the largest soil sampling geochemical survey ever carried out in Australia.

Five two-man teams traversed the area on half kilometre spaced lines, and took soil samples every 250 metres. The lines were on foot, and compass and hip chain were used to navigate through country which included some patches of very thick mulga scrub. A hip chain is a device strapped to the hip, inside the device there is a spool of cotton thread, the end of the thread is attached to a shrub and as one walks ahead, the thread plays out, and a counter shows the measured distance. Hip chains were unexpectedly accurate, but due to GPS technology are now entirely obsolete.

Micah Hudson, Grant Granites and myself joined the survey. We were accommodated at the Barrow Creek pub, later to become famous because of the Peter Falconio disappearance.

Tennant Creek is closer than Yuendumu to Barrow Creek. On week-ends, friends and family of the crew came from Tennant Creek to join us. The pub owner wasn't half bad on the drums. A mining engineer from Tennant Creek brought a van full of musical instruments and amplifiers. Back then I myself was more than bearable on the trumpet. So after a bit of lubrication at the bar we fired up. Hudson slowly wound up a guitar until reaching his Jimmy Hendrix climax. Grant would occasionally sip a beer and then back to the bass guitar. He was on fire. Greg, the geologist in charge, sidled up to me at the bar. "Had musical ability played a part in YMC's recruiting?", he asked. I avoided eye contact as I told him with a straight face that everybody in Yuendumu played music like that and then I had another beer.

Yuendumu Mining was on a roll and pursued an active campaign of applying for exploration licences whenever prospective ground became vacant. In 1995 at Yuendumu we did what was probably the first ever presentation to Traditional Land Owners in an Aboriginal language, and I suspect there hasn't been one since. Central Land Council officers were clearly uncomfortable with Robin Granites' address and not used to not being in control. If all was as it should have been, the land council weevils should have been impressed and delighted, instead they were put out and quite hostile as they reluctantly had to accept the written translation they were provided with. Yuendumu Mining's applications were approved by the Traditional Land Owners.

With the price of gold having reached a new peak and Yuendumu Mining Co. having built up a significant portfolio of exploration licences and licence applications, which included some highly prospective ground, we saw a window of opportunity to float an Aboriginal controlled gold exploration company on the stock market. The first such ever. We even registered a company: Aboriginal Gold NL. We had no capital so we sought the assistance of our Joint Venture partners, the Normandy group.

Posgold paid for Purnpajardu's and my airfares to Adelaide. There we waited at reception in the glass cage HQ in Hutt Street. It wasn't even certain that the assembled board of Directors and high level managers would have time to see us, but eventually we were led in. Normandy's CEO, Robert Champion de Crespigny was there, looking out the window. He suddenly halted the proceedings and shot out of the room. He came back, chuffed with himself. He had sprung a new employee smoking on the footpath below at the front of the building, and told him that if he caught him again, he would sack him. A scene reminiscent of Donald Trump's reality TV show 'The Apprentice'.

Robert having thus asserted his authority, it was now my turn to proceed with my presentation of our Australian Stock Exchange dream. *"Before I start I'd like to know what have you done to my mate Geoff Stewart?"* I asked, anticipating the loud laugh this elicited from those present. Purnpajardu and I had entered the dog-eat-dog world of corporate Australia, where stabbing someone in the back is a cause for mirth. A week earlier Geoff Stewart had been deposed as the chairman of North Flinders Mines and been replaced by a Normandy appointment. I then continued with a well articulated presentation. A carefully prepared map showed our tenements and geological potential and our hopes. Purnpajardu then fielded a few questions as to what all this would mean to Warlpiri people. It all went smoothly.

The question was then asked: *"Why should we help Aboriginal Gold, when it will be competing against us?"* I told them that firstly we felt flattered that they perceived us as potential competition. *"Why you should help us is that it is in Normandy's best interests to be seen as a friend of Aboriginal Australia, seeing as most of your operations are on Aboriginal Land."* Furthermore I told them that should we succeed in finding an ore body, the value of the neighbouring tenements held by them would be enhanced. There would be a better chance of finding

additional ore bodies in the region and it would rationalise the necessary infrastructure should mining go ahead. Everyone would be a
winner.

The price of gold went down, the window closed, and Aboriginal
Gold NL ended up a faded dream. Problems with Yuendumu Mining's
relations with some Traditional Land Owners hadn't helped and neither
had the Central Land Council been very supportive. Instead of
perceiving Yuendumu Mining Co. as a potential partner in the
economic betterment of Yapa, the Central Land Council saw us as
competing for their clients, their 'natives'. They never took Yuendumu
Mining Company seriously and preferred to deal with well heeled
outsiders. I failed to 'sell' ourselves, not through lack of trying.

We never found El Dorado.

Haystacks...

The art of mineral exploration is to combine observation with knowledge, so as to efficiently home in on a target. I've already mentioned that Yapa, through their upbringing and the spacial orientation of their languages and thinking, have phenomenal powers of observation. Yuendumu Mining Company sought to use this attribute in its own exploration efforts.

Gold is often associated with arsenic in nature, something to do with their atomic structures. In a typical gold deposit for each gram of gold there are kilograms of arsenic, something to do with their relative abundance in the earth's bowels.

The chances of finding commercial mineral deposits by prospecting willy-nilly across a vast expanse of country, are like the proverbial snowflake in hell, especially after almost two centuries of Australian gold rushes, during which probably every significant mineral occurrence sticking out of the ground has been found. Before looking for the needle, it is best therefore to look for the haystack. In the case of gold it is far easier to look for rocks containing anomalous arsenic.

The gold deposits at the Granites Gold Field, occur in what has been named the Dead Bullock Formation. We selected a few areas which had been mapped by government geologists as the Lander River Beds Formation. These are the same age and believed to be analogous to the Dead Bullock Formation.

In one such area we took soil samples by using Yuendumu Mining's unique leap-frog method. We had two vehicles, one GPS, and a crew of six. There were †A. Winwood-Smith, Micah Hudson, Harry Jangala Collins, Grant Granites, Dougie Wilson and yours truly. Each vehicle had a Yapa driver and a Yapa navigator, and a Kardiya pen-pusher. I explained to the crew the aim of the exercise. The soil samples were to be taken from spots which 'drained' as large an area of rocky outcrop as possible, such as at the base of two converging scree slopes. It was like stream sediment sampling but without streams.

At relatively high speed the first vehicle set off with the navigator shouting,

"*Kakarrara...yatijarra....jingi-jingi...Karlarra...*"

(east....north.... straight ahead....west....) till it stopped at the first sampling site. Whilst a sample was taken, the GPS was read and the numbered sampling 'ticket' written up (colour, vegetation etc.). Meanwhile the second vehicle leapfrogged past the first sampling site and selected the next site. The first vehicle then caught up with the other crew, who were busy sampling, quickly read and recorded the GPS reading, and then took off to site number three. They would be leapfrogged by the other crew en route to sampling site number four and so forth. In one afternoon we took 54 samples covering a 20 square kilometre area. The navigators had done an incredible job. When plotting the samples on a map I came to realise that it would have been impossible to improve on site selection, and it had all been done 'on the run' in a flash! Maximum coverage with a minimum number of samples. When the assay results came back one quarter of the samples had greater than eight parts per million (ppm) of arsenic. Ppm - parts per million - is grams per metric tonne. We had found our first haystack.

AWS had read in Michael Terry's book 'Sand and Dust' (Published in 1937) that 'West of Davenport' on one of his expeditions, they had got 'colours' (traces of gold). Using explosives, Terry and his party had excavated a pit on a quartz reef and found 'pyrites of arsenic' (arsenopyrite) but almost no gold. Mt. Davenport is the large hill at the Vaughan Springs Homestead (Pikilyi). On a visit to Adelaide, AWS called into the South Australian Museum, where he was given access to Michael Terry's notebooks and journals, from which he copied relevant information. Michael Terry's party had watered their camels at a water hole at the fork of two creeks. We purchased two air photos being all we could afford on our tight budget and identified several creek confluences. We calculated the Australian Metric Grid coordinates of the most likely one of these. This calculation was quite tricky, but none the less, we set off with optimism with our GPS to the calculated spot.

When we got there we were only eighty metres from a beautiful full water hole at the confluence of two dry creeks, which we subsequently found out is named Mijirlparnta, not to be confused with Mission creek near Yuendumu, also Mijirlparnta. Mijirlparnta is an often used Warlpiri name for semi permanent waterholes because the name is derived from the Warlpiri word for red river gum resin. From there we followed AWS's notes, *'one and a quarter miles north-north-east'* where we found that the outcrops were of a much younger and non-prospective formation, the Nicker Beds. Not far from there, is the area we'd previously leapfrog sampled. Next we headed to the location within our haystack, where sampling had yielded the highest arsenic value - 76 ppm.

At the base of a scree slope we duly found our sample pin marker, a steel pin with a coloured plastic 'flag'. There, in plain sight at the crest of a hill, no more than two hundred metres away, was a mulga post stuck upside down in a prospecting pit. On the post had been carved 'MT SOG BN' and a date - 15th May 1933. We had located Terry's find, almost sixty years later on 2nd March 1993. The initials were Michael Terry, Stan O'Grady and Ben Nicker. Terry's Find is almost exactly 30 km due west of Vaughan Springs. The Warlpiri name for the area is Yujukupurntu, I betcha Michael Terry and his mates didn't know that.

The nurse in charge at Nyirrpi clinic, Colin Watson, was a good friend of AWS. One day in conversation with † Banjo Tex, Colin mentioned Terry's Find, that AWS had told him about. Banjo recalled that when he was a lot younger, he used to regularly travel to his homeland Nyinyirri-Palangu (Ethel Creek) on the back of a donkey. On one such trip he spotted a mulga post planted at the crest of a hill. When he investigated he found some Kardiya markings carved into the post. Banjo thought these markings might be secret or sacred, so out of respect, he speared the post into the pit so it couldn't be readily seen. This is the orientation we found it in.

Terry's Find subsequently became part of the Mount Doreen Joint Venture with Posgold. Posgold spent a considerable amount of money sampling and drilling the area but didn't find any needles in our haystack.

Terry's pit - photo A.Winwood-Smith

A sign of the times...

An in your face manifestation of the Intervention's dog whistling on grog etc. was the previously mentioned festooning of the countryside with 'No Alcohol No Pornography' signs which popped up like mushrooms after a rain. On the way to Nyirrpi, one of these offensive signs was spray painted with 'INTERVENTION, THE WHITE WAY, NOT THE RIGHT WAY' and on the way to Alice Springs one of the signs had 'KEVIN Rudd Kuna Rurrpa' sprayed on it. Very clever that, KR and KR. *Kuna rurrpa* means 'arsehole' or something like that. It's a term of abuse.

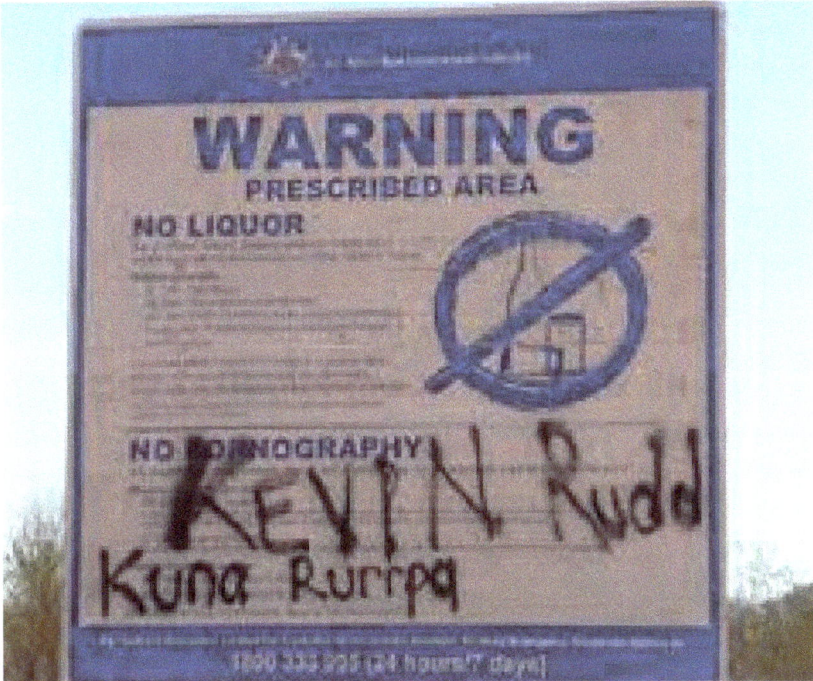

Valerie Martin told me that some older women had asked her what this 'pornography' was all about and when she told them, they reacted with loud Eeeee!!!!s - a Warlpiri version of Yuck!!!! They had never heard of it. I don't think there is a Warlpiri word for it.

Canberra, whence the Intervention emanated, was known to have a thriving pornography industry. In Yuendumu we painted over our No Pornography sign with IF YOU WANT PORN GO TO CANBERRA. I've never seen the Central Desert Shire move so quickly. Within days our sign had been taken down. When I confronted the Shire Services Manager about this, she told me that some people might find our sign offensive. I asked her what she thought about the sign we'd painted over, and which had been there for ages; might it not have offended some people? She said, *"I know nothing about that."*

Sounds familiar? The Nuremberg Trials: *"I knew nothing, I was only following orders."*

We parodied the quarantine bins at state borders and airports, you know the ones. *"Place your fruit and plant matter in this bin."* We installed empty, opened 44 gallon, aviation fuel drums at our airstrip and at the entrance to Yuendumu, with a sign: *"Welcome to Yuendumu - Pornography drop off point."*

I was to be disappointed when I frequently and with anticipation checked the bins - nothing!

The bins didn't last and were soon removed. Even in Yuendumu there are individuals lacking a sense of humour.

I've already told you how Yuendumu's river of grog had been reduced to a mere trickle, yet this did not give the Intervention pause when they imposed alcohol restriction on the Yuendumu 'Prescribed Area'. This was a cynical act of duplication. In most 'Prescribed Areas' more or less effective legislated alcohol restrictions had already been in place for a very long time.

It was never clear to us if both sets of liquor laws were in force concurrently or if the new Federal laws trumped the NT Laws. This was not made any clearer by the fact that the NT Liquor Commission never stopped accepting applications for, and issuing or renewing Liquor Permits to Kardiya. The new laws had a curious exemption. The laws did not apply to recreational fishermen. An Australian tradition is to go fishing on a boat with fishing tackle, bait, and 'an Esky full of piss' to use an Australian colloquial expression. It may be a coincidence, but I believe Nigel Scullion, our recent past Minister for Indigenous Affairs, was the President of the Amateur Fishermen's Association of the NT in 2007.

A lawyer friend suggested we could go fishing and 'get on the piss' in a 'tinny' on the Yuendumu sewerage ponds. All we'd have to do is dangle a fishing line overboard to make it legal.

In February 2010 we received an email:

"I am giving up alcohol this February to raise as much money as I can for FebFast, to raise funds to help reduce alcohol and other drug related harms in young Australians. Please click on this link to visit my very own fundraising page to find out all about it. Please dig deep to sponsor me. It only takes a few seconds. Spread the word and send to as many people as possible. Or if you're brave enough why don't you take up the challenge and give up alcohol in February with me."

The email was from the Intervention appointed Yuendumu based Government Business Manager. The Federal Government's front man. We were flabbergasted. Until that moment we all had naively assumed that the Intervention alcohol restrictions applied to both Yapa and Kardiya, to *ngalipa* - to all of us. We didn't have to give up grog as we already had, decades ago, or at least we said we had.

FRANK BAARDA

Did we generously donate to the good cause? Have a guess!

Welcoming the Intervention - Willowra, 2007

338

Gobbledygook...

At Moe High School my brother and I were put back a year for the simplistic reason we couldn't speak English. The all too common assumption that if you don't speak English you must be dumb, is particularly damaging to those Aboriginal Australians who start school knowing only their other-than-English mother tongue. The assumption creates an unfair atmosphere of low expectations. Luckily for Ted and me, after our first term, Mr. Hollingsworth, one of the more enlightened teachers at Moe High, had us moved up to our own age group.

Bless Mr. Hollingsworth, our English teacher; it was he who introduced me to the Ancient Mariner, the Jabberwocky, the Big Rock Candy Mountain, and Alan Marshall's 'I Can Jump Puddles'.

Mr. Griggs another Moe High School teacher would have become a basketball player if he hadn't taken up teaching. He was thin and around seven foot tall and had a loud very deep voice, like a foghorn. He was our science teacher. On one occasion Mr. Griggs, after throwing a piece of chalk at me, and me blankly staring back at him, came charging up to my desk, grabbed me by the scruff of the neck, pulled me up and, whilst vigorously shaking me, blurted out in his deep bass voice, *"Babba-goo, bubble-doo, blubber blubber blue, hubarb moo, blub blub blub glue, gobbledygook..."* He hadn't quite finished when the lad sitting next to me interjected, *"He doesn't speak English, Sir."* Mr. Griggs then put me down like a sack of potatoes and, mumbling, returned to his lectern to resume his science lesson.

I've already told you that bilingual education is an obsession of mine. As per usual, others can say it so much better than I can. In 1958 T.G.H.Strehlow wrote:

> *"Above all, let us permit native children to keep their own languages,- those beautiful and expressive tongues, rich in true Australian imagery, charged with poetry and with love for all that is great, ancient and eternal in the continent. There is no need to fear that their own languages will interfere with the learning of English as the common medium of expression for all Australians. In most areas*

of Australia the natives have been bilingual, probably from time immemorial. Today white Australians are among the few remaining civilised people who still think that knowledge of one language is the normal limit of linguistic achievement."

I know that bureaucratic battles are boring but consider the politics of bilingual education at Yuendumu school to be of such importance that I'm going to ask for your forbearance as you struggle to stay awake through the next few pages.

Bilingual education, often referred to as 'two way education' has had its ups and downs in the Northern Territory. Hard work, commitment and conviction by Yapa and Kardiya school staff and community members, greatly hampered by bureaucratic and professional ignorance and sabotage has resulted in a chequered bilingual history at Yuendumu school.

Bilingualism was embraced in Yuendumu in a flurry of optimism in 1974. Within a few years the number of Government schools with bilingual programmes in the NT grew to over twenty in many languages.

It was on Christmas day in its inaugural bilingual year that the programme in Yuendumu suffered its first major setback when a batch of newly created Warlpiri reading material, which had been sent to the Government Printer in Darwin, was destroyed by Cyclone Tracy. There was no electronic backup back then. They had to start all over again.

There followed a roller coaster ride when the programme was continuously buffeted by the sociological and politically opportunistic winds of change. Just like in a classroom, where the blackboard is wiped clean before the next lesson, the NT Education Department often wipes existing policies and starts with a new initiative, more often than not just before the next election. They can't help themselves. The Education Department is forever rolling out new policies and initiatives and reinventing the wheel.

I'm reminded of the Billy Bragg song 'Moving the Goalposts':

> *... He's been up all night moving the goalposts ...*

♫ ♫ ♫

So much harder to score goals when the goalposts keep moving, but we keep trying.

From time to time the Department would, without consultation or warning, unilaterally declare that bilingual education wasn't working and would be either terminated or phased out.

When they first tried to shut down bilingual education, they hadn't counted on Jeannie Egan. Jeannie organised several trips to Alice Springs by Yapa school staff and their supporters, who almost literally jumped on the Department's main office front desk. From memory the Department wasn't forewarned about these sorties and with egg on their departmental faces, backed off when they realised Yapa wouldn't. Until the next battle, but for now, we had kept bilingual education.

The low point in Yuendumu was reached when a new school principal, on being presented with the Yuendumu School Languages Policy, declared, *"We won't be needing this,"* and then tore up the two page policy, little caring or realising that he was tearing at Yuendumu's social fabric.

Es un pedazo del alma que se arranca sin piedad...
(It's a piece of the soul, torn out without pity), from 'Veinte Años', a
1920s Cuban classic song by Maria Teresa Vera.

♫ ♫ ♫

The high point in Yuendumu's bilingual struggles was potentially reached when after four years of negotiation the Remote Learning Partnership Agreement (RLPA) was about to be signed. A 'partnership' is supposed to be an arrangement between equals. That is what partners are: equal, *'lipurlu'* (level) in Aboriginal English.

Lajamanu, Willowra, Yuendumu and Nyirrpi schools comprise the Warlpiri Triangle (initially there were three schools) which had negotiated the RLPA with the NT Department of Education. Considerable effort and resources over a four year period had resulted in what I consider to be the most meaningful cross-cultural negotiated agreement I have ever come across. The main thrust of the RLPA was that Warlpiri and English were to have equal status in a two way learning environment, they were to be *lipurlu.*

Then in October 2008 came the bombshell announcement by Marion Scrymgour, the NT Minister of Education, of the imposition of the 'Four Hours English Only' policy. Teaching during the first four hours of the school day, the time when children are at their most alert and receptive, was to be conducted in English only. Marion is an Aboriginal woman, raised in Darwin, her first language, English. She is the latest CEO of the Northern Land Council.

Sometime after Marion's announcement, a meeting was held in Alice Springs to discuss the proposed RLPA signing ceremony in Lajamanu. Items on the agenda included, on what date the signing would take place and which officials should be invited. Barbara Martin had heard a whisper of what was to come and insisted that Wendy and I attend. Warlpiri people are reluctant to say 'no', It is rude, and runs counter to Warlpiri good manners. Barbara wanted us to come along to back them up, as she foresaw that saying 'no' was what was about to happen. It turned out Yapa didn't need our backup. Seldom have I heard Yapa so eloquently and forcefully say 'NO!!'

It became apparent at this meeting that the wording of the RLPA had without warning and without discussion been altered to comply with the new 'Four Hours English Only' policy. Not many words were changed on the rewritten RLPA but these made all the difference. Delegates at the meeting pleaded and argued for the RLPA to be changed back to what had been agreed to, back to *lipurlu.* It was as if we'd come to this meeting expecting to sign up for a mansion only to be offered a shit-house. When the Department representatives would not revert to the pre- 'Four hours English only' version, the Warlpiri

Triangle refused to sign the altered agreement and cancelled the proposed signing ceremony.

I've just revisited my RLPA file and guess what I found amongst the fine print? The last item on the 'Background' introduction:

> *"The parties acknowledge that a legal or fiduciary relationship is not created by signing this agreement and neither party has the authority to act on behalf of the other. Furthermore, this agreement will not be legally binding on either party."*

Weasel words, smoke and mirrors - "Peace for Our Time."

The RLPA is but a faded memory of what might have been. New Kardiya and younger Yapa school staff members have never heard of the RLPA and neither have most Education Department officials.

The RLPA has been officially buried, without a headstone. Out of sight, out of mind.

The 'Four Hours English Only' policy virtually killed bilingual education in the only nine remaining Government schools in the NT that still had a 'two way' language programme. Yirrkala school in northeastern Arnhem Land was the only school that refused to comply and that continued uninterrupted with their bilingual education. Yirrkala had signed their RLPA just in time. Areyonga school took the NT Education Department to the Human Rights Commission and won, but that is another story. Some Kardiya teachers who had seemingly been in favour of bilingual education at Yuendumu, suddenly turned against it and saw the new policy as licence for them to appoint themselves as the language police:

"You're not allowed to talk in Warlpiri in the morning." "You must only speak English before lunch." "You can't sing Warlpiri songs or read Warlpiri books in the first four hours." Racists showing their true colours! Well, the Warlpiri and their allies are not yet fully conquered. The Teachers Union was contacted, and they in turn contacted the NT News. *"Language Gestapo"* read the headline.

During a "bush cabinet" meeting in Yuendumu, Marion Scrimgour met with us to apologise. She didn't really apologise, she stood by the policy which she had introduced, and only regretted not having consulted with us and given us prior warning. She wanted us to know that the policy did not forbid people speaking in Warlpiri. The memory of the days when "speaking in language" was forbidden are part of the Warlpiri psyche and when she munificently announced that we were permitted to speak Warlpiri, you could have cut the air with a knife. I'll never know if Marion was aware of the offence her remark had caused to Yapa at this meeting.

The extreme nonsense of the language police was nipped in the bud, but all the same for far too long, our trained experienced Yapa teachers such as Yamurna, Nancy Oldfield, sat passively observing and doing very little for the first four hours every day, while their Kardiya team teaching partners struggled to impart knowledge using English only.

Three and a half years after its introduction and just before an election, the policy was quietly dropped, but the Department did nothing to repair the damage caused by the 'Four Hours English Only' policy, damage which is yet to be fully repaired. Someone once said that when you put a tank in reverse, the flattened ground doesn't immediately spring back to its former glory. At a school council meeting, the principal at the time, stated that the jury was out on bilingual education. The legacy of the 'Four Hours English Only' policy, is that English has remained as the dominant teaching language and Warlpiri culture and literacy get a smaller slice of the time allocation, than in former years. But we are working on raising it back up. Yamurna who had been relegated from teacher to observer, is now our Assistant Principal. Things are looking up.

History is replete with examples of book burning. Such was narrowly averted at Willowra, 150 km north-east of Yuendumu, when the 'Four Hours English Only' heavy artillery monolingual barrage was launched against bilingual education in the NT. The then Principal of Willowra school decided that the room containing Warlpiri reading material should, as it was no longer needed, be converted into a staff tea room. The books were to be dumped at the rubbish tip where they would end up being burned. An alert visiting Education Department whistle blower, narrowly averted this from happening. Supporters of bilingual education are forever required to keep on their toes and put out countless brush fires. This is very tiring and time consuming.

The National Assessment Program - Literacy and Numeracy or NAPLAN replaced MAP tests throughout Australia in 2008, the same year in which the NT's 'Four Hours English Only' policy was first enforced. The annual tests of years 3, 5, 7 and 9 aim at providing a snapshot of students' current reading, writing, language and numeracy skills. MAP testing I'm told, was less ominous than the NAPLAN tests which replaced it.

When Yuendumu school was told that funding would depend on numbers of NAPLAN tests administered, all children were required to fill in the tests, even when they obviously could not read English at all. They were mostly multiple choice tests so they could just tick or cross or colour in boxes and because of this the students got some of the questions right, thus giving the impression they actually knew some of the answers. Sitting the tests did little for children's self confidence and their keenness to attend school.

A few children who were progressing with Warlpiri and English literacy and thought they were doing well in reading, actually cried when they found they couldn't read any of the test.

Bilingual education has been blamed for persistently low NAPLAN results in remote communities. This is despite the no-brainer, that any child will perform poorly when tested in a language they don't fully understand. Students in the most elite Melbourne schools would fail miserably should they be tested in Warlpiri. Frank Zhao, a mathematical genius, who was Geelong Grammar's 2019 Dux, wouldn't stand a chance in Warlpiri. How could this self evident fact receive such scant consideration? Suggestions that tests in Warlpiri might prove more meaningful and more useful to Yuendumu school are lead balloons that fall on deaf ears. The current tests are a complete waste of time.

Het haalt toch niets aan als vragen gesteld worden in een taal die men niet kan verstaan.

See what I mean?

As if the 'Four Hours English Only' policy hadn't happened and the RLPA hadn't existed, the Department of Education pulled a new rabbit out of the hat. Ta-dah!

The Community Driven Schools policy!

A special School Council meeting was called in late 2013, at which two Education Department weevils, tasked with rolling out the new initiative, explained the new policy to us. They asked us who in the community we thought they should consult to find out what the community wanted from Education. *"Us ,"* we said. *"We are the appointed representatives of the community and we take a particular interest in Education matters." "Yes, but who in the community should we talk to?" "Us, "* we insisted. *"You need go no further than this room."* They took no notice and repeatedly asked us who in the community they should talk to.

Before the meeting Barbara Martin had pointed to one of the officials and reminded me that he'd been the main negotiator of the RLPA. I turned to Joe Blow as Barbara had called him and said:

> *"Weren't you involved in the Remote Learning Partnership negotiations? It was absolutely brilliant! You could save yourself a lot of trouble. No need to reinvent the wheel. Just blow off the dust and cobwebs and there, all nicely thought out and in the agreement, is all you need to know regarding community wishes and aspirations."*

With the wind duly taken out of their sails, the meeting ground to a halt. The weevils then offered to come back to discuss the matter further. Francis Kelly piped up:

"We are sick and tired of talking to messengers, we want to talk to the Minister, the Education boss and our local member."

No, we definitely didn't want the weevils to return and waste our time again. Thus it was arranged that Bess Nungarrayi Price, our local member at the time and originally from Yuendumu, Peter Chandler, the then Minister for Education, and Ken Davies. the then Chief Executive of the Department of Education, would come to Yuendumu. An accident in Katherine which resulted in the death of a Nungarrayi, Bess' skin sister, meant that Bess couldn't come and the meeting was cancelled.

If the mountain will not come to Muhammad, then Muhammad must go to the mountain. In April 2014, a delegation from the Yuendumu School Council went to see Ken Davies in Darwin. We went to push for the reinstatement of bilingual education in light of the Department's new policy of Community Driven Schools.

The delegation consisted of Elizabeth Katakarinja, Barbara Martin, Tess Ross and myself.

Ken expressed surprise: *"Have you come especially to see me?"* First time he'd heard of us. He either didn't know about the proposed meeting which had been cancelled or he'd forgotten. Tess and Barbara, both veterans of the fight for bilingual education showed Ken a batch of Warlpiri reading material. Turns out we didn't have to sell bilingual education to Ken, after all he'd started his NT career as a teacher in Papunya he told us. Only one problem, the policy of Community Driven Schools was being held in abeyance, pending the release of the Wilson Report, so Ken, whilst impressed with us, and on-side, couldn't promise anything. The Wilson report was the latest such report to look into Education in the NT. We suspect these reports are pre-written before token community consultations take place, and we often find out about these enquiries after the deadline for submissions has expired.

I seem to remember through the mists of time that soon after we saw Ken, we came to realise that he'd already read the Wilson Report, which is why he wouldn't promise anything. Which is also why he chose to give us false hope, to get us off his back and make us go away happy. Thus operate career bureaucrats.

We were to see Ken Davis once more when he and some other officials turned up and met with the Yuendumu School council. We were mistaken when we assumed the party had come to Yuendumu in response to our delegation. Our Darwin sortie was not mentioned, it was as if it had never happened. Instead we had to sit through a power point presentation by someone lobbying for our school to become independent by switching from the NT Government to a Church body. This proposal, which was supported by the Department, despite the carrot of increased funding, was not at all well received. We were being asked to swap our umbrella for a raincoat. Independent from what? At this meeting we were also pressured to adopt Direct Instruction. As we understood it Direct Instruction was not designed to embrace bilingual education and as applied in Australia it is in fact an 'English Only' method, and we told them so.

It was at this meeting that Anna Lennie a school council member who had her own two Kardiya children attending Yuendumu School told the visitors that:

> *"When there is a Kardiya teacher in front of the class the Yapa children roll around muck about and are generally distracted whilst my children sit quietly paying attention. When there is a Yapa teacher in front of the class, the Yapa children sit quietly paying attention and my children roll around muck about and are generally distracted."*

Years of academic research and learned papers from around the world, years of tilting at the bureaucratic windmills yet Anna managed to, in a few words, describe how bilingual education functions in reality.

In September 2016 Ken Davis became the CEO of the newly created Department of Territory Families. He is now in charge of the dingoes. Back to square one:

> *"Yes, but who in the Department should we talk to?"*

Oxymorons…

The Warlpiri schools receive significant support from the Warlpiri Education and Training Trust (WETT), which derives funding from mining royalties. From Warlpiri money. Some Yuendumu Yapa teachers were in Canberra doing a presentation on the good work being done by WETT when the Wilson report was released. Word came back to us that our delegation was very happy in that the Wilson Report had supported bilingual education. They obviously had not read between the lines.

This from the Wilson Report:

"The review supports the teaching of literacy in first language where feasible. For Priority 1 schools, the department should mandate early literacy approaches in English including phonemic awareness, phonics."

No kidding, this oxymoronic pair of sentences are conjoined in the report.

Furthermore: *"The curriculum should be delivered in English."*

If you skip the next bit, you won't miss much. They are weasel words. These are some of the Wilson Report recommendations:

1. sustained teaching of first language, including literacy, to Indigenous children for whom English is not their first language, where feasible and where a trained teacher is available;

2. training of Indigenous first language speakers to teach the language both as fully trained teachers and on a Limited Authority to Teach basis;

3. provision of English language learning from the start of school;

4. delivery of the curriculum in English; and

5. the active presence of trained first language-speaking adults in the classroom where the curriculum is delivered in English to Indigenous students whose first language is not English.

In other words Yapa teachers were going to be allowed to witness the delivery of a curriculum in English. Whoopy poop!

The School Council seized on *"The review supports the teaching of literacy in first language, where feasible…"* We unilaterally declared teaching in Warlpiri at Yuendumu to be feasible.

A very common misconception is that bilingual education is teaching children two languages.

Many opponents of bilingual education say that children can learn Warlpiri at home and there is no need to teach them Warlpiri in school. This is a furphy, just think about it, did you learn about Shakespeare, the periodic table and calculus at home? Did you learn to speak English at school? Regrettably many high level Education Department officials fail to understand the distinction between learning a language and using it to learn.

Another very important principle that should be recognised and applied but usually isn't, is that an unqualified Warlpiri speaker is far more able to communicate with and impart knowledge to Warlpiri children than is a fully qualified English only language speaker. English is a foreign language to a young child whose mother tongue is Warlpiri. For them, just like it had been for me and my brother at Moe High School, English is gobbledygook. For very young children it takes a few years for such a child to begin to fully understand what an English speaking teacher is saying, especially when dealing with languages that are so vastly different. The Kardiya teacher may as well be speaking in tongues or in Swahili. Without an effective bilingual programme, this results in years of educational development being lost. Most children never catch up.

Another common misconception is that a linguist is someone who just speaks the language, whereas linguists are professionals who studied a great deal about languages, just as geologists are professionals who studied a great deal about rocks.

I recall an example about this misconception about linguists. During the second Gulf War, I listened to a radio interview with an Australian soldier who'd been assigned to Australia's role in evacuating wounded Iraqis to the Gulf States for medical attention. *"We are going to need a lot more linguists,"* said the soldier.

I see the role of a linguist in a bilingual school to be like that of an architect who designs a building, rather than builds it, or better still that of an orchestra conductor. The Warlpiri brass and the English strings, and there stands the conductor waving a tiny baton, and out pours beautiful music. To those who don't know any better the conductor doesn't appear to be doing a great deal.

Without a linguist a bilingual programme works in the dark because the Kardiya teachers usually don't know much or sometimes nothing at all of the local vernacular language, and Yapa teachers' command of English is often inadequate. Thus when 'hard' language is encountered in stories or information, the choice becomes to either replace the 'hard language' with simple language or leave it as is, possibly not understood and meaningless. Pitjantjatjara teachers used to complain that they didn't want their kids learning 'Missionary Pitjantjatjara', a simplified version of the language or 'baby talk'.

All linguists who have worked in Yuendumu School have quickly learnt Warlpiri.

After much lobbying by the school council Yuendumu school now has a full time qualified linguist and a Yapa/Kardiya teaching team in every classroom. There is however no guarantee that the linguist position will be continued

At the first School Council meeting held after the pandemic outbreak, the school linguist outlined by video link, the progress that had been made on developing the Warlpiri theme cycle and we were told that Yapa staff now outnumber Kardiya staff members. If true, the latter hasn't been the case since decades earlier during the 'Welfare' training allowance and the CDEP wages subsidy days. This is nice, but the battle for Yapa staff to receive the same privileges as Kardiya staff, such as free electricity, has been fought for decades, and is yet to be won.

On the same day as the School Council meeting (29th April 2020) the NT Minister for Education, Selena Uibo, herself a Yapa ex-teacher, announced that in 2021 the RATE (Remote Aboriginal Teacher Education) programme would be re-introduced.

In the past the RATE programme was highly successful in training Yapa to become class teachers without the need for them to leave their communities for extended periods. External teacher training was fraught with often insurmountable difficulties. One such difficulty was to quote Geoffrey Blainey 'the tyranny of distance'.

So often have we been disappointed in the past, that we await with bated breath to see if the new RATE programme will be as effective as the old RATE programme. We fear that the programme will yield teacher training the same as for mainstream schools, the same non-Warlpiri oriented focus and the same high English literacy hurdles.

Another unmet need is specialist training of mainstream Kardiya teachers to work in remote indiginenous language speaking communities. When I recently called into the school printery (the BRDU- Bilingual Resources Development Unit) there, seated around a large table, there was a group of Yapa school staff working on a school matter, not a Kardiya in sight. Self-determination in action Yuendumu School has some way to go to reach its former zenith of bilingual education but we are slowly getting there.

Hallelujah, hallelujah, hallelujah! Yati, Yati, Yati!

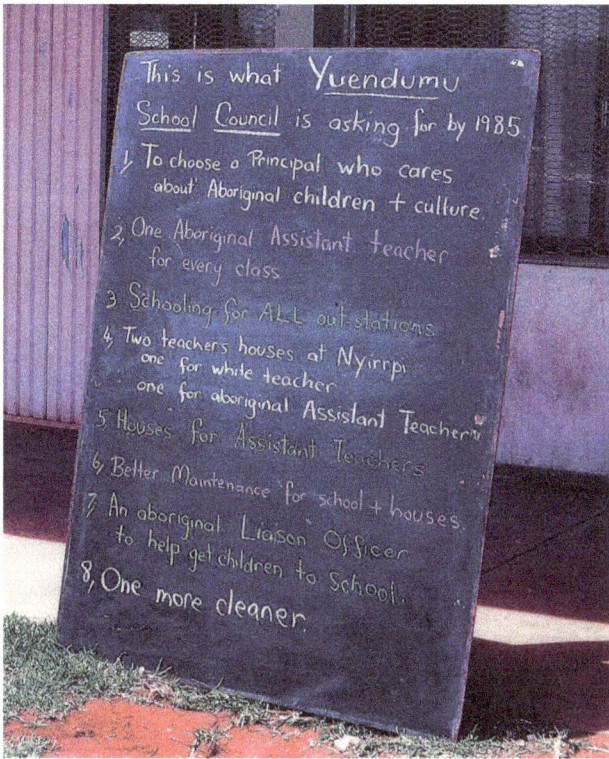

1984 sign in front of the school office - list of requests to bring to the attention of visiting Education Department officials.

I'm in the doghouse now (Buddy Jones-1939)

🎵🎵🎵

A true story my father told me from his childhood memories:

"When our mother had to go to the hospital, my sister Femmie and I went to stay at Onkel Fritz and Tante Lina's. Onkel Fritz Nierhaus was a communist who had married mum's sister. They had seven children: Änne, Friedrich, Gerhard, Willie, Rika, Lina and Christineke. Tante Lina always confused their names, and would use nearly all of the names whenever she addressed any one of them. They were as poor as church mice, and the children were always hungry. One evening a large roast appeared on the dinner table. Femmie and I looked at each other... Waltman, Onkel Fritz' dog, was never seen again."

Don't know why, but whenever dad told me about his aunt Lina, it made me think of the Old Lady who lived in a Shoe.

Dogs are an important feature of community life. I've already told you of the Yuendumu dogs being the second largest contingent of witnesses at the Warlpiri Land Claim hearings and of our kidnapping dog Chocolate, and of Dougie, Shirley Martin's star-picket towing prize winning dog at the inaugural Yuendumu School dog show. And then there are Rosie Fleming's dogs being well looked after at the Art Centre, and then there was the policeman who was asked to leave after he'd gone on a dog shooting spree.

I can't think of a single time when dogs weren't an important part of Yuendumu quotidian existence.

In Alexis Wright's book 'Tracker', someone described † Tracker Tilmouth's job interview style when he was Director of the Central Land Council. One question he invariably asked was:

"Do you like dogs?"

Anyone who has ever visited a remote Aboriginal community will know that this is a very pertinent question to ask. Honest, if you don't like dogs, forget about paying us a visit.

If Tracker decided the applicant was going to be hired he would conclude the interview with "*Don't forget, you've come to work for us, not to save us.*" Also very pertinent.

As Yapa settled down on communities so too they adopted dogs into their families. Dogs breed much faster than dingoes and soon dog overpopulation became problematic. This worried Kardiya society and still does. To Yapa, culling is not an acceptable solution.

Wendy recalls that during the 'Welfare days' she'd joined a group of Yapa women who were discussing the latest incidences of the police shooting sick dogs. When Wendy let it be known that she agreed with the ladies that the police ought to seek dog owner's permission before shooting dogs, a very old lady conspiratorially beckoned to Wendy and showed her a hairless dog she was clutching to her bosom hidden in her blouse. "*Yurrkunyu-kujaku,*" (for fear of the police) she whispered. Her dog had a skin-name and a name, Marjorie.

†Shorty Jangala Robertson was a dignified old widower and one of Yuendumu's most successful and hardworking artists. His paintings have been sold worldwide and he generously distributed his considerable income amongst numerous relatives.

You could hear Shorty coming. As Shorty wandered about on his social rounds he was preceded by a phalanx of dogs. Shorty's dogs jealously guarded his space and his travels were punctuated by dog skirmishes. His dogs however never bit a human and were a picture of canine health. Shorty looked after them and they looked after him. They were *marlpa* (company). They were *warlalja* (family).

When we arrived in Yuendumu there were many mangy, hairless, skinny, sick dogs. Gradually dogs have become better looked after, more healthy and less starving. At our shops, sales of dog food have increased dramatically over time. In 2010, I wrote:

> "*In three decades Yuendumu society has undergone inspiring changes. Much reduced violence and alcohol abuse. Greatly improved*

nutrition and hygiene. Eradication of petrol sniffing. Higher status for women. Establishment of a world class art industry. And yes, better dogs."

Yuendumu's better dogs and the owners of the better dogs are much indebted to Gloria Morales and to Warlukurlangu Artists. In 2004 Gloria, the co-manager of the art centre, started to treat ticks and scabies and feed hungry dogs, take unwanted puppies to the RSPCA and take dogs to Alice Springs to have them desexed. She did this of her own bat and at her own expense. Later when it became apparent that this endeavour was much appreciated and worthwhile, Gloria started to receive assistance both physical and financial, and her initiative has since expanded into the fully fledged Warlukurlangu Artists dog programme.

Affiliated to the dog programme, is the not for profit Aussie Desert Dogs which finds homes for puppies and dogs all across Australia. You can choose a Yuendumu dog from their website, which has photos and stories. You pay for inoculations and your dog arrives by plane.

In the last two decades the Yuendumu dog population has halved and the dogs are twice as healthy!

Very recently the Watson family had a dog who started to bite people. There was no alternative, the dog had to be euthanised. The family arranged for Gloria to put the dog down. They dug a grave, made up a cross and the family said their final goodbyes and prayed. The family believes their much loved dog has gone to heaven. After all heaven wouldn't be heaven without dogs. I wonder if they get wings.

Barking up the wrong tree...

As previously mentioned, on the coat-tails of the Intervention, the assets of the Yuendumu Community Government Council were seized when it was swallowed up by the Central Desert Shire. As of 1st July 2008, the local council effectively ceased to exist. The area covered by the shire exceeds that of a small European nation and the Shire's Alice Springs head office, falls outside of this area. The Shire employs more than one hundred staff in Alice Springs, but not one single Warlpiri is employed there.

One of the first moves by the newly appointed Yuendumu Shire Services Manager (SSM) was an attempt to reintroduce the previously rebuffed 'limit of two dogs per household' policy.

When our son Joe heard about this policy he demonstrated his mathematical nous when he instantly proclaimed, *"Yuendumu is going to need a lot more households."*

I felt compelled to warn the SSM about the Pandora's box he was opening and sent him a lengthy email discussing the role of dogs in Yuendumu society. Couldn't help myself, I concluded the email stating that I feared he was, *"barking up the wrong tree."* I should have let sleeping dogs lie.

Later, I learned that my email was widely read at the Yuendumu Shire office and that much laughter had ensued. The SSM was not amused. That is an attribute that some people put in positions of power seem to share, an unwillingness to laugh at themselves, an inclination to take themselves way too seriously.

For years Yuendumu Mining Company (YMC) used to dig new trenches at the rubbish dump with our bulldozer. These were $5,000 - $15,000 contracts let by the Yuendumu Council.

One of the first contracts let by the Intervention was a $200,000 contract to erect a fence around the rubbish dump as well as to do some clean-up and trenching work. Alice Springs contractors completed the job in under two weeks. With that kind of money YMC could have replaced its ailing bulldozer and completed the contract, and have money left over, but we weren't asked. The Shire has since decided that an excavator is more suitable than a bulldozer to dig new trenches. YMC didn't own an excavator.

I should have learned by now that being a smart arse can turn around and bite you on the bum. I'll be doggone, no more rubbish dump contracts for YMC.

Our SSMs, GBMs and the GECs who replaced the latter continue to bark up the wrong tree.

A hallmark of the Control Control Control freaks in charge is that they are dogmatic.

The word 'shire' soon acquired negative connotations. Myself, I kept looking out for hobbits and rued the non-appearance of a Gandalf. Just as the Intervention became 'Stronger Futures' and 'Closing the Gap', so too the Central Desert Shire became the Central Desert Regional Council. But we're not fooled. We can spot a wolf in sheep's clothing from many *lingka* away. Many of us defiantly insist on referring to the 'Shire'. We don't call them the Council, the 'Council' is the one they took away from us.

As part of the Shire's attempt at ingratiating themselves with the locals they now controlled, they instituted a regional council consisting of delegates from the various communities.

Early on Ned Hargreaves became a council member. Ned, a good if not always polite talker, had been complaining about problems with his house so I said to him, *"Well now you should get things sorted at the next council meeting."* When he came back I asked him how he got on with his housing problems. He said, *"We weren't allowed to talk about that. It wasn't on the agenda."*

At a Local Implementation Plan meeting held in July 2010 dogs suddenly reappeared on the agenda. The 'limit of two dogs per household' policy, again reared its canine head. The Interventionists are like a dog with a bone. Dogged they are. The authorities' propensity to put the 'limit of two dogs per household' policy forward again and again, epitomises the unrelenting inflexible approach in their pursuit of total control. No matter how often members of the community object to a proposal the authorities, like a dog returning with a stick, keep coming back with it. At this meeting Lottie Napangardi said, *"People here love their dogs, they are family,"* and the policy was again rejected.

Don't worry, the policy will be back! Eventually it will become law, and like all such laws it will be broken and ignored.

At the Nyirrpi shop, the following notice appeared:

The Vet will be at Nyirripi next Monday 8/8/11 The Number of dogs need to reduce (sic) on Community and the Mangy Dogs need to be destroyed
    If you hide your dogs from the Vet
    I will have the Police Shoot your Dog
    Please help clean up the Community

The notice was signed 'Peter'. For all it's worth Peter, the Shire's Nyirrpi Shire Services Manager, didn't last.

The notice was met with the protest, derision and ridicule it deserved and was soon removed.

The notice itself didn't worry me so much. We all need a laugh from time to time. Far more ominous to me was that some people would have seen nothing wrong with the notice. Also somewhat worrying was that although, not very likely, it wasn't entirely impossible that the Police may have carried out the command.

Back in Native Welfare days, when scabies was rife in the community, some health authority sent a message: "Burn all their blankets and shoot all their dogs." Some dog shooting did go on but the Superintendent decided that blanket burning was going a bit too far.

Whenever authoritarianism, despotism, fascism, and other manifestations of humanity's darker side, pop up in this the land of the 'Fair Go', I worry.

Paraphrasing that famous Pastor Niemöller quote:

"First they came for the dogs…"

Landlords and Tenants...

When we traversed El Salvador in 1971, I was told by a local that 97% of the land was owned by 3% of the population. Recently on television, Stephen Fry in Central America informed me that fourteen families own virtually all the land in El Salvador.

In Australia 100% of Aboriginal land is controlled by mainstream society. Land Rights are rights only in name and on paper. Salvadorans and Australian Aborigines have this in common in that they both got the short end of the stick.

Many of you will be familiar with Midnight Oil's 'Beds are Burning' song:

♫ ♫ ♫

The time has come to say fair's fair
To pay the rent, to pay our share
The time has come, a fact's a fact
It belongs to them, let's give it back

You'll also recall Rosie Fleming being dismissed as a 'crazy old lady' at the first Yuendumu meeting at which the Intervention sought 80 year leases, when she asserted that 'You Government people' didn't own the land. The Commonwealth later changed this to 40 year leases with an option for the government to extend the leases by another 40 years. Tricky that, the Federals sought the option to extend, yet the community would not be granted an option to refuse extension! Smoke and mirrors. Whilst pretending to seek less, they were seeking and eventually got more.

The Federal Government joined the NT Government to introduce the $647 million Strategic Indigenous Housing and Infrastructure Program (SIHIP). The programme would be implemented subject to the Government securing adequate land tenure. In Yuendumu negotiations started with a $4 million carrot - $2 million for a small select group of Traditional Land Owners and $2 million for 'the Community'. The community was divided, those wanting to take the money and those who considered land inalienable. When negotiations stalled, the bribe was replaced with a different tack. $18 million had been set aside for refurbishment or demolition of existing houses and construction of a modest number of new houses.

"If we are not granted secure tenure we will not build any new houses nor will we carry out maintenance and repairs on existing houses" was the non-negotiable ultimatum. The Commonwealth was offering to build some new houses and to repair and maintain existing houses that they would own and the NT Government would manage. Strictly speaking they were offering nothing. They were offering Yapa the 'opportunity' to become tenants on their own land in what had been largely their own houses. They were what colloquially are known as 'Indian givers'. Yuendumu, was 'last man standing' when it came to caving in to FaHCSIA's sleight of hand blackmail. A pyrrhic victory.

In the first five years of SIHIP not a single Aboriginal residence had been built in Yuendumu. During that period a multi-million dollar state of the art Centrelink building with impenetrable security was assembled like an IKEA piece of furniture from five semi-trailer loads of material which arrived from Bendigo in Victoria. Similar Centrelink facilities were installed in several NT communities and it is my understanding that these buildings are leased by the Commonwealth and are owned by a syndicate of investors who have since on-sold their investment to other absentee landlords. The security arrangements at these Centrelink agencies seem to me over the top as I can't imagine anyone breaking in to steal unemployment benefit application forms. Also during this period a flash modern house, accommodation for visiting student doctors, arrived on the back of two semi-trailers from, I don't know whence, and also on the back of semi-trailers from Queensland two duplexes to house Kardiya teachers arrived, but not a single Yapa residence.

Concurrent with but not to be confused with the Federal campaign to secure long term leases on residences, the NT Government sought

40 year leases for their infrastructure such as the school, the police station, the power house and the clinic. At a community meeting Yapa suggested that these leases should be conditionally approved. In exchange for acceding to the leases, housing should be provided for Yapa teachers and Yapa police, bilingual education should be reintroduced, a Yapa person should be trained to run the power house (as had been the case in the past) and so on. At a subsequent meeting an NT Government spokesperson said that having such conditions on the leases would make them unworkable and offered to negotiate a Partnership Agreement instead. We knew all about 'partnerships' such as the previously mentioned aborted Remote Learning Partnership. Goes without saying that without linking the leases to the suggested conditions, such an agreement would be unenforceable and not worth the paper it was written on. Negotiations stalled. The government persevered and applied the ratchet principle of negotiations, as well as a bit of divide and rule. Eventually the leases were granted unconditionally and without even a toothless Partnership Agreement. They got what they wanted, they often do.

Right from the outset residences in Yuendumu were regarded as belonging to Yuendumu. To *ngalipa*, to all of us. All dealings regarding rent and repairs were initially through the Yuendumu Housing Association and later through the Yuendumu Council. Allocation of houses was by consensus. For example if Yapa vacated a house because of a death in the family, a coat of paint later and another family would move in. Disputes and arguments would be resolved internally between families, often arbitrated by the Council.

Yapa rules not always understood by Kardiya would be applied. It worked. Yuendumu was a community and was communally owned. It was also communally run, decisions reached by consensus. Over time housing stock increased. Funding came from various sources. DAA, ADC, ATSIC, ABTA, GMAAAC (the 'Big A's' I used to call them) local organisations and others.

Election after election we would be told by politicians: "*Vote for me I got you x number of houses.*"

As a prelude to increased outside control, the local perception of communal home ownership was gradually eroded. Far be it for me to claim I understand Yapa and Kardiya laws, let alone the distinctions and contradictions between them, but I believe what has happened in the case of Yuendumu, is that whereas Yapa law recognises broad groups as having communal 'ownership' of places, a small select group of Yapa belonging to a subset of the total group was instead increasingly recognised by the Central Land Council, as being the Traditional Land Owners (TLOs) of Yuendumu.

This select group of TLOs was based on a narrow legalistic application of the Aboriginal Land Rights (Northern Territory) Act 1976. In other words on Kardiya law. More and more decisions were made under the guidance and control of government agencies and the Central Land Council, who would claim to be acting on behalf of the TLOs and to have obtained their consent. In exchange for a rubber stamp, these TLOs are granted preferential treatment in housing and other matters. What irks many Yuendumu people, is that the increased rents most families pay to Territory Housing are the source of lease rents which are paid out to a select few families. The supposed TLOs get the crumbs of the mainstream economy cake. These crumbs at times are substantial and cause much resentment jealousy and conflict within the community.

If it wasn't so serious, you'd have to laugh. This remote control is taken to ludicrous extremes. When recently a small bus-stop shelter was erected at the front of Yuendumu clinic by the Central Desert Regional Council, a ream of paperwork was required and a CLC anthropologist had to come out to consult with the TLOs to make sure it wasn't a sacred site before erection could proceed. Such erections used to be verbally approved without red tape by local council members. There is no such thing as bureaucratic or administrative Viagra to enable functional erections.

Sacred Sites protection is now an almost entirely Kardiya run and legislated enterprise. Near a recently sealed stretch of the Tanami Road, not far from Yuendumu there stand a number of *yurrkali* (blood-wood - *Eucalyptus terminalis)* which are part of a jukurrpa. Despite the contractors having been told this, they knocked one down, and it is rumoured they had to fork out $30,000 in compensation. Much care was taken to avoid a costly repetition. Thus a number of trees ended up standing like sore thumbs on the cleared road shoulders. These trees aren't faring so well. One died of loneliness and stood out for all to see for quite a while. Eventually it was chain sawed down and cut up - dirty linen removed.

The Wikipedia entry on Yuendumu includes, *"and is a community largely made up of the Warlpiri and Anmatyerre Aboriginal people."* This is news to me. Yes, sure, Yuendumu is close to Anmatyerre land, and yes, sure the Jukurrpa songlines cross the invisible boundary, and yes, Warlpiri/Anmatyerre intermarriage goes back to time eternal, but the population of Yuendumu is predominantly Warlpiri and has been so since Yuendumu's inception. This was never a problem, until recently. The Warlpiri and Anmatyerre people are very close, I would be told, and this would be illustrated by two flat outstretched hands being held touching each other side by side. I was told they were *lipurlu*. The controversial alleged TLOs of Yuendumu are partly of Anmatyerre descent. Divide and rule in action.

With the Intervention came the final assault on local independence. Most existing residences were appropriated regardless of what funding had been used to build them in the first place. At present Territory Housing which comes under the Department of Local Government Housing and Community Development, controls 118 Public Houses and 35 Government employee houses in Yuendumu. Zodiac Business Services is a privately owned company which was specifically set up to take on the controversially granted Tenancy Management contract. Tangentyere Council, an Alice Springs based Aboriginal organisation took on the Housing Maintenance Officer (HMO) contract. The HMO comes out to Yuendumu and assesses necessary repairs and maintenance and with the exception of very minor repairs handballs the jobs to a panel of registered Alice Springs contractors. YKNAC our local outstation resource organisation didn't get a look in.

I recently had a conversation with the Kardiya HMO. He told me that local TLOs gave him a hard time and made unreasonable demands on him. I asked him who these TLOs were, a moot point, they weren't part of the CLC recognised small clique of TLOs. I told the HMO that the antagonism he was experiencing was understandable in view of the history of home ownership in Yuendumu. *"But these houses belong to the Commonwealth!"* he retorted.

Thus is history rewritten. Yet one more of the many examples of the previously mentioned orwellian 'erasure of the past' that Yuendumu is cursed with.

Let me remind you of the lyrics of the 'Beds are Burning' song:

The time has come to say fair's fair
To pay the rent, to pay our share
The time has come, a fact's a fact
It belongs to them, let's give it back

Well that's exactly what has happened - Yapa have given it back and are paying the rent. I somehow feel that Rob Hirst, Jim Moginie and Peter Garrett had something else in mind when they wrote that song.

What's good for the goose...

Income quarantining was one of the main planks of the Intervention. Quarantining sounded rather authoritarian, so the Northern Territory Emergency Response (NTER) soon euphemistically changed this to Income Management. Under Income Management, in the Prescribed Areas, 50% of welfare payments could only be spent in duly authorised outlets (not many to start off with) and not on restricted goods such as alcohol, tobacco, gambling and pornography.

I've mentioned but not elaborated on the Peter Yu review which had given us such false hope.

The first recommendation under the heading 'Welfare Reform and Employment' in the October 2008 NTER Review Board Report, simply stated:

"The current blanket application of compulsory income management in the NT cease."

If you type 'cease synonyms' into the Google search engine in less than one second you get:

'Bring to an end, bring to a halt, bring to a stop, end, halt, stop, conclude, terminate, finish, wind up, discontinue, desist from, refrain from, leave off, quit, shut down, suspend, break off and cut short.' They left off abort. None of these are ambiguous and the application of any one of these would have satisfied us.

It wasn't to be, Income Management was to stay, and is still with us to this day. When Income Management proved to be an administrative nightmare, fairly soon the Basics Card was introduced and now of course we have the looming Cashless Debit Card. It proved very easy for the Basics Card to be abused, especially in Alice Springs where income management licenced merchants weren't too fussy and didn't know the card holders. A person other than the card holder might go shopping with it and for example go to a supermarket with a shopping list and then supply the goods at half price to a Kardiya waiting around the corner and then head to the casino or the pub with the proceeds. Another side-effect of Income Management is that it gave rise to a thriving alcohol and tobacco black market. Income Management had the counter intuitive effect of causing drinking by Yapa to spike. That is what happens with forbidden fruit. When people had been responsible for their own money they acted more responsibly. Surprise!

Income Management is supposed to be about helping people in managing their money but in fact it is about others controlling their money. Centrelink are in charge of implementing Income Management which it does from overseas, Hobart Tasmania.

Centrelink's motto is *'Centrelink Giving You Options'.* Centrelink, one of the most inflexible and incompetent government agencies, with their control of Income Management, does nothing of the sort. In fact it has taken away Yapa options. I must apologise, I can't help myself, but the motto with its contradiction, made me think of *Arbeit Macht Frei* (work sets you free), the slogan crowning the gates to Auschwitz.

In Don Watson's very funny book 'Bendable Learnings' (2009) I find the following:

"The Centrelink contact point for statistics, previously known as the Knowledge Desk is now known as the Business Intelligence Front Door."

Quite a feat, using 'intelligence' and 'Centrelink' in the same sentence, *n'est ce pas?*

Don Watson also quotes from a Centrelink brochure on multicultural services:

"If you cannot read, this brochure tells you where to get lessons."

Yuendumu society is often presented with Catch-22 situations like in Centrelink's multicultural brochure.

The Yuendumu Community Council obtained a key cutting machine. Then Council employee, Lorry put up a notice: *"If you've lost your key, come and see Lorry who'll cut you a new one."* Fair enough and if you were unable to read Lorry's sign you could always refer to the Centrelink brochure first to find out where to get reading lessons.

Subsequently, when asked to duplicate a bundle of keys, Lorry placed them one by one in the machine and on handing them over was surprised when shown that both the originals and the copies were all blank. He'd placed them in the machine back to front and duplicated a set of blanks. We gave him blank stares. So often have Yapa been unfairly stereotyped that I feel compelled to point out that Lorry is a Kardiya.

I received a phone call from someone at Centrelink in Alice Springs. Their team had come across a bogged vehicle with ten people. Micah Hudson was bringing his family to Yuendumu for the Sports Weekend. I was given the GPS coordinates and told they were on the Newhaven Road. I checked the GPS coordinates on a map and it turned out they were on the Nyirrpi Road. When I rang the fellow at Centrelink to tell him this, he was adamant that it was the Newhaven Road. Much later he called back to apologise and confirmed that it was indeed the Nyirrpi road. It turned out the vehicle wasn't bogged. It had stalled whilst crossing a large pool of water on the road, and it had a weak battery. From a Warlpiri perspective, not knowing what road you're on is almost inconceivable. Not knowing the difference between bogged and a flat battery, isn't too useful either.

The 500 pages of the Intervention (NTER) legislation includes a whole section on Income Management. It is based on the offensive one size fits all assumptions that all welfare recipients in these places don't know how to look after their money, don't know how to look after their children and spend all their money on grog and pornography. Thus, to add insult to injury, the people sent out to manage people's incomes and control their lives are from a Warlpiri perspective extremely stupid, almost beyond belief.

Centrelink and some other Yuendumu organisations seem to attract these intellectual pygmies.

You've all heard the phrase *"Lies, damned lies, and statistics."*

FaHCSIA carried out a survey of community stores. The survey reported an increase in sales of food including fresh food. FaHCSIA claimed this would over the longer term, support healthier families and communities. The Yuendumu Mining Store which suffered a 40% drop in sales resulting from the imposition of Income Management, for which it wasn't licensed, was not included in the survey. Incidentally Yuendumu Mining's sudden drop in turnover set in motion the slide which would eventually lead to its insolvency. All stores surveyed had a monopoly on Income Managed sales. In Yuendumu surveyed sales of food were thus confined to the only Income Management licensed store, the newly installed so-called 'Intervention Store', which I dubbed the third store from the fifth column, and thus increased numerically from zero at a rate of a notional mathematically calculated infinity percent.

Neither were food prices mentioned in the survey's media release. In the 1920's German Weimar Republic of my father's childhood, sales of food expressed in German Marks had skyrocketed, just as have food sales in present day Venezuela expressed in Bolivares. At the time of writing a loaf of bread costs around half a million Bolivares.

A survey by an NT Government nutritionist showing that the 'Intervention' store was the most expensive food store in Yuendumu was suppressed and the nutritionist threatened with legal action.

So what does the imposition of Income Management cost? According to a January 2013 report by the Australian National Audit Office:

"For a customer living in a remote area, the departments estimate that the cost of providing Income Management services is in the order of $6,600 to $7,900 per annum."

Is this value for money? I don't think so.

When Income Management was introduced, the Little Sisters of Jesus were quietly and on the sly offered exemption. They declined. *"If we are to be exempt, all other Yuendumu pensioners should be exempt,"* was their exemplary response.

BasicsCard
PIN APPROVAL ONLY

5029 4900 1350 7495
VALID TO 06/2024
John Citizen

Another planet...

By stealth, a new word has crept into the lexicon, 'governance'. The word doesn't seem to exist in Warlpiri. We are dealing with semantic attack, yet another arrow in the assimilationist quiver. Thus the thumbscrews of control keep getting tightened.

Legislation and political and bureaucratic pressure make it increasingly difficult, nay impossible, to avoid registering any new Aboriginal organisation as an Aboriginal Corporation. These AC's are registered with the Office of Remote Indigenous Corporations (ORIC) whose main task is to ensure compliance with the governance rules. ORIC came under the Department of the Prime Minister and Cabinet, and has since been reassigned to the newly created National Indigenous Australian Agency (NIAA). I wouldn't dare to suggest that this arrangement is open to the possibility of being abused to further certain political agendas. Suffice it to say, I cannot get rid of a mental picture of Damocles' sword, except that in this case the Sword of Damocles is overhanging the powerless.

If you are a masochist, I suggest you go to the ORIC website and familiarise yourself with their Rule Book template. Definitely the Sword of Damocles!

Andrew Fisher became Andrew Stojanovski when he married Vesna Stojanovska. Andrew is the author of 'Dog Ear Cafe: How the Mt. Theo Program beat the curse of petrol sniffing.' When Andrew first arrived in Yuendumu he set up a teepee at west camp. This earned him the nickname 'Feathers' which later fell into disuse when it was replaced by Yakajirri, an honorific name bestowed on him by Darby Ross as this had been Darby's father's name.

When, in 1993, Andrew first got involved with the 'Petrol Sniffing Prevention Programme' (PSPP), he received virtually no official support. Yuendumu Mining Co. could barely afford the credit for rations, fuel and vehicle repairs it regularly extended to PSPP, whilst the latter awaited irregular and uncertain government funding.

The PSPP, like the Night Patrol, had started to a large extent as an unofficial Yapa volunteer initiative. Yapa on foot would spring sniffers in action, tip out their petrol cans and escort them back to their families. In the year 2000, the PSPP was incorporated as the Substance Misuse Aboriginal Corporation (SMAC).

Ironically, funding only became readily forthcoming when there were almost no petrol sniffers left. The funding of Yuendumu's substance abuse prevention programmes exhibited what I believe in mathematics is called an 'inverse exponential correlation'.

When Traditional Land Owners Peggy Nampijinpa and her husband † Johnny Japangardi 'Hooker Creek' made their homeland available, the focus of the fight against petrol sniffing shifted from Yuendumu to Mt. Theo (Puturlu) outstation about 100 km to the north. SMAC became known as the Mt. Theo Programme and sniffers were exiled to Mt. Theo to be rehabilitated. In 2007 Andrew, Peggy and Johnny were awarded the Order of Australia Medal for their pioneering work on the Mt. Theo programme.

Peggy wasn't too pleased when soon thereafter she was put on Income Management by the Intervention.

In due course the Mt. Theo programme grew into WYDAC the Warlpiri Youth Development Aboriginal Corporation. WYDAC currently has sixty six sources of income. Government agencies, philanthropic and charity organisations all with differing agendas and imperatives and all requiring individually tailored reports to acquit their munificence. There is no, "Here is the money, we'll trust you to do your best with it, no strings attached", about it. Cheque writers refuse to relinquish control. It is all governed by governance under ORIC's watchful eye, thus making it virtually impossible for Yapa to ever take over running these organisations.

Don't get me wrong, some very devoted, professional, altruistic, admirable people have, and still are, working for WYDAC, and it's not without a tinge of jealousy that I write about WYDAC. Trying to manage Yuendumu Mining Company, the last four decades, I have utterly failed at sourcing outside financial assistance, something WYDAC has excelled at. That was the price Yuendumu Mining paid for independence and relevance.

WYDAC spends an inordinate amount of time and effort on unravelling the labyrinthine tangle of attached strings and red tape. Time and effort which would be better spent on developing Warlpiri youth. Rummaging through old papers whilst packing up my office, I stumbled on the 'WYDAC Strategic Development Report January to June 2013'.

Lest I bore you, I'll only present a few snippets for you to get the drift of the fifty eight page small type report. Yes, fifty eight small type pages with copious charts:

Item 2.4 (Page 8) Life Pathways: "Young people supported to develop employment life pathways so as to participate strongly in community life." Don't ask me what that means exactly.

The section on the Yuendumu Community Swimming Pool has a twenty line table which tells me that in the half year reported on, there were 7055 activities of which 5937 were public activities as distinct from group activities. An adequate profusion of activities, and ignorance of the mathematical concept of 'significant numbers'.

Verily vital information. Information Yuendumu and its pool could not function without.

The report also tells me that the main aim for the pool is to:

"Improve physical and mental health outcomes for young people through exercise." More to the point would be, *"To provide a place for people to swim."*

Says nothing about the physical and mental health outcomes for those Kardiya, tasked with meeting the requirements of the new governance regime. A governance regime emanating from a different planet to that on which Yapa reside, but one that they have become completely subjugated by.

Mark Moran has spent a lot of time at the cross-cultural coal face. Some of his experiences and insights are written up in 'Serious Whitefella Stuff', a book well worth reading. At WYDAC last year, Mark delivered a week-long workshop dealing with the cross cultural administrative disconnect which pervades remote Aboriginal Australia.

Mark told me that, at his workshop Yapa participants tended to fall asleep

Mark likes Yuendumu. Mark wrote this in a parting email to me:

'*....when one of the world's most complex public administration systems meets one of the world's most resilient cultures."*

Short and sweet folks, that is Yuendumu!

FRANK BAARDA

She don't like that kind of behaviour ...

♪♪ ♪♪ ♪♪

Reckless- James Reyne 1983

There is no doubt in my mind that intolerance of cultural and ethnic diversity is very much a part of the psyche of present day Australian society. The same mindset, which led to the Nazi horrors and the massacres of the Australian Frontier Wars, and sadly other atrocities in many other parts of the world, can be found in contemporary Australia. It is the same xenophobic ethnocentricity, the same arrogant conviction that 'we' are better than 'them'. That 'they' are *untermenschen* (less than human).

When this attitude is not carried to the extremes of ethnic cleansing, it is manifested in a conviction that 'they' must become like 'us', otherwise 'they' are doomed. If you want proof of this, consider that Australian Prime Minister John Howard was to proclaim at Ntaria (formerly Hermannsburg) on 28th August 2007, two months after he launched the Intervention: *"Aboriginal Australians, to have any future at all, will have to join the mainstream."* Subsequently, in February 2011 Prime Minister Julia Gillard when presenting the third Closing the Gap report to Parliament echoed John Howard and stated that *"Indigenous Australians have to change their behaviour if the Closing the Gap initiative is to succeed."*

How to deal with this bi-partisan myopia, which seems unable to give consideration to the possibility of the authorities changing their own behaviour instead, has been staring us in the face for over half a century?

> *"In Australia, our ways have mostly produced disaster for the Aboriginal people. I suspect that only when their right to be distinctive is accepted, will policy become creative."* - Kim Beazley Sr.

Witness

We have had the unusual privilege of witnessing immense changes in Yuendumu, both for better and for worse. Changes to the social fabric and political circumstances. Changes to the physical layout and daily life in the community. Changes to the power structure.

A lot happens in forty-eight years and I felt that as a witness to these changes, it is important that I attest to what I have observed and learned.

What stands out starkly has been the steady, unrelenting, deliberate, systematic suppression and crushing of Warlpiri cultural differences.

What stands out even more starkly has been the Warlpiri resilience, their passive resistance to changes they have not consented to and their success in maintaining their unique ways of being, seeing and believing, in spite of enormous pressure to conform from all levels of the English speaking world.

This pressure is often not malevolent but derives from a deeply held, uncompromising, ethnocentric conviction that the English ways are superior and offer a quality of life no other culture can match. These assimilationists feel it their duty to "save" the Aborigines from what they perceive to be a life of unfortunate primitive backwardness and disadvantage. Little do they realise.

The grave injustices being visited upon Aboriginal Australia by institutionalised coercive disempowerment and control need to be exposed and debunked. This story is my modest contribution to this debunking.

Solutions

For every complex problem there is a solution that is simple, neat and wrong. - H.L.Mencken

If you've stuck with me this far, thank you. When I obsess and have a rant about the injustices being foisted upon remote Aboriginal Australia, I sometimes get pulled up - *"It is all very well for you to bring up these issues, but you offer no solutions. What do you think needs to be done?"*

I usually say that it would be presumptuous and arrogant of me to offer solutions, especially when there are so many great recommendations in all those voluminous reports, resulting from countless hours of consultation and meetings, by and with Aboriginal people, now apparently consigned to archives. Aboriginal Australia has been shouting to the rooftops at every opportunity. Kardiya society has chosen not to listen. Instead they have applied what Mahatma Ghandi so eloquently described during his 1922 Sedition trial:

> *" ...They do not know, that a subtle but effective system of terrorism, together with an organised display of force on the one hand, and the deprivation of all powers of retaliation or self-defence on the other, has emasculated the people and induced in them the habit of simulation ... This awful habit has added to the ignorance and self-deception of the administrators..."*

In her book 'Grog War' Alexis Wright points out that whereas the guns and spears of the frontier may well have disappeared there is a *"contemporary war where the weapon is the English language"* and that Indigenous people are forced *"to counteract each attack on their lives with this historical weapon of their oppression."*

I won't bore you with the long list of historical protests, demands and pleas which have fallen on deaf ears. They can all be summed up as an assertion of, and a demand for Yapa rights to true self-determination and respect.

Indigenous Australia has offered countless solutions and recommendations which have mostly been ignored, not followed through, or occasionally appropriated and poorly implemented. A prime example is the Uluru 'Statement from the Heart', with its very modest appeal, that Aboriginal people have a voice in matters that directly affect them.

The red compacted skeletal soil, the hard baked ground of Central Australia is called *pati*. The Warlpiri word for ears is *langa*. I have heard bureaucrats and politicians referred to as *langa pati* .

Aboriginal Deaths in Custody 1987
  339 recommendations

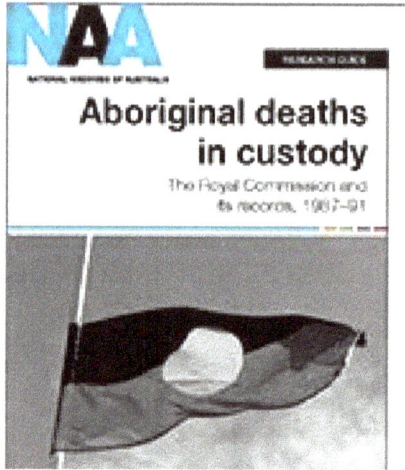

Recommendation #339

The Process of Reconciliation - That all political leaders and their parties recognise that reconciliation between the Aboriginal and non-Aboriginal communities in Australia must be achieved if community division, discord and injustice to Aboriginal people are to be avoided. To this end the Commission recommends that political leaders use their best endeavours to ensure bi-partisan public support for the process of reconciliation and that the urgency and necessity of the process be acknowledged.

Bringing them Home 1997
  54 recommendations

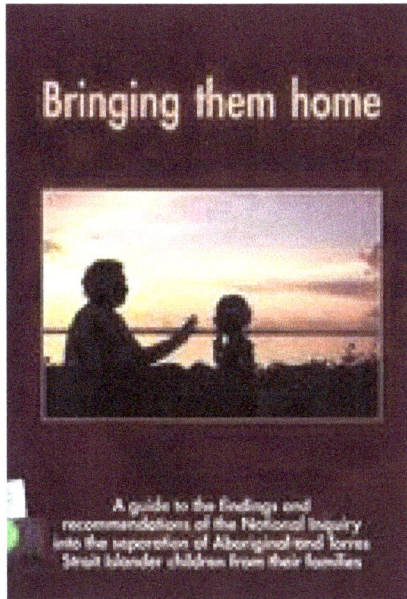

Recommendation #8A

That state and Territory governments ensure that Primary and Secondary school curricula include substantial modules on the history and continuing effects of forcible removal.

Little Children are Sacred 2007
97 recommendations

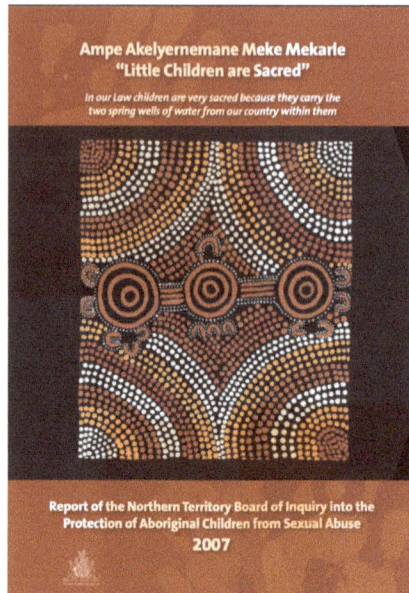

The first recommendation concludes with:

It is critical that both governments commit to genuine consultation with Aboriginal people in designing initiatives for Aboriginal communities.

The elephant in the room...

Countless meetings and discussions have taken place between Yuendumu community members and leaders and government or opposition representatives or representatives of other outside bodies such as the land council.

The most pressing objective raised by the Yuendumu community during such dialogue is the reinstatement of our own local council. Under the present arrangement of administrative rules and laws, such a re-empowerment is impossible and demands are stonewalled or ignored and locals fobbed off with empty promises or weasel words

Another example of how local wishes and demands are ignored is when community members request police on communities stop wearing guns. We are told that police are entitled to wear guns, and they can't be forced not to, it is their choice. The possibility of sending only officers who are prepared to go unarmed to communities, isn't countenanced.

On a national level, the Aboriginal and Torres Strait Islander Commission (ATSIC) was for better or for worse the most representative pan-Indigenous body that Australia ever had.

ATSIC was established in 1990 by the Hawke Labor government. In 2004 Prime Minister John Howard declared *"...we believe very strongly that the experiment in separate representation, elected representation for indigenous people has been a failure..."*

In 2005 ATSIC was abolished with bipartisan support. The government had once again thrown out the baby with the bath water.

Australia is the only English speaking ex-colonial power that has not negotiated a treaty or treaties with its original inhabitants and their descendants, and that hasn't got a Bill of Rights.

Campaigns to have Australia's first people recognised in the Constitution and to negotiate Treaties are on a never-ending treadmill, the latest conspicuous manifestation of which is the Uluru Statement from the Heart. A large and varied group of Indigenous people sat down under the shadow of Uluru (Ayers Rock) and cobbled together a powerful English language statement requesting a 'voice to Parliament' only to have the statement summarily dismissed by Prime Minister Malcolm Turnbull on the specious grounds that it would be an unacceptable, *"third tier of government."*

It was nothing of the sort. The statement includes, *"We call for the establishment of a First Nations Voice enshrined in the Constitution."* *"In 1967 we were counted, in 2017 we seek to be heard."*

The elephant in the room is ATSIC, which could never have been so cavalierly dismantled if the First Australians had been recognised in the Constitution. Neither would the West Australian government have got away with evicting the people of Oombulgurri off their lands. Oombulgurri residences were subsequently bulldozed, yet another case of throwing the baby out with the bathwater.

Oombulgurri - Lest we forget

Yuendumu then and now…

The Yuendumu Settlement we fell in love with in 1973 was the westernmost permanent outpost along the Tanami Track. There was a 292 km. stretch of dirt road to the nearest town. There were no phones, no TV, and a few houses and street lights in the central Kardiya area. It became a community with houses for Yapa (never enough), bitumen roads, many more Kardiya bosses and workers, and many people on sit down money. Now we are a growth town, essentially a service provider for Yapa, who are excluded from participation in the running of their community by ochre cards, literacy based certificates and a tangle of red tape. There are some jobs for Yapa but they're never in charge. Yapa belong to a culture evolved to conserve energy and there is no chance for a little sit down in today's work force. The main reason people leave work, is that they don't like to be bossed about and told off. They don't need to work for money. In the old days it didn't matter how long a job took as long as it got done. Today, you work like a Kardiya or not at all. Yuendumu is now firmly held in the grip of the Kardiya world.

As we return from Alice Springs and after hours of darkness, drive over the rise on the Tanami Road, which reveals the twinkling lights of Yuendumu, I still experience the same thrill I remember from my childhood when the ship I was on approached a harbor. Although what used to be a six hour trip now only takes three there is still that wonderful feeling of almost being home.

What used to be a dangerous, unmarked curve at the men's museum near the entrance to Yuendumu, now has several signs including a large, faded, rather patronising "Look for people" sign.

The welcome arch is no longer at the edge of Yuendumu and has seen better days. The Yuendumu Football Club Magpies shield at its apex is missing. Before reaching the arch, there is now Yuendumu's largest building, the lit up police complex and you may also notice the barbed wire topped walls of the women's safe house and a few more duly fenced in residences.

Also missing is the aroma of smoke from countless mulga wood campfires. Those convivial open air gatherings or card games which you could join if you so wished. Gatherings at which sometimes old people would tell Jukurrpa stories.

Many of the houses and buildings had minimalist fences and there were many alleys used by barefoot pedestrians as shortcuts. The alleys have almost disappeared and the fences have expanded into unfriendliness. With the sealing of roads and the gravelling of footpaths, walking barefoot can be a painful exercise. No foot prints appear. You can no longer see who walked this way before you today.

The influx of Kardiya with a low opinion of Yapa, and the imposed system of bureaucratic control has put paid to the Yuendumu where everybody knew everybody, and to a community that it was a joy to be a part of. Cross-cultural social interaction is but a shadow of its former self.

Still all is not lost. Yapa are extremely good at remembering people, much better than we Kardiya. In Alice Springs and Yuendumu or wherever, I am continuously greeted with a smile and the children are an absolute delight as they enthusiastically wave at us and call out our names as we drive in to Yuendumu as we unwind the car window and wave back. On returning from holidays our Warlpiri friends and family give us such a warm welcome. They are as glad to see us back, as we are to be home. They often give us a big hug.

Resilience

On our return from annual holidays last year, we saw large numbers of Yuendumu residents drifting back from Balgo across the Western Australia border. Teeth euphorically glistening out of red ochre smeared faces, they had just taken part in the annual Jilkaja business during which a significant number of boys, including some from Yuendumu, had been initiated into manhood. I've been told that 2,000 participants came from Western Australia, and 2,000 from Central Australia. Whatever the actual numbers, it was many. Kardiya were not involved in making this happen.

This year it was Yuendumu's turn. When shopping in Yuendumu one had to be patient as both shops were full of ochre smeared visitors and locals. Despite the concerted assault on Yapa identity by the ethnocentric behemoth, which is Kardiya society, there, in a parallel universe, resilient Yapa 'business' refuses to be extinguished.

Yuendumu Magpies at the MCG- June 2009 (Photo- PAW)

The glass is half full …

The day before the Australian Electoral Commission's mobile polling team was slated to come to Yuendumu, Wendy and I had to travel to Alice Springs because we had an appointment with the bank. On the way, at Tilmouth Roadhouse, we ran into a team from the Alice Springs ABC radio station. They were planning to do a live broadcast that afternoon from Yuendumu with an emphasis on the up and coming NT election. They took the opportunity to record interviews with us, as long standing residents of Yuendumu. We both told of what we did in Yuendumu, what we thought of the place and its people and why we were happy to stay there as long as we had. To the inevitable political questions we told them that the Environment and Aboriginal Rights were our top priorities. I suggested that the most important immediate thing our leaders could do was to seriously revisit the Uluru Statement from the Heart.

On our way back from Alice Springs we turned on the car radio and tuned into the ABC's live Yuendumu broadcast. A twelve year old lad was asked what was Yuendumu like? *"Perfect,"* he answered. What was his favourite thing in Yuendumu? *"Football,"* was his answer. What was his football team like? *"Excellent,"* came the reply.

Yuendumu, a perfect place with an excellent football team, what more could one wish for.

Ngulajuku - That's all

Agradecimientos

As I cobbled this story together, I became increasingly aware that whereas a book usually has one author, there is a veritable army of people helping to make it all happen. People who contribute anything from a useful comment or suggestion, some relevant additional information or recollection, some pertinent advice, a reality check, to many hours of selfless editorial labor. The author is like a soloist in an orchestra which provides anything from the tinkling of a triangle to a grand piano in full flight.

The Orchestra

Alan Cashin, Alan Oshlack, Alexis Wright, Amiuus Lennie, Andrea Hull, Andrew Stoyanovski, Andy Kelly, Andy Minko, Andy Sutherland, Anna Lennie, Ann Mosey, Beatrice Ruby-Kerr, Bentley James, Bill McKell, Blim Nolan, Bob Gosford, Brian Gray, Bruno Wilson, Cecilia Alfonso, Christine Godden, Claudia Rowe, Courtney Singleton, David McCubbin, David Marks, David Moore, David Nash, Derreck Williams, Diane Tripp, Donovan Baarda, Donovan Rice, Fiona Walsh, Forrest Holder, Francis Kelly, Frank Jung, Gloria Morales, Grant Granites, Harry Blagg, Harry Nelson, Howard Tankey, Ian Viner, Jack Waterford, Jan Bauer, Jason Woods, Jayne Irvine, Jenny Baarda, Jeremy Drew, Jim Allender, Jim Kable, Joe Baarda, Joe Blake, Jon Altman, Kate Thompson, Kay Smith, Kieran Finnane, Kim Mahood, Lee Cataldi, Liam Campbell, Lisa Watts, Malcolm Wall, Margit Bowler, Margot Rosenbloom, Mark Moran, Martin Flanagan, Mary Laughren, Matthew Egan, Max Walker, Melinda Hinkson, Micah Hudson, Michael Harries, Neil Murray, Otto Sims, Patrick Davies, Rebecca Toll, Robert Graham, Robin Granites, Rod Horner, Rod Moss, Roger Fidler, Sam McKell, Simon Fisher Sr, Steve Hodder, Steve Swartz, Tamsin Wagner, Ted Baarda, Ted Egan, Thalia Anthony, Tommy Watson, Tony Hoskins, Tony Juttner, Vic Cherikoff, Warren Williams, Wendy Baarda, Yasmine Musharbash, and any others who may have slipped through the cracks of my geriatric memory.

ABOUT THE AUTHOR

Frank Baarda was born in 1943 in Holland. He spent his primary school years in Argentina. When he was twelve years old his family returned to the Netherlands and after two years emigrated to Australia. He spent most of his teenage years in Moe, Victoria. He met his wife at the University of Melbourne where he studied geology. He worked as a field geologist in Australia during the 1960s nickel boom, then in Canada and the Canadian Arctic as a well-site geologist. They returned to Australia by road to Panama and then by ship across the Pacific. In 1973, after two years in Darwin, Frank and his family arrived at their predestined Yuendumu.

The cultural, geographic and linguistically diverse background to Frank's life has given him a distinctive perspective on and appreciation of Yuendumu and its people.

In memory of Harry Jakamarra Nelson 1944 - 2021

A teacher in two worlds

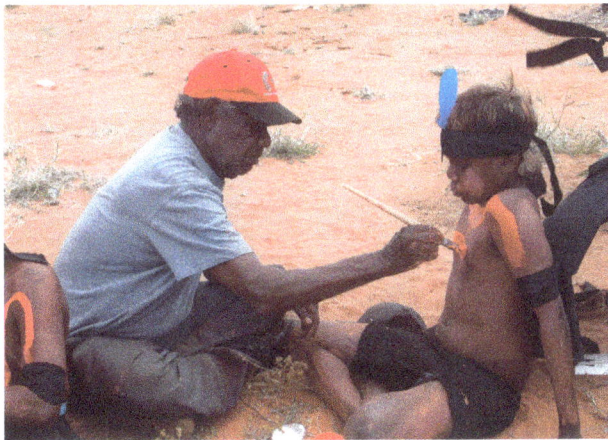

www.ingramcontent.com/pod-product-compliance
Lightning Source LLC
Chambersburg PA
CBHW041254040426
42334CB00028BA/3012